Reflective Social Work Practice

Thinking, doing and being

Reflective Social Work Practice demonstrates how social workers can creatively and consciously combine 'thinking, doing and being' when working with individuals, families, groups, communities and organisations, and when undertaking research.

The book discusses conceptual and theoretical aspects of reflective practice and presents a new, cohesive reflective social work practice model. It explores the themes of thinking (theory), doing (practice) and being (virtues). By defining 'being' in terms of virtues, the authors provide new perspectives for improved learning and practice in social work.

Each chapter features reflective exercises, examples, review questions and activities to engage and challenge the reader. Extended case studies throughout illustrate how a holistic approach to social work can enhance practice and enrich the quality of services delivered to people and communities.

Written by authors with extensive professional experience in social work, *Reflective Social Work Practice* is an invaluable resource for social work, human services and welfare students, educators and practitioners alike.

Dr Manohar Pawar is Professor of Social Work at the School of Humanities and Social Sciences, Charles Sturt University (New South Wales, Australia), and is President of the Asia-Pacific branch of the International Consortium for Social Development. He has more than 30 years of experience in social work education, research and practice in Australia and India.

Dr A.W. (Bill) Anscombe is Course Director for Social Work at Charles Sturt University. He has been involved in social work since 1973 and has had a practice career at multiple levels in the areas of corrections and child protection. He has worked jointly in social work while also holding significant university teaching and research responsibilities.

Reflective Social Work Practice

Thinking, doing and being

Manohar Pawar

A.W. (Bill) Anscombe

CAMBRIDGE
UNIVERSITY PRESS

477 Williamstown Road, Port Melbourne, VIC 3207, Australia

Cambridge University Press is part of the University of Cambridge.

It furthers the University's mission by disseminating knowledge in the pursuit of education, learning and research at the highest international levels of excellence.

www.cambridge.org
Information on this title: www.cambridge.org/9781107674349

First published 2015

Cover designed by Marianna Berek-Lewis
Typeset by Integra Software Services Pvt. Ltd.
Printed in China by C & C Offset Printing Co. Ltd.

A catalogue record for this publication is available from the British Library

A Cataloguing-in-Publication entry is available from the catalogue of the National Library of Australia at www.nla.gov.au

ISBN 978-1-107-67434-9 Paperback

Contents

About the authors

Dr Manohar Pawar is Professor of Social Work at the School of Humanities and Social Sciences, Charles Sturt University (New South Wales, Australia) and is President of the Asia-Pacific branch of the International Consortium for Social Development. He has more than thirty years of experience in social work education, research and practice in Australia and India. He is the lead chief investigator of research funded by the Australian Research Council's Discovery Project, which focuses on virtues and social work practice. Professor Pawar has received a number of awards, including the citation award for outstanding contributions to student learning (2008, from the Australian Learning and Teaching Council), and Quality of Life Award (2001, from the Association of Commonwealth Universities). Current areas of interest include international social work, development and social policy, social consequences of climate change and water, social work education, informal care and ageing, NGOs and community development. Some of his recent publications are:

Pawar, M. (2014). *Social and Community Development Practice*, New Delhi: Sage

(2014). *Water and Social Policy*. Basingstoke: Palgrave Macmillan

(2010). *Community Development in Asia and the Pacific*, New York: Routledge

Pawar, M. & Cox, D. (eds) (2010). *Social Development: Critical Themes and Perspectives*, New York: Routledge

Cox, D. & Pawar, M. (2013). *International Social Work: Issues, Strategies and Programs* (2nd edn), Thousand Oaks, CA: Sage

Lyons, K., Hokenstad, T., Pawar, M., Huegler, N. & Hall, N. (eds) (2012). *Sage Handbook of International Social Work*. London: Sage

Dr A.W. (Bill) Anscombe is Course Director for Social Work courses at Charles Sturt University. He has been involved in social work since 1973 and has had a practice career at multiple levels in the areas of corrections and child protection. He has worked jointly in social work while also holding significant university teaching and research responsibilities. Additionally, he has undertaken research projects in areas that include educational, Indigenous, community, multicultural, organisational, religious, private, government and non-government agencies. With Professor Pawar, he is a Chief Investigator in the Australian Research Council's Discovery Project on social work and virtues. Dr Anscombe has been awarded an Australian Government National Volunteer Award and a 2012 Humanitarian Award by the Refugee Council of Australia/STARTTS. He is a director of four small and medium-sized not-for-profit organisations.

Acknowledgements

Conceptualising this book and the ideas in it has been an intellectually fascinating, gratifying and curious exercise for us. We are grateful for our own life experiences, our socialisation into the social work profession and our working life at Charles Sturt University (CSU). Each one of them has significantly contributed to making this book. Wonderful social work and other professional colleagues with whom we work every day within and outside the university and students who listen to our lectures and ideas, read our study material, and challenge us are important in initiating and completing any intellectual endeavour, and particularly a book such as this. The ambition of achieving excellence in scholarly teaching and research set by our own CSU is a crucial benchmark; one that we all strive to accomplish. This book is a small step towards achieving that ambition. CSU's Special Study Program and a research fellowship of the Institute for Land, Water and Society were useful to focus on in this book project, and we appreciate CSU's support through those schemes.

Isabella Mead, Commissioning Editor, Cambridge University Press (CUP), was efficient and effective in commissioning the book, organising reviews and reading the manuscript. It was a pleasure to work with Isabella and the production team at CUP. We are grateful to them. We would also like to thank peer reviewers for their constructive comments and suggestions.

Most importantly, we would like to acknowledge the love, support and sacrifice of our families – our parents, wives and children. Without them we would not have been able to complete this book.

Finally, we would like to encourage, appreciate and thank readers of this book as the meaning they are going to derive from what we are saying is important for them and to us, and we hope it helps them derive greater meaning from their thinking, doing and being. For any shortcomings in this book we are responsible.

Manohar Pawar and A.W. (Bill) Anscombe

Introduction

WE ARE PLEASED to introduce this book to you, the reader, and we invite you to read it critically, creatively and constructively. You may ponder why, given that there are many books on social work practice methods, you should read this one. This is a book with a difference. Generally, social work literature is dominated by theory and practice issues, and practice and theory or thinking and doing, and doing and thinking. These are important, but they are mostly bereft of being. The main focus of this book is how to conceptualise and apply being in social work practice along with thinking and doing. We strongly believe that conscious and explicit use of being enhances the quality of social work practice. So the motto of the book is how to improve oneself and practise better by focusing on being.

This is not to suggest that social workers and social work practice are not doing well. More than a century of professional social work presence in the world – and its continuous spread – testifies to its need and the quality of work performed by thousands of social workers. However, what seems to dilute that effort or make it inadequate is the ever-growing social problems and needs, increased complexity and a 'patchwork' of responses to those problems. Poverty, unemployment, increasing inequality, inbuilt and entrenched structural exploitation at a global scale (e.g. the global financial crisis, outsourcing of work, the migration of capital to the detriment of labour, all under the ideological umbrella of market forces, managerialism, liberalisation and privatisation) on the one hand and, as a consequence, increasing social instability and risk, drug, alcohol and mental health issues, homelessness, family disorganisation or breakdown, child abuse and neglect, youth unemployment, gender discrimination, domestic violence, the situation of the disabled and the elderly on the other hand, seem to suggest that we need something more than thinking and doing and doing and thinking, theory and practice and practice and theory.

Such social problems and needs are complex both at macro and micro levels. At all levels, including individual, family and community, they need complex responses in terms of commitment, judgement and decisions. Instrumental approaches appear effective, but they are failing in many ways. We believe building being along with thinking and doing will strengthen the social worker and the social work profession to take bold steps, to take right decisions and to pursue them to enhance the well-being of individuals, families and communities, and society in general. Towards that goal, this book has attempted to develop the concept of being and a reflective social work practice model that blends thinking, doing and being. It also demonstrates the application of the model across social work practice methods, such as work with individuals and families, groups, communities, human services organisations and social work research.

Readership

This book is based on our practice in social work and teaching experience in the Bachelor of Social Work, Master of Social Work and related human-services courses. Its content is relevant to educators and students of social work, social welfare and human services. It is equally interesting and useful to social work practitioners, youth/welfare/human services workers and trainers, in both government and non-government organisations. It can be used as a textbook in social work theory and practice courses and/or subjects, and it can also be used as an important reference in the relevant social work methods subjects, depending upon the need. Although most of the examples are drawn from the Australian context, the reflective social work practice model blending being, thinking and doing can be used in any country's context. Hence the scope of the book is global.

Organisation

The book is organised into eight chapters. Recapitulating historical roots and definitions of social work, chapter 1 presents our understanding of contemporary social work practice and discusses the concepts of thinking, doing and being. It shows how being is neglected in social work and needs to be strengthened. By discussing conceptual and theoretical aspects of reflective practice, in chapter 2 we develop the reflective social work practice model that blends being, thinking and doing. It also includes an analytical framework that explicitly captures being in various phases of practice. The next five chapters show the application of the reflective practice model on the methods of social work practice. Chapter 3 shows how the model is useful while working with individuals and families. The application of the model for group work practice is discussed in chapter 4. The use of the model for community practice is discussed in chapter 5. With the strength of the model, how social work research can assume an empowering, enabling and action-oriented approach is discussed in chapter 6. Chapter 7 demonstrates the application of the model in the welfare administration and organisational context. The final chapter reflects on the contents of all seven chapters in terms of thinking, doing and being, and contemplates future directions for social work practice.

▦ Special features

For pedagogical purposes, the book has some useful features. Each chapter has clearly posted learning objectives and key themes and concepts at the beginning. A summary of the chapter and questions and exercises are presented at the end. In addition, a number of reflective questions are posed in the text of the chapter, although an answer is not provided in the text for every reflective question. A social worker's thinking, doing and being related to the practice case and personal reflections are separately analysed and presented in each chapter. We believe these features should facilitate learning and teaching with ease.

▦ How to read this book

The book is written in a simple and readable style to facilitate its use by students, educators and practitioners. Although the chapters are logically sequenced, readers may read any chapters according to their interest. However, we suggest that you read as follows. To have a broad overview of social work and the social work profession, and of expected social work standards and to understand the concept of thinking, doing and being, read chapter 1. To understand the meaning and variants of reflective practice, reflective practice theories, and our reflective social work practice model, read chapter 2. Some understanding of the reflective social work practice model is necessary to properly follow the content of the remaining chapters. Thus understanding the model in chapter 2 is a prerequisite for following the remaining chapters. But the model may be modified according to your practice requirements. If your social work theory and practice subject combines all the social work methods, the whole book can be used as a textbook. If you are studying each social work method as a separate subject/course, we recommend that you read it as follows: for work with individuals/casework subject/unit, read chapters 2 and 3; for a group work subject/unit read chapters 2 and 4; for a community organisation and development subject/unit read chapter 2 and 5; for a research methods subject/unit, read chapters 2 and 6; and for a welfare administration/human service organisation subject read chapters 2 and 7. To gain an understanding in summary of all chapters and future directions of social work practice, read chapter 8.

▓ Feedback

Peer reviewers of this book indicated that it is both introductory and in depth. It is so – as it begins from simple concepts and moves to complex issues. To some extent it is because of the nature of the subject, being, that we are looking at. We also believe that readers need to be challenged to know more with rigour. For some concepts and readings, you may need to take additional reading to facilitate a better understanding. The reviewers also commented that 'the book provides a different perspective to social work training by emphasising the being, which is often not a focus of the training'. As reviewers have recognised and commented, we have tried something new and different, and we are conscious that it is far from perfect and that our model and the analysis of being can be improved. To better meet your needs and needs of practice with any future editions, we would appreciate your feedback on the book.

We wish you an intellectually stimulating and challenging read.

1

Contemporary social work practice: thinking, doing and being

IN THIS BOOK we attempt to develop the concept of being in the context of social work theory and practice. We will demonstrate how being can be applied across all practice methods:

- working with individuals and families
- working with groups
- working with communities
- social work research
- social services administration and management.

On the basis of our experience and reflections, we believe that the explicit development and use of being in social work strengthens both the practitioner and the practice. This emphasis on being enhances the quality of engagement with people, communities and their institutions. It can better help practitioners to meet needs and resolve issues, thereby developing stronger communities in which individuals and families can thrive.

▦ Chapter objectives

The main objective of this chapter is to discuss contemporary social work practice in terms of broad trends in social work education, practice and the profession, and the place and importance of 'being' within it. After studying this chapter, readers should be able to reflect on the following:

- the meaning(s) of social work
- a history of social work
- broad trends in social work education and practice
- Australian social work and professional development
- the concepts of thinking, doing and being and how these are connected and/or disconnected in practice.

Main themes and concepts used

Some of the core ideas discussed in this chapter are the meaning of social work as an evolving concept and a brief history of social work. By examining the evolution and development of professional social work in the past 120 years, it identifies broad trends in social work education and practice in terms of remedial and developmental social work, as well as some emerging approaches. It then discusses how social work education and practice has evolved in Australia and contributed to these trends in social work. Further, it discusses how social work has developed as a profession. It asks whether (and how) the profession is based on thinking in terms of theory and a body of knowledge, doing in terms practice and skills, and being in terms of virtues. Reflecting on contemporary social work practice, we suggest that the concept of 'being' in social work is neglected and underdeveloped and that it does not have an explicit equal place in practice along with thinking and doing.

This chapter will cover some core concepts and terms used in social work, including Charity Organisation Society, Settlement House, clinical/remedial social work, developmental social work, profession and professional body, accreditation standards, thinking, doing and being. Although most of these concepts are discussed to some extent in this chapter, we recommend that you develop familiarity with them early on.

The meaning(s) of social work

What is social work? To begin with, we must recognise that there is no universal and singular definition of social work. However, it is important to ask the question in order to better understand one's identity as a professional social worker. There is an ongoing debate and concern about what social work is. In terms of language, the term 'social work' is not owned by the social work profession. Many people who work in communities and assist others as volunteers, community leaders, politicians, religious or spiritual leaders and so on often claim to be social workers and proudly say that they do social work. The prefix 'social' seems to make things too trivial, general or diffused.

REFLECTIVE EXERCISE 1.1

Consider your own responses to the question: what is social work? What is your general understanding of social work?

The root of the word 'social' is found in Latin, where *socius* (noun) means not only 'ally, confederate' but also, by extension, 'sharer, partner and companion'. Its adjective *socialis* means 'of or belonging to companionship, sociable, social'. Another Latin word associated with *socius* is *socio*, which means 'to join or unite together, to associate: to do or hold in common, to share with'. *The Shorter Oxford English Dictionary* lists four meanings for the word 'social' that emphasise respectively belonging, mutuality, group living, and activities to improve conditions of a society by addressing problems and issues (Pawar & Cox 2010a). From these meanings it is clear that the commonsense meaning of social work is work done in association or companionship for others and not for oneself. Its foundation is not individualistic but groups, sharing, mutuality and confederation.

The use of the term 'social work' and/or professional social work by professional bodies and social work practised by non-professionals and professionals has created confusion in some communities. Some people wonder about the difference between the two. Although the degree of this confusion may differ from one place to another, its existence, and its contribution to the 'social work identity issue', cannot not be denied. Has 'professional social work' departed from the original meaning of 'social'? Some social workers, both emerging and established, continue to raise the question of what is social work and whether what they are doing constitutes social work. As it is a troubling question, often producing a discomfiting response, the meaning of social work as defined by professional social work bodies keeps changing and evolving to suit the given socioeconomic, political and cultural context. For example, Gibelman (1999) shows how the social work profession in the United States developed and used different definitions of social work at different times. Similarly, the Australian Association of Social Workers (AASW) has developed, adopted and used different definitions of social work. In an earlier version, the AASW (1999) in its code of ethics stated:

> The social work profession is committed to the pursuit and maintenance of human well-being. Social work aims to maximise the development of human potential and the fulfilment of human needs, through an equal commitment to: working with and enabling people to achieve the best possible levels of personal and social well-being and working to achieve social justice through social development and social change.

Later, in its 2010 version of the code of ethics, the AASW (2010) adopted the following social work definition agreed by the International Federation of Social Workers (IFSW) and International Association of Schools of Social Work (IASSW) (IFSW & IASSW 2004): 'The social work profession promotes social change, problem-solving in human relationships and the empowerment and liberation of people to enhance well-being. Utilising theories of human behaviour and social systems, social work intervenes at the points where people interact with their environments. Principles of human rights and social justice are fundamental to social work.' Although this internationally agreed definition of social work has been adopted by the AASW, some argued that this definition of social work is individualistic, Eurocentric and universalistic, and does not makes sense for some countries and cultures. Responding to these and similar criticisms, international professional bodies IFSW and IASSW called for further debate and discussion of the definition of social work. In January 2014, the IASSW (2014) board has approved the following new definition of social work:

> Social work is a practice-based profession and an academic discipline that promotes social change and development, social cohesion, and the empowerment and liberation of people. Principles of social justice, human rights, collective responsibility and respect for diversities are central to social work. Underpinned by theories of social work, social sciences, humanities and indigenous knowledges, social work engages people and structures to address life challenges and enhance well-being.

The inclusion of some new elements such as social development, indigenous knowledges, diversity and collective responsibility seem to be in response to the critique of the earlier definition. Looking at this evolving concept of social work, one may argue that the meaning and definition of social work will be questioned from different cultural and ideological perspectives, and the debate and discussion should continue as the meaning keeps evolving to capture what it does where, when and how. But, interestingly, such debate and questioning may not exist in 'social work' carried out by other people in communities (non-professional social workers). Many people and organisations in communities (e.g. volunteers, community leaders, religious leaders, faith-based organisations, and NGOs) state that they do 'social work', and most people and communities seem to simply accept it. Then why are we, professional social workers, so much concerned about defining and redefining social work? Are we concerned about our 'status' as professional social workers? Are we troubled about our boundaries? Therefore are we concerned about our identity? Do these questions focus more on 'self' rather than on others? It is important to reflect on these and similar questions while thinking about the meaning of social work and to contribute to further debate and the construction of meaning. Perhaps the consideration of the origins of social work might help in this meaning-making process.

REFLECTIVE EXERCISE 1.2
Compare your own responses to the question 'what is social work?' with the above definitions of social work.

▓ Origins of social work

The origins of social work are complex and controversial. The history (or histories) of the practice vary across different cultures and periods. In order to trace its origins, a critical question we need to ask is: where do we begin? The history of social work and its interpretation will be contested and articulated differently depending upon the way social work is understood and the parameters set around such an understanding. It is reasonable to assume that during different periods (ancient, medieval and modern), in different societies and communities, people and (religious) groups in formal and informal ways have been kind and helpful to each other, particularly in a crisis (Pawar 2014a).

Human history goes back thousands of years, and we may not have records of early social work practice. For example, the existence of Aborigines in Australia for thousands of years and their social work practices are not known to us. Activities like social work were carried out by religious missionaries before and during colonisation. The spread of human values such as compassion, love, kindness, generosity, sacrifice and so on can be traced in human history. Unearthing that kind of broadly under-stood social work history is an important research task that needs to undertaken. However, here the origins or history of social work do not include such a past, although it is important and should be acknowledged. We discuss a one-sided history of the origins of professional social work known to us and available in the literature below.

The Charity Organisation Society model

In the West, following the Enlightenment, reason, the Industrial Revolution, techno-logical innovation and industrialisation, life significantly changed from the sixteenth to the eighteenth centuries. Rural to urban migration, poverty, destitution, sickness and the situation of children and the elderly in urban centres in the midst of wealth creation were disturbing phenomena that attracted voluntary efforts of both individuals and organisations such as charity societies and settlement houses in the UK and USA. Both religion and rationality influenced their work as churches were significantly engaged in addressing social issues by developing children's aid societies and similar efforts to help the needy long before formal social work training began. Payne (1997) notes that casework originated in the attempts of the London Charity Organisation Society (COS), formed in 1870. The first almoner (medical social worker) was appointed in 1895. According to Rowlings (1997: 113), knowledge, skills and the value-based first school of social work were established in the UK and the Netherlands in 1896, in Germany in 1899 and France in 1907. Based on the UK's COS model, the first COS was founded in

New York in 1877, and it spread to other US cities. COSs tried to systematically organise voluntary charity efforts through 'friendly visitors' who looked into poor families and corrected individual behaviour (Leighninger & Midgley 1997: 10). The COS in New York offered the first formalised training program as a summer school in 1898. Later it became the School of Philanthropy in 1904 and School of Social Work at Columbia University. Later, several social work schools were established in the United States. In the first decade of the twentieth century, social work emerged as an occupation. Mary Richmond's role in the COS and her conceptualisation of social work and publication of the book, *Social Diagnosis* (1917) have significantly influenced the nature and development of the social work profession (Stuart 2013).

'Good works' and settlements

Another origin of social work may be traced to evangelical Christianity and Victorian 'good works', which had an approach of 'we care for everyone who comes'. Through this approach shelters for orphans and oppressed women were provided and university settlements were established (Payne 1997). Following London's first settlement house, Toynbee Hall, Jane Addams and Ellen Gates Starr founded Chicago's Hull House, the most famous settlement in the United States, in 1889. Settlement workers tried to organise and mobilise poor people to improve social and economic conditions by changing policies and provisions. This origin within social work is linked to community organisation and development (Payne 1997; Leighninger & Midgley 1997: 10; Stuart 2013), but has mostly remained in the background of social work education, practice and the profession.

The casework approach

During its first twenty to thirty years, from 1890 to 1920, social work gradually became established as an occupation and profession in Western countries, and Mary Richmond's casework approach became a torch light for social work education and practice. It was a kind of consolidation period for developing social work knowledge and skills for the profession, and the consequences of World War I, among other things, lent themselves to such practice. During the following twenty to thirty years, from 1920 to 1950 or 1960, the Western social work education, casework-oriented medical model spread to many developing countries and colonies, and the model continues to dominate in the twenty-first century.

Therefore the foundation of professional social work education and training in Australia was laid under the influence of the British and the North American models. On the two models Lawrence (1976) commented: 'Although both followed medical social work practice, American schools were strictly professional and concerned with techniques of social casework and the British two-year social study diplomas focused on social and economic issues.' Under these influences and with the initiative of voluntary bodies such as hospital almoners, private trusts, Christian missionaries and training boards, social work professional training in Australia had begun during the 1920s (Mendes 2005; Nash 2009) and was mostly based in large cities. Later universities assumed a leading role in providing social work education and training (Lawrence 1976), initially leading to certificates and diplomas (Norton 1976). The impact of the Martin Committee gradually helped many universities to offer a four-year or equivalent full undergraduate degree, Bachelor of Social Work (BSW). As in many countries, social work education and training in Australia has gradually expanded at its own pace. As of 2013, about twenty-eight Australian universities provided four-year social work degrees or the equivalent at the BSW level, and many of them also have introduced a two-year masters degree as the first professional qualifying degree, Master of Social Work (MSW). Before we look at the some of the features of and issues relating to professional social work in Australia, it is important to become familiar with the broad trends in social work education and practice over a period of about 120 years of professional social work.

REFLECTIVE EXERCISE 1.3

'To understand the nature of social work in Australia, it is important understand the origins of social work in the UK and USA.' Discuss.

Broad trends in social work education and practice

From origins of professional social work, two broad trends may be categorised and analysed. The first is individual (one-to-one) casework-based, medical/remedial/pathologically oriented social work practice that may be traced to COS work referred to above. The second is developmental social work and its variants, such as community organisation and development, policy practice, macro practice, empowerment and strengths-based practice, structural social work and so on, which may be traced to settlement house work. It is important to understand these two trends or traditions in social work education and practice. But they are not antithetical to each other, although their framework and focus are different, and are important from their own perspectives.

Clinical and remedial social work

The individual (one-to-one) casework-based, medical/remedial/pathologically oriented social work practice model focuses on the individual, the problem, clinical diagnostic tools and results. It treats the symptoms the way it is done in medical practice; that is, study, diagnosis and treatment. It holds the individual responsible for the problem or situation, thereby assuming the passivity of the person. Richmond's book, Social Diagnosis (1917), guided this kind of practice for a long time. This model was also described as Band-Aid social work (Tomlinson 1978). This medical/remedial model of social work exerted a significant influence in the USA and UK and in many developing countries at least for the first fifty years, approximately until 1950. Even today it is a dominating social work education and practice model in many countries as most of the practice has its variants, such as engagement, assessment and intervention.

Although many social workers successfully and effectively use this model, and it might have helped a number of people over the years, its adequacy and coverage was questioned because it did not help to stop or prevent problems and reach out to all those who need it. Given the magnitude of the need and problems people and communities were facing, this approach was not adequate and effective as it did not address the causes and did not look beyond the individual level. The number of trained social workers from such a perspective was and is not adequate. It was necessary to move beyond the medical/remedial model and the individual (i.e. one-to-one casework) to focus on groups, communities and institutions to address structural issues so as to help meet needs and resolve issues at the individual, group, community and institutional levels. Hence in the 1950s and 1960s, beyond casework practice, group work, community organisation, welfare administration and research were recognised as the other methods of social work practice, although the medical/remedial model has continued its dominant presence both in education and in practice as a practitioner-driven phenomenon.

Developmental social work

The developmental social work model and its variants, such as community organisation and development, policy practice, macro practice and empowerment, is the one that focuses beyond the individual level and looks with the participation of the concerned at addressing causes, which are often located in social, cultural, economic, political and institutional structures. It focuses on recognising and building strengths (Pulla 2012) and capacities at all levels – individual, community and institutions – with resource mobilisation and utilisation for the well-being of groups and communities. Hence the main focus of the developmental model of social work would be, for example, poverty alleviation, employment generation, infrastructure development by mobilising people and by bringing necessary policy and institutional changes. In essence, developmental social work focuses on social change by employing a range of approaches such as social development, social planning, advocacy, lobbying, social and judicial activism, social mobilisation and people's participation. Many social work educators and practitioners have asserted the relevance of developmental social work (e.g. Cox 1995; Midgley 1995, 2014; Midgley & Conley 2010; Cox & Pawar 2013; Pawar 2000). In most social work courses, group work, community organisation and development, welfare adminis-tration/social policy and research subjects have been taught as methods of social work. However, somehow these methods and the overall developmental social work have remained at the periphery, with the casework model remaining domi-nant, even today, in most of the schools.

In analysing these two broad trends, it is important to point out that it would be oversimplistic to understand all casework as medically or remedially oriented and group work, community organisation and development, and the other variants as developmental. It is important to understand these two distinct trends and their orientations and limitations. It also may be noted that the medical/remedial model or some of its elements can be applied at group work and community development practice and that the developmental model can be used in casework practice. For example, institutional (government) intervention in the Northern Territory in Aboriginal communities appears remedial and pathological. Many aspects of neo-liberal and managerial policies and practices have elements of the remedial model, which is blaming the victim or the individual for their situation. On the other hand, the developmental model can be used in casework practice from empowerment and strength perspectives. Hence the move from medical/remedial-oriented practice to developmental-oriented practice is needed, irrespective of the level at which it is practised.

REFLECTIVE EXERCISE 1.4
Discuss the main differences between clinical/remedial social work and developmental social work.

Variants of developmental social work

Since around 1990 several new strands have emerged within social work, which are significant and may be considered as different variants of developmental social work. These are:

- radical social work (Fook 1993; Ferguson & Woodward 2009; Mullaly 2006)
- critical social work (Allan, Briskman & Pease 2009; Fook 2012)
- feminist social work (White 2006; Dominelli 2002)
- empowerment and strengths-based practice (Lee 2001)
- reflective practice (Martyn 2000; Knott & Scragg 2013; Webber & Nathan 2010)
- human rights and social justice (Ife 2012; Reichert 2011; Mapp 2007; Wonka 2007)
- anti-oppressive and anti-discriminatory practices (Dominelli 2003; Dalrymple & Burke 2006; Baines & Benjamin 2007)
- social development (Midgley 1995, 2014; Midgley & Conley 2010; Pawar & Cox 2010b)
- ecological or green social work (Dominelli 2012; Gray, Coates & Hetherington 2013; Australian Social Work 2013; Pawar 2014b)
- international social work (Cox & Pawar 2013; Healy 2008; Hugman 2010; Lyons et al. 2012; Healy & Link 2012).

Although these strands can be used across all methods of social work, by and large social work education and practice seem to be clinging to casework/remedial practice and primarily focusing on work with individuals. These variants are mostly discussed from the theory and practice and practice and theory points of view by neglecting being. Focus on developing being along with thinking and doing may help to focus on developmental social work.

The developmental social work model is well reflected in the agenda of internationally leading professional social work organisations, namely the International Federation of Social Workers (IFSW), International Association of Schools of Social Work (IASSW) and International Council on Social Welfare (ICSW). Since 2010 these three professional bodies have come together and set the global agenda for the future. Social development has come into their vocabulary, and it is the future agenda of these organisations and the social work profession, although the International Consortium for Social Development had recognised the significance of social development since 1970s. These organisations' global agenda for social work and social development are:

- social and economic inequalities within countries and between regions
- dignity and worth of the person

- environmental sustainability
- importance of human relationships.

In later discussion they have identified shared commitments and a renewed determination to promote social work and social justice. The representatives agreed that:

- the full range of human rights are available to only a minority of the world's population
- unjust and poorly regulated economic systems, driven by unaccountable market forces, together with non-compliance with international standards for labour conditions and a lack of corporate social responsibility, have damaged the health and well-being of peoples and communities, causing poverty and growing inequality
- cultural diversity and the right to self-expression facilitate a more satisfactory intellectual, emotional, moral and spiritual existence, but these rights are in danger owing to aspects of globalisation which standardise and marginalise peoples, with especially damaging consequences for indigenous and first nation peoples
- people live in communities and thrive in the context of supportive relationships, which are being eroded by dominant economic, political and social forces
- people's health and well-being suffer as a result of inequalities and unsustainable environments related to climate change, pollutants, war, natural disasters and violence to which there are inadequate international responses (Jones & Truell 2012).

The conference organised by the three professional bodies in 2012 focused on the action and effects of the social work and social development agenda, and in 2014 they focused on social work, education and social development. These developments initiated by professional bodies seem to suggest that the future of social work lies in developmental social work. It would be interesting to see how these broad trends and current developments are reflected in professional social work in Australia.

REFLECTIVE EXERCISE 1.5
What is the global agenda for social work and social development? Do you agree or disagree with the agenda? Discuss.

■ Professional social work in Australia

As stated earlier, Western transplanted social work in Australia began in the 1920s, and it has developed over a period of nearly a century with some unique features. In this section, we explore some of these features in brief.

1. Gradual growth of the profession

Like in many other countries, professional social work in Australia grew gradually. It took about twenty years, from the 1920s to the 1940s, to organise itself into a professional body. How it professionalised itself and the activities of the professional bodies will be covered below. Its gradual and slow growth in terms of social work education and training, and the number of social workers it trained, was not adequate to meet needs and issues in the field. Even today, sufficient numbers of trained social workers are not available to meet certain industry sector personnel needs, for example child protection, mental health, aged care, disability and NGOs where non–social-work-trained workers have been employed. It is important to reflect on this situation.

2. International recognition of educators, practitioners and researchers

Australian social work educators, practitioners and researchers have made significant contributions to social work knowledge that have been recognised internationally. For example their contribution to radical social work (Fook 1993), reflective practice (Fook 2004, 2007), critical social work (Hick, Fook & Pozzuto 2005; Allan, Briskman & Pease 2009), community development (Ife 2013; Pawar 2010), rights-based social work practice (Ife 2012) strengths-based practice (Pulla 2012), human rights, social justice and action (Briskman, Latham & Goddard 2009), general social work theories and skills (Gray & Webb 2013; Connolly & Harms 2009; Healy 2005, 2012; Maidment & Egan 2004; Harms 2007), sustainability and ecological social work (McKinnon 2013; Pawar 2013, 2014b), human services practice (Alston 2009; Chenoweth & McAuliffe 2012; Ozanne & Rose 2013), international social work (Cox & Pawar 2013; Hugman 2010), social work ethics (Bowles et al. 2006; Hugman 2013; Gray & Webb 2010) are noteworthy and useful.

3. Remedial/clinical social work practice still the norm

Despite this unique and valuable contribution to the theory and knowledge base of social work, by looking at social work training and practice overall we get an impression that, by and large, most social work in Australia is still remedial or clinical and focuses on working with individuals.

4. Contradictions in anti-discriminatory and anti-oppressive practices

In theory, social work in Australia looks reflective and critical, but in practice we are not sure to what extent it is reflective and critical. Similarly, in theory it talks about anti-discriminatory and anti-oppressive practices, but in practice it often appears discriminatory and oppressive as it works for such structures and organisations. For example, if it is anti-discriminatory and anti-oppressive, what contribution has it made to change the Aboriginal contexts in practice during its hundred-year existence? In the same vein, what contribution has it made to multicultural issues and the social integration of immigrants and refugees in practice?

5. Racism and social work practice

Does social work practice have an element of racism? It has mostly focused on white social work (Walter, Taylor & Habibis 2011), and Aboriginal Australians continue to remain an excluded group in their own country.

6. Poverty and unemployment

Although it claims to follow social justice, human rights and critical practice, has it directly engaged in addressing poverty and unemployment issues?

7. Gender and social work practice

Social work engages more women than men in practice to deliver social work services. Why should mainly women bear this kind of work and why do men not also engage in similar work in equal numbers?

These and similar features and questions tend to make us think that social work in Australia, in terms of critical social work, human rights, social justice, anti-discriminatory and anti-oppressive practice, pays 'lip-service' more than it provides practice. Growing inequality (class), poverty and unemployment, racism and gender are important entrenched structural factors that diminish the quality of life of people and communities. Social work efforts in practice need to address these structural factors. Such critical features of professional social work help us reflect on the relevance of transplanted social work from the West and the role of social workers in terms of their thinking, doing and being in addressing local issues. Awareness of it seems to exist, but without substantial action. To further reflect on this situation and above questions, it may be useful to look at the social work professional body and the other related bodies and the roles they play in the development of the profession and practice.

▤ Professional development of social work

Is social work a profession? The professional status of social work may be debatable, particularly in the context of deprofessionalisation processes such as identity crisis, the role of other professions, the market and privatisation, the diminishing welfare state, fragmentation, and the nature and scope of its own activities and historical legacies (Rogowski 2010). Despite these processes, social work's professional status is based on the evidence that it has its own body of knowledge built on interdisciplinary social sciences and practice, formal training leading to university qualifications, techniques and skills for practice, vocation in terms of paid employment and career, and a professional body to maintain and monitor standards. Despite such confirmed professional characteristics, it seems to lag behind other professions such as law, engineering and medicine. Since it is a unique profession, one wonders whether it is appropriate to compare it with such professions.

Although social work appears to meet the professional requirements, it is a profession with a difference. Unlike the other professions, which tend to mystify people (clients) and create distance and hierarchy (giver and receiver) with expertise and sophistication, the profession of social work and social workers are supposed to stand with people as their partners and work together by breaking the barrier of giver and the receiver to achieve goals set by the people themselves. Do social work professional bodies and social workers work with people as equal partners, or do they try to behave like 'experts', creating a feeling of giver and receiver? Reflecting on this critical question, now let us look at social work professional bodies and professional development of social work in Australia.

Australia is one of the few countries in the world where social work is relatively well organised, with a professional body known as the Australian Association of Social Workers (AASW). It took nearly twenty years to organise this professional body as social work formal training had begun in different states in the 1920s. Under the leadership and vision of Norma Parker the AASW was established in 1946 as a membership body. For a while the AASW also worked collaboratively with the Australian Association of Almoners. However, the almoners later described themselves as medical social workers. While space does not permit delving into historical details, some scholars (Lawrence 1965; Osburn 1999; Mendes 2005) have noted that social workers mostly focused on casework practice, although there was need and demand for social action and community work, and the association was preoccupied with membership eligibility, accreditation standards and the identity of the profession. Due to the changing socioeconomic and political context and growing demand by employers, a new cadre of community and welfare workers were recruited, but they did not have professional social work training and were not members of the AASW, although they did identical work in the field. Whereas the AASW focused on accreditation standards and proper training of social workers, the Australian Social Work Union (ASWU), which emerged in 1976, accommodated community, welfare and youth workers (Thorpe & Petruchenia 1985: 179–98), worked for better industrial conditions and focused on social action and social change activities (Connolly & Harms 2009: 372). The historical divide between social work and welfare, community and youth work and these workers' identical work has continued the confusion in the community about what they do and how they are different.

Before going into further detail about the AASW, it is important to be aware of other similar organisations that have emerged along with the development of the AASW. In 1956 the Australian Council of Social Services (ACOSS), the peak body of the community services and welfare sector, was established. The ACOSS 'aims to reduce poverty and inequality by developing and promoting socially, economically and environmentally responsible public policy and action by government, community and private sectors; and by supporting the role of non-government organisations in providing assistance to vulnerable people and groups in Australia and contributing to national policy-making'. (For further details visit the website: http://www.acoss.org.au/about_us/who_we_are/)

In 1969 the Australian Institute of Welfare Officers was established as a professional body for welfare and community workers. Later it changed its name to the Australian Institute of Community Welfare Workers, and its present name is the Australian Community Workers Association (ACWA). The ACWA's main purpose is to support community workers in every sphere of their work. Its website (http://www.acwa.org.au/about) provides details of its membership, accreditation, code of ethics and continued professional education.

To enhance the quality of social work, welfare work and community development education as a contribution to the well-being of the Australian community, the Australian Association for Social Work and Welfare Education (AASWWE; renamed Australian and New Zealand Social Work and Welfare Education and Research) was established as a membership body, which publishes its own journal, holds annual conferences and provides small research grants (for details visit: http://www.anzswwer.org/).

The National Coalition of Aboriginal and Torres Strait Islander Social Workers Association (NCATSISWA) was established in 2003 to bring together Aboriginal and Torres Strait Islander social workers as a professional body, to exchange information and ideas and to network for the benefit of Aboriginal and Torres Strait Islander communities.

In 2004 the Australian Council of Heads of Schools of Social Work (ACHSSW) was established as a representative body with the overarching aim of promoting the development of social work through education, research and active engagement in the policy and practice arena. To achieve its aims, it regularly holds meetings, discusses relevant issues and meaningfully engages with stakeholders (for details visit: http://www.achssw.org.au/home).

Although the AASW was established much earlier than these organisations, their agenda later became similar, although with a different focus. It may be reasonable to infer that members of some of the other organisations came together to establish them to address certain tasks and needs that AASW was not able to do and/or it excluded some members on the basis of professional training, accreditation standards and so on. However, the AASW tries to maintain cooperative relationship with these organisations, regularly holds discussion with the ACHSSW, sometimes develops joint submissions on relevant issues (e.g. with the NCATSISWA) and holds conferences together with these organisations. Despite the fact that for professional social work and social workers, it is a national body with about 7000 members, perceptually it has not yet attained the status of a peak body such as ACOSS. Whatever its current status and some difficult moments in its development, it has consistently carried out some important functions for its members and for the profession. The details of the AASW vision, mission and objectives and what it does are available on its website (http://www.aasw.asn.au/whoweare/about-aasw). It mainly promotes and regulates the social work profession. To do so, among other things, it establishes, monitors and improves practice and ethical standards, and develops reviews and accredits the education standards for social workers. As building blocks for the profession, these standards are important, and it may be useful to review current standards in brief.

Australian Social Work Education and Accreditation Standards 2012

Australian Social Work Education and Accreditation Standards 2012 (ASWEAS) are detailed on the AASW website (http://www.aasw.asn.au/document/item/3550). With a preamble, the ASWEAS are organised into eight sections. It states broad principles and the minimum standards in regard to social work education content and learning outcomes, structure of the program and its delivery, and organisational and governance arrangements. It also provides procedures and guidelines for accreditation and related policies. Although all sections are important for implementing the accreditation standards, for the purpose of our analyses the third section, relating to educational content and learning outcomes, is important. The AASW requires specific content relating to mental health, child well-being and protection, cross-cultural practice and practice with Aboriginal and Torres Strait Islander peoples and communities in all social work programs (3.3). Foundational knowledge from social sciences to understand society and individual (3.3.7) is needed. In addition, the educational content needs to include interdisciplinary knowledge, skills and values for practice (3.3.1), knowledge of ethics, particularly the AASW code of ethics (3.3.2), method of and skills for social work practice (3.3.3 and 3.3.4), understanding the overall context for practice (3.3.5), different fields of practice from micro to macro levels and field education (3.3.6 and 3.4.) and knowledge of and work with interdisciplinary professional teams (3.3.8).

According to the principles of social work education, the above areas of education content are expected to develop 'attributes of thinking, being and doing'. It also states: 'These attributes are informed by core values, including social justice, human rights, human dignity and equity – "attributes of being".' It also suggests preparing graduates to be self-initiating, critically reflective and innovative. Further it adds 'reflective and reflexive practice, structural analysis, critical thinking and ethical professional behaviour as the core attributes to equip a social work practitioner to enter practice across the range of social work settings, fields of practice and methods' (AASW 2012: 4).

Although the AASW accreditation standards as the minimum requirement are important and necessary to maintain and improve social work education standards, they have come under considerable criticism. The main criticisms are that the standards are too prescriptive, too restrictive in terms of the four core areas as they exclude other important similar areas (e.g. the disabled, the aged or refugees) and that they are too generic and do not allow for any specialisation. Further, there is a great variation in their implementation. They frequently refer to commitment, values and effectiveness, but there is no clear direction or discussion as to how to develop them. For example, most of the standards are around thinking in terms of knowledge component and skills in terms of doing, but very little on being, and being is described in a confusing way under the principles of social work education.

REFLECTIVE EXERCISE 1.9
Do you think all your subjects in the social work course fit into the accreditation standards? Explore.

■ AASW practice standards

Another set of standards developed by the AASW along with the accreditation standards are practice standards (details at the website: http://www.aasw.asn.au/document/item/4551), and both are closely connected. The aims of the practice standards are to provide a basis of expected standards of practice and for applying standards across the diversity of practice, a guide to practice and its assessment and for planning ongoing professional development. It also briefly includes the nature and scope of and the framework for the practice standards. According to the practice standards, any professional social work practice must be based on values and ethics, professionalism, cultural responsiveness and inclusiveness, appropriate knowledge and its application, including communication and interpersonal skills, recording and sharing information, and professional development and supervision, irrespective of whether the practice relates to work with individuals, families, groups and communities, social policy practice, management, leadership and administration, education and training, and research and evaluation (AASW 2013).

There are eight practice standards relating to values and ethics, professionalism, cultural responsiveness and inclusiveness, gaining knowledge and applying it, communication and interpersonal skills, recording and sharing information, and professional development and supervision. There are several indicators under each standard.

Most of the practice standards focus on 'doing', although knowledge for practice and the application of knowledge to practice emphasise 'thinking'-related activities. There is very little on the 'being' of a social work practitioner and its role in effective practice. However, some of the indicators from values and ethics and professionalism practice standards, such as critical reflection and examination of personal and professional values and ethics, integrity and accountability, modelling social work values, acting in a principled and accountable manner, maintaining appropriate professional/personal boundaries, declaring conflicts of interest and deciding to use appropriate methods can be linked to the being of a social worker, although practice standards and indicators are not explicit about this. One of the three values, professional integrity, on which practice standards are based, is not clearly spelled out. What better drives these practice standards?

REFLECTIVE EXERCISE 1.10
Compare and contrast your field placement activities with practice standards. What similarities and/or differences can you notice?

▦ AASW code of ethics

The social work code of ethics is fundamental to the accreditation and practice standards. Every social worker needs to carefully study the social work code of ethics (details of which may be viewed at http://www.aasw.asn.au/document/item/740) to understand the meaning of social work, its aims, objectives, values and principles. The minimum ethical standards or guidelines for practice are important. Values such as respect for persons, social justice and professional integrity influence social workers' practice. The code also states social workers' responsibilities relating to ethical practice, clients, colleagues, workplace, education and research. It emphasises acquiring knowledge for practice and provides guidelines for resolving ethical issues (see AASW 2010).

Most of it focuses on what social workers should do by adhering to stated values and ethical practice processes. However, the code does not well discuss how social workers themselves should develop so as to practice better. It often states the profession's and social workers' commitment to values and aims of social work, and ethical practice. How can one prepare more committed social workers? In an indirect way, under professional integrity, the code states that 'The social work profession values honesty, transparency, reliability, empathy, reflective self-awareness, discernment, competence and commitment'. There is also emphasis on quality of service and improving it, judgement in terms of decision-making and accountability. Merely valuing these qualities or virtues in a code of ethics is not adequate. It is crucial to focus on developing them in social workers, which appears to be missing in the code of ethics and the social work profession and practice. In addition, all those social workers who are not members of the AASW are not obliged to follow the code. But certain qualities are important to all social workers. Hence, the next section discusses this missing element in terms of 'being' of social workers along with thinking and doing.

◼ Thinking, doing and being in social work practice

As referred to under the principles of education above, in social work education and practice social workers often refer to a commonly used phrase, 'thinking, doing and being'. It is important to understand each one of these terms and how they are connected to (reflective) social work practice.

Thinking

When social workers generally use the term 'thinking' along with doing and being, they tend to understand it as (social work) theory/knowledge and how they apply such theory and knowledge in what they do. The understanding of theory/knowledge in terms of thinking involves cognitive processes (the biological/neurological processes of the brain that facilitate thought). Thinking or theory/knowledge has two interlinked components: first, the object or content of thinking and, second, the way we think about (process) the content. The components of thinking, content and process can be further delineated as follows in table 1.1.

Table 1.1 Key elements of the content and process of thinking

Content	Existing knowledge
	Existing theory
	Existing understandings and frameworks including personal and professional knowledge
	Contextual issues related to both general matters (paradigms, rules, legislation) and specific matters (this client, this community, this problem, these strengths)
Process	Usual thinking
	Critical thinking
	Critical reflection
	Systemic/logical thinking
	Lateral/creative thinking

The content of social workers' thinking can include existing knowledge, theory (e.g. psychological or political theory, systems theory) and models and frameworks (e.g. solution-focused models, narrative therapy, models of community development, understandings about violence, bonding and attachment). It also includes personal and professional knowledge (e.g. what could I personally and professionally bring to this situation and what the professional/organisational imperatives are; the AASW code of ethics) and knowledge about the context (e.g. whether it is a matrilineal or patrilineal society or neither; background and issues of clients and communities; child protection laws, etc). It may also include the logical extension of a particular course of action, including short- and long-term probable or possible consequences. For example, if we do so, is it a precedent with short- and long-term implications? It will necessarily involve thinking about the potential rewards and potential consequences and an assessment of the probability of their occurrence and the severity of their occurrence. This has elements of risk-predicting philosophy but is different in that it is both an intuitive and systemic assessment rather than only an actuarial assessment. The content component of thinking also recognises that the subject matter of the thinking may not be entirely and accurately known, nor strictly logical or correctly sequenced.

Critical thinking

How social workers think about the content that is the process of thinking, in terms of critical, reflective, logical and lateral thinking, is crucial for their practice. Critical thinking is a process of determining the authenticity, accuracy or value of something. It is characterised by the ability to seek reasons and alternatives, perceive the total situation, and change one's view on the basis of evidence. It is sometimes called 'logical' or 'analytical' thinking. Critical thinking consists of mental processes of discernment, analysis and assessment. It includes all possible processes of reflecting upon real or imagined possibilities in order to form a solid judgement that reconciles the evidence with common sense and the set of known circumstances. Critical thinking, according to Brookfield (1987: 1), involves a process of 'calling into question the assumptions underlying our customary, habitual ways of thinking and acting and then being ready to think and act differently on the basis of the critical questioning'. Critical thinking and critical reflection appear to go together. According to Fook and Gardner (2007: 51), critical reflection is a structured process designed to 'unsettle the fundamental (and dominant) thinking implicit in professional practice in order to see other ways of practising'. This concept will be further developed in the next chapter.

Systemic thinking

Systemic thinking is a social approach that uses systems theories to create desired outcomes or change. It is an approach to problem-solving that views certain 'problems' as a part of the overall system. Solutions to the problems may lie within or outside the system, and focusing on the problems may only further develop the undesired element or problem and negate possible solutions. Logical thinking classifies the structure of statements and arguments, both through the study of formal systems of deduction and inference and through the study of arguments. Logic is also commonly used in argumentation theory and is a step-by-step and convergent approach to thinking (Cox & Willard 1982). It is closely related to reasoning. Reasoning is the mental process of looking for reasons for beliefs, conclusions, actions or feelings. It includes both inductive (drives from particularity to generality) and deductive (drives from generality to particularity) reasoning. Human beings have the ability to engage in reasoning about their own reasoning through introspection and self-reflection.

Creative or lateral thinking

Creative (often termed 'lateral') thinking is a novel way of seeing or doing things that is characterised by four components:

- fluency (generating many ideas)
- flexibility (shifting perspective easily)
- originality (conceiving of something new)
- elaboration (building on other ideas).

De Bono (1985) defines lateral thinking as methods of thinking concerned with changing concepts and perception. Lateral thinking is about reasoning that is not immediately obvious and about ideas that may not be obtainable by using only traditional step-by-step logic. It is a divergent approach. He characterises thinking under six 'hats', which allow for consideration of facts and data (white hat), emotions and intuition (red hat), logical negative approaches (black hat), positive and optimistic thinking (yellow hat), creative thinking (green hat) and process control thinking (blue hat).

Divergent and convergent thinking

We consider inductive and deductive reasoning, critical thinking or reflection, systemic or logical thinking and lateral or creative thinking as complementary – in a powerful partnership – that leads to better theory building and better practice. Social workers require thinking that is both inductive and deductive as well as divergent and convergent. Divergent thinking uses the creativity (lateral approaches) to play 'what if?' – establishing multiple scenarios and ideas to consider as hypotheses. Convergent thinking uses sound reasoning and common sense to analyse possibilities and to select the hypothesis with the greatest potential on the basis of a set of criteria for expected outcomes. These skills (and others) enable social workers to assess unfamiliar scenarios, to generate plausible options for action, to evaluate client capacity and to arrive at well-reasoned and defensible judgements (Crisp et al. 2004; O'Hara & Webster 2006).

REFLECTIVE EXERCISE 1.12
What is your understanding of thinking? What do you think of the way the concept of thinking is discussed here?

Doing

When social workers refer to 'doing' along with thinking and being, generally it refers to what social workers do or perform in practice. Thus 'doing' also refers to roles of social workers and skills they employ in performing those roles. It may also be noted that some of the skills, such as demonstrating empathy, genuineness, warmth and so on, are embedded in 'being' and that it is difficult to separate them except for heuristic purposes. A number of social work texts (e.g. Hepworth, Rooney & Larsen 1997; Lister 1987; Mowbray 1996; Trevethick 2012) list 'doings' of social workers in terms of roles and skills. As an example, drawing from Zastrow's (2010: 16–18) description of roles of social workers, table 1.2 shows what social workers do in practice. The AASW practice standards and code of ethics, as stated earlier, often refer to these roles and skills.

Table 1.2 Roles and skills (doings) of social workers

Enabling	Involves helping to articulate their needs, clarify and identify problems, explore solutions and develop capacities to deal with future problem-solving more effectively.
Brokering	Involves linking individuals and groups with the services or personnel that they need.
Advocating	Involves information collection arguing for the correctness of client's needs and requesting and challenging institutional decisions that limit or deny services.
Empowering	Involves social workers developing the capacity of clients to understand their environment, make choices, take responsibility for those choices and to influence their life through the organisations and environments in which they live.
Activism	Is concerned with social justice, inequality and deprivation and seeks to bring basic institutional change by shifting power and resources to disadvantaged groups. It may involve confrontation, conflict, negotiation, community organisation and mobilisation.
Mediating	Involves intervening in disputes between parties in order to help them find compromise, reconcile differences and reach contractual or covenantal agreements. Mediation involves remaining neutral and making sure that both parties in a dispute understand their positions by clarifying, recognising miscommunications and helping the parties present their case clearly.
Negotiating	Is somewhat like mediating, and brings together those who are in conflict over one or more issues in order to arrive at a compromise and mutually agreed solution. A negotiator may be aligned with one side or the other.
Educating	Involves information-giving and teaching new and adaptive skills. Initiating calls attention to a problem or a potential problem and involves the social worker recognising the likely outcome and consequences in the future.
Coordinating	Involves bringing different components into focus. Often now referred to as case management, coordination involves ensuring that there is no duplication of services or conflict in objectives or, where there is conflict between objectives, that the conflict is managed effectively.
Researching	Involves seeking out appropriate information, evaluating that information, applying it to practice settings, assessing the merits and shortcomings of interventions or of services. Researching can be at an individual level (e.g. researching a client's health situation) or at the mezzo or macro levels.
Group facilitating	Involves leading others through a group experience with a therapy group, education group, a self-help group or many other forms of group.
Public speaking	Involves informing others of the availability of services or advocating the development of new services. This public speaking may be an interagency meeting, in the press, on radio or television, at forums, conferences or in small networks.

It may be noted that the social workers' doings in terms of roles and skills are largely (but not exclusively) process-oriented rather than being specifically 'outcome'- or even objective-oriented. The 'doing' of social work varies from practice situation to practice situation and from client to client. Finally, the list is neither exhaustive nor inclusive of all roles and skills.

Being

Although social workers often use the phrase 'thinking, doing and being', the concept of being is not as clear as the concept of 'thinking' and 'doing'. Social work literature and practice often refers to thinking and doing and doing and thinking; that is, theory and practice and practice and theory in a binary form to the neglect of being. The meaning of 'being' differs according to different disciplinary traditions. For example, in the discipline of philosophy, 'being' has existential and metaphysical connotations. There is a need to develop the concept of being in the social work discipline and use it on a par with thinking and doing. When social workers refer to 'thinking, doing and being', what do they mean by 'being'? The dynamic concept of being may be constructed in terms of the physical/organic, mental/emotional, social/relational and spiritual/existential dimensions of it. Being involves recognising that humans are both shaped by and are shapers of the environment – physically, socially, ecologically and spiritually (see figure 1.1).

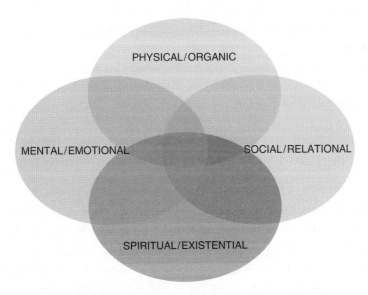

Figure 1.1 Dimensions of being

Understanding the self or 'being' of the social worker (and the 'client') is clearly important. The terms 'being', 'self', 'identity', 'integrity' and 'character' are sometimes used interchangeably in different contexts. Being involves concepts of personhood and the self. The use of self is not a new concept in social work, but it is widely located (O'Connor & McDermott 1997; Payne 1997a; Hepworth, Rooney & Larsen 1997), variously defined and ambiguous (Dewane 2006: 543). It is useful to identify and delineate aspects of the self (Zubrzycki 1999).

Interestingly, the concept of the use of self is not applied to 'clients' or others involved with social workers. Muran et al. (2001) provides an analysis of the term 'self' while Dewane (2006: 544) operationalises the use of self under five headings:

- use of personality
- use of belief systems
- use of relational dynamics
- use of anxiety
- use of self-disclosure.

Davies (1994: 174–5) describes a worker's self as 'an identifiable person ... her idiosyncrasies ... her height, her age, her sex, her ethnic origins, her temper, her energy, her prejudices – these are the qualities she has to work with, for better or worse'. Heydt and Sherman (2005: 25–6) argue that the self is an instrument and in fact the primary instrument that a social worker has to facilitate change. They say that the conscious use of self purposefully and intentionally allows for 'his or her motivation and capacity to communicate and interact with others in ways that facilitate change ... the skilled worker is purposefully making use of his or her unique manner and style in relating to others and building positive helping relationships with clients is fundamental to social work practice'.

Arnd-Caddington and Pozzuto (2006: 109) assert that the term 'use of self' has developed from the recognition of the importance of the relationship between a social worker and the client, and state that 'over time the concept of relationship has evolved into the term "use of self"'. The term 'use of self' has been applied to honesty and spontaneity (Davies 1994), to genuineness, vulnerability and self-awareness (Edwards & Bess 1998) and to mindfulness of one's belief system and judicious self-disclosure (Dewane 2006). These can be criticised as the self as an object. Constructionist psychotherapies would address the self as non-concrete and non-continuous (Gergan 1999; Lax 1996). Gergan, for example, says that 'the concept of the self as an integral, bounded agent is slowly becoming untenable' (1999: 202). Lax considers the self as a product of interacting with others. Arnd-Caddington and Pozzuto (2006: 135–6) citing Mead (1934) argue: 'The self has a character which is different from that of the physiological organism proper. The self is something which has a development; it is not initially there, at birth, but arises in the process of social experience and activity, that develops in the given individual as a result of his relations to that process as a whole and to other individuals within that process.'

Virtue ethics and being

The above discussion suggests that self is an important part of being and that it is developed over a period of time in interaction with others. The social work profession, education and training need to interact with workers in such way that it develops a 'social work self' in them. One significant aspect of self-development and being is character, qualities or virtue development, which is closely connected to virtue ethics. The conscious construction of being based on virtues is important because social work thinking and doing are dominated by deontology (the study of what is morally obligatory, permissible, right or wrong) (Kant 1964), which focuses on moral rules for action based on reason and rationality, objectivity, impartiality, unbiasedness, duty and respect for others, and the ethic of consequentialism (based on the tenets of hedonism – maximising pleasure and minimising pain) and utilitarianism (the greatest happiness of the greatest number of people). Here the consequence or the outcome is more important, although the action or the process of producing the outcome has to be morally right. These ethical frameworks focus on rule-bound actions and outcomes and ignore the actor.

Countering the influences of deontology and consequentialism or utilitarianism and to overcome their weaknesses, McBeath and Webb (2002) contend that social work ethics – and thereby practice – needs to significantly draw on virtue ethics. Social workers on a daily basis deal with complex, unpredictable and uncertain situations, and ways of doing or intervening in such situations cannot be defined and prescribed in terms of strict rules, procedures, duties or conduct. Rather than focusing only on the action and outcome, it is useful to focus on the actor. What social workers are is as important as what they do. Once the core virtues are developed in them, those virtues will help them to effectively deal with unpredictable and uncertain situations.

McBeath and Webb (2002: 1020) state: '... virtue ethics can be used to offer an account of the modes of moral existence shaping *the being* of a good social worker. More simply then, the basic question is not what is good social work, but rather what is a good social worker?' A small number of social work ethicists are also of the view that virtue ethics is relevant for social work practice (see Hugman & Smith 1995; Banks 2006; Bowles et al. 2006). The virtue theory is broadly influenced by the Platonic and Aristotelian notions of what is excellent (*areté*), what is practical and wise (*phronesis*) and what typifies human flourishing (eudaimonia), although Aristotle first emphasised the good of the larger community, then the good of the individual (Aristotle 1976). Aristotle's doctrine of mean provides the basis for virtues. The prudence or temperance of a worker helps to choose between two extremes in a balanced way that suits the situation.

Hence, for the purpose of this book, being means virtues of social workers and virtue-led social work practice. Macbeith and Webb (2002: 1020) observe:

> The virtues are the acquired inner qualities of humans – character – the possession of which, if deployed in due measure, will typically contribute to the realisation of the good life or 'eudaimonia'. The role of the virtuous social worker is shown to be one that necessitates appropriate application of intellectual and practical virtues such as justice, reflection, perception, judgement, bravery, prudence, liberality and temperance. This 'self flourishing' worker, in bringing together the capacity of theoretical and practical action, makes possible a hermeneutic or interpretive praxis best appraised in dialogue with fellow practitioners and clients.

Seligman (2002: 132) and researchers involved in the positive psychology movement identify twenty-four virtues that they divide into six groupings. These are:

1 wisdom and knowledge (creativity, curiosity, open-mindedness, love of learning, perspective)
2 courage (bravery, persistence, integrity, vitality)
3 humanity (love, kindness, social intelligence)
4 justice (citizenship, fairness, leadership)
5 temperance (forgiveness and mercy, humility and modesty, prudence, self-regulation)
6 transcendence (appreciation of beauty and excellence, gratitude, hope, humour, spirituality).

Further, from a theological perspective similar virtues have been discussed. For example, eight virtues can be elicited from Buddhism's Noble Eightfold Path: right viewpoint, right values, right speech, right actions, right livelihood, right effort, right mindfulness and right meditation. In his book *Mere Christianity* the philosopher C. S. Lewis, who is arguably the most widely read Christian theologian of the twentieth century, refers to seven virtues – four of which he calls pivotal or cardinal virtues – and three as theological virtues (2001: 71–3). The cardinal virtues (which are also known as the four classical Western virtues and were listed at least by Plato) are:

1 prudence (by which Lewis means practical common sense and having the ability to think about what you are doing and what will come of it)
2 temperance (by which he means going to the right length and no further)
3 justice (by which he means fairness, including honesty, give and take, truthfulness, keeping promises), and

4 fortitude (by which he means courage).

The three theological virtues are (Lewis 2001: 113–29):

1 charity (by which he means love in the Christian sense, which includes forgiveness and that sense of doing the best for someone else)

2 hope (by which he means the continual looking forward to the eternal world – not as a form of escapism but as a means of giving direction and purpose), and

3 faith (by which Lewis means holding on to things that your reason has accepted in spite of changing emotions and feelings).

We believe that these and similar virtues are relevant for developing the being of social workers. As mentioned earlier, some aspects of professional integrity can be developed as virtues of social workers. These are social workers' commitment to values and aims of social work, and ethical practice, honesty, transparency, reliability, empathy, reflective self-awareness, discernment, competence, judgement in terms of decision-making, accountability and quality service.

It is unrealistic and artificial to separate thinking, doing and being, and to underplay being by just focusing on thinking and doing. Thinking, doing and being are closely connected (see figure 1.2), and being is central to thinking and doing. Being in terms of virtue-led practice can better drive thinking and doing and doing and thinking. The sequence also needs to be reversed so that we first focus on building being, which will lead to theory and practice and practice and theory reflective integration and to creating good and happy communities and individuals.

Hence, in social work being may be understood as a dynamic and developing total state of a social worker, who consciously learns to continuously reflect on self and others with a view to raising critical self- and social awareness, internalising values and cultivating virtues to effectively synthesise thinking and doing and doing and thinking to achieve better outcomes for people and communities. In the contemporary professional social work practice, explicit and focused cultivation of virtues as a significant

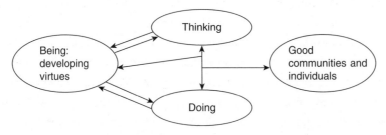

Figure 1.2 Linking being, thinking and doing

aspect of social workers' being is missing. In this book, we attempt to show how such a being can be developed and employed in all social work practice methods.

REFLECTIVE EXERCISE 1.14

What are your views about the way being is defined and discussed in this chapter? Do you think being is underdeveloped and underrecognised in social work? If being needs to be described in terms of social workers' virtues, what kind of virtues social workers should have?

Conclusion

The main objectives of this chapter were to discuss the meaning and history of social work, broad trends in social work education and practice, the development of the social work profession in Australia and the concepts of thinking, doing and being. Accordingly, we have critically discussed the meaning of social work as an evolving concept and shown how the meaning has changed over time to respond to criticisms and to include all perspectives. Social work is work done for others and not for oneself. It is problematic to discuss the origin and history of social work. The origin of professional social work has been traced to voluntary efforts through the development of charity organisation societies and settlement houses in the UK and USA. Early professional social work training began in Europe in the late nineteenth century and in Australia in the 1920s. Two broad trends may be identified and analysed in the development of professional social work. They are the dominance of the remedially oriented medical model of social work and developmental social work and the recent focus on a social development agenda.

Seven critical observations have been made about professional social work in Australia, which has made significant contributions, but many issues remain to be addressed. Social work as a profession is relatively well established in Australia, although it appears to have had a troubled history. It has excluded some workers who do identical work. It appears that since the AASW as a professional body was not able to address certain needs and issues and/or excluded certain groups, many other professional bodies (ACOSS, ACWA, NCATSISWA, AASWWE, ACHSSW) have emerged, although the AASW cooperatively works with most of them. The AASW mainly promotes and regulates the social work profession by establishing, monitoring and improving practice and ethical standards and by accrediting education standards for social workers. Our review of the AASW accreditation and practice standards and code of ethics suggested that these focus in an imbalanced way on thinking, theory and knowledge and doing – on practice to the neglect of being – virtues of social workers. Towards addressing this gap, the final section of the chapter has discussed the concept of thinking, doing and being, and has shown how these are closely connected and how being drives thinking and doing. It is important to build the being of social workers in order to enhance the quality of social work practice.

▦ Questions and exercises

1 Critically reflect on the definitions of social work.
2 Try to describe the meaning of social work as understood by you.
3 How and why does the meaning of social work matter for a social worker's identity?
4 Do you think the history of social work should be restricted to professional social work, or do we need to look at the broader and deeper history to understand social practices of the past?
5 What are the major historical influences on Australian social work education and practice?
6 Discuss the important differences between the medical model and developmental model of social work.
7 What are your views on the social work and social development agenda? Do you think it fits the development of social work?
8 What are the main features and issues of professional social work in Australia?
9 What do you think can be done to move or expand from remedial to developmental social work and many of its elements such as human rights, social justice and critical, anti-discriminatory and anti-oppressive practices?
10 View the websites of relevant professional organisations, review their aims and objectives, and critically compare them with AASW aims and objectives.
11 Critically review the AASW code of ethics and practice standards and refer to them as often as you need to.
12 What is your understanding of thinking, doing and being?
13 Which social work roles do you like?
14 Try to describe your being. What are the virtues you think you need to strengthen?
15 Do you think a focus on being helps to improve practice?

2

A reflective social work practice model: blending thinking, doing and being with PEOPLE

B EING REFLECTIVE IS an important and useful virtue. Reflective practice has been often referred to in social work education and practice and the AASW code of ethics, and for many social workers it has become a common phrase. As reflective practice is both a virtue and a practice approach, it needs to be properly understood, internalised and practised. Hence, the core ideas contained in this chapter are the conceptual and theoretical basis of reflective practice and a reflective social work practical model that focuses on explicit use of being in practice along with thinking and doing. The content of this chapter is useful and applicable to any social work theory and practice subjects, whether they are offered in an integrated manner, combining work with individuals, groups, communities and organisations, or as separate study units. As an example, to demonstrate the use of the reflective social work practice model blending being, thinking and doing will be applied to social work practice methods in chapters 3 to 7. These chapters will show students and practitioners how to use reflective practice with a focus on being, thinking and doing in their work.

▦ Chapter objectives

This chapter discusses the meaning, significance and theoretical bases of reflective practice and a reflective social work practice model blending being, thinking and doing. After studying this chapter, readers should be able to reflect on:

- the meaning of reflection, reflective practice, critical reflective practice, reflexivity and reflexive practice
- significance and the use of reflective practice in social work
- theoretical bases of reflective practice
- a reflective social work practice model blending being, thinking and doing with PEOPLE.

▦ Main themes and concepts used

The main theme of this chapter is reflective practice and a model for reflective practice in social work. It first discusses the meaning of reflective practice and related concepts such as critical reflection, critical reflective practice, reflexivity and reflexive practice. Then it looks at the significance of reflective practice and why social workers should use it. The next section covers the range of theories that underpin reflective practice. In the latter half of the chapter, we present a reflective social work practice model that draws on thinking, doing and being and delineates into participants, environmental scan, objectives, participation processes, labour and evaluation, which we abbreviate as the PEOPLE model. As part of the model, it includes a framework – based on being, thinking and doing, and doing and thinking – for reflection and analysis. The model is useful for reflective social work practice across any methods of social work practice.

▦ Meaning of reflective practice and its variants

Despite some confusion and ambiguity, reflective practice has become an increasingly influential idea in social work education and practice (Wilson 2013). One way of reducing the confusion and ambiguity and of developing clarity is to define various phrases related to reflective practice. Consider the following terms:

- reflect
- reflection
- reflective practice
- critical
- critical reflective practice
- reflexivity and reflexive practice.

Let us first look at the terms 'reflect', 'reflection' and 'reflective practice'. The *Oxford Dictionary*'s meaning of 'reflect' is to think deeply about, or remind oneself of, past events. Thus reflection is thought or memory of past events (Cowie 1993). The term 'reflection' is derived from the Latin term *reflectere*, meaning 'to bend back'. It is bending back to the past event, nowhere else. In social work education and practice, reflective practice connotes practitioners, with self- and social awareness, going back to their practice experiences and thinking about such experiences in terms of what the problem, need and context were. What, how and why did I do about the problem or need or context? Are there better ways of bringing 'thinking, doing and being' together to see better outcomes?

According to Fitzgerald (1994: 67), reflection is 'the retrospective contemplation of practice undertaken in order to uncover the knowledge used in a particular situation, by analyzing and interpreting the information recalled'. We have revised this definition to further improve it. Reflective social work practice is the retrospective contemplation of practice undertaken in order to uncover the knowledge used, skills used and the doing, and the being or self used in a particular situation, by analysing, interpreting and reinterpreting the information recalled to improve and/or replicate the practice if relevant and applicable. Simply, reflective practice is a learning approach; learning by doing and learning to do better and create knowledge through reflections.

Reflections on, in and for practice

Three further variations on reflective practice are reflections on practice, reflection in practice and reflection for practice. 'Reflections on practice' refers to social workers reflecting on their practice event after that event is completed, to derive learning and new understanding from the event. 'Reflections in practice' refers to social workers reflecting in the process of a practising event, which may be based on their intuition, creativity and practice wisdom as decisions are taken in the moment (Schon 1983; Atkinson & Claxton 2000). Pierson and Thomas (2010: 434) describe it as 'the more immediate ability to review what one is doing when it is being done. This skill requires practitioners to be able to "take time out" and not be pressed into poor decisions through unthinking habitual behaviour or because of, for example, immediate pressures from service users or management.' Critiquing the above two types of reflection, Thompson and Pascal (2012: 317) add the third type, namely, reflection for practice. 'It refers to the process of planning, thinking ahead about what is to come, so that we can draw on our experience (and the professional knowledge base implicit within it) in order to make the best use of the time resources available to us.' Such an addition appears important, but it creates a problem for the original concept of reflection that is thinking about the past event. If it is to include forethought, the dictionary meaning of reflection has to be expanded or a new term, 'foreflection', needs to be coined.

Critical reflection and critical reflective practice

It is also common to see the use of the phrases 'critical reflection' and 'critical reflective practice'. Do these terms make any difference in understanding and practising reflective social work practice? The term 'critical' has two meanings, and both can be used simultaneously and separately. Depending upon the context, readers need to understand how it is used. The first meaning is the well-emphasised dictionary meaning. 'Critical' simply means crucial or very important. It also means identifying weaknesses and strengths (although the dictionary refers to looking for or pointing out only faults).

In addition, it means the art of making judgement on literature, art and so on (Cowie 1993). If we perceive social work practice as an art, passing judgement (undertaking evaluation) on such practice involves criticalness. Critical also includes being systematic, analytical and rigorous (Rolfe, Jasper & Freshwater 2011). In this sense, for any professional practice, reflective practice has to be critical irrespective of the use of the term critical.

The second meaning of the critical reflective practice is ideologically oriented and theory laden. Here the term 'critical' is linked to Marxist thoughts on economic conditions and class struggle, and their derivatives. Through critical reflective practice, social workers look at class, race, gender and similar issues and factors, and reflect on and in their (power) relationship in causing deprivation, oppression, discrimination, violation of human rights and injustice for individuals, families and groups and communities, and work towards transforming structural relationships through anti-discriminatory and anti-oppressive practice to enable, empower and emancipate people and communities. Thompson and Thompson (2008) refers to this as breadth dimension of the critical, and their depth dimension of the critical includes being able to look beneath the surface of a situation, to see what assumptions are being made and what thoughts, feelings and values are being drawn upon.

Rolfe et al. (2011) link critical reflection to Habermas' (1987) 'critical science'. They state: 'For Habermas, to be critical is to be aware of, and alert to, the external and internal constraints and forces that prevent us from seeing the world as it really is.' Critical reflection involves addressing such constraints and facilitating the transformation. Social work has an inbuilt element and requirement of self- and social awareness that calls for both self- and social analysis, which is also referred as critical reflective practice, although many social workers have been undertaking such an analysis long before critical reflective practice emerged.

Critical reflective practice also refers to research. Rolfe et al. (2011: 6) suggest that 'critical reflection is a way for practitioners to add to their evidence-base by conducting research into their own practice'. They claim 'critical reflection as a collection of methodologies and methods similar to existing and established research methodologies and methods for generating data, constructing knowledge and applying it to practice'.

Critical reflective practice is also associated with postmodern thoughts as it offers another and/or an alternative way of creating knowledge for practice, distinct from modernism – reason, technical rationality and positivism. For example, Fook (2002; 2004: 20) has tried to bring together critical postmodern thoughts and critical reflective practice to develop a broader framework for analysis and understanding, which allows for multiple and diverse construction and deconstruction of similar situations. Such an approach has the potential to point out and address dominant and exploitative power relations and structures.

Reflexivity and reflexive practice

Finally, two more terms to be understood are reflexivity and reflexive practice. In the reflective practice literature, the terms 'reflective' and 'reflexive' have sometimes been used interchangeably and sometimes used separately (Thompson & Pascal 2012). This mix-up has caused or has the potential to cause confusion for readers. The dictionary meaning of 'reflex' is an involuntary or automatic action (e.g. sneezing or shivering) made instinctively in response to a stimulus. It denotes self-directed action or activity. In reflection, you go back to the past event, and in reflexivity you turn to action. Reflective practice also has an action element, and reflexivity also has an action element, except that the latter is involuntary or automatic. Then what is reflexivity and reflexive practice in the context of reflective practice? Bruce's (2013: 120) analysis suggests that reflexive practice is a part of reflective practice 'as it encourages the development of greater awareness of the underlying assumptions that influence the way we make sense of situations'. Citing Sheppard (2007), Bruce states: 'It is this high degree of self-awareness, role-awareness and awareness of the assumptions that inform our perception of situations that is a distinguishing feature of reflexive practitioners.'

Reflexivity is commonly used in research methodology, particularly in ethnography. From the research perspective, Koch and Harrington (1998) have identified four forms of reflexivity. These are:

1 sustaining objectivity in the positivist tradition
2 raising questions about how knowledge is generated and validated through epistemology
3 a critical standpoint, in which researchers locate themselves within political and social positions, and
4 a feminist standpoint, in which researchers embody and perform the politics of the researcher–participant relationship (Rolfe et al. 2011: 185).

To Fook (1999: 45), reflexivity is 'an ability to recognize our own influence – and the influence of our social and cultural contexts on research, the type of knowledge we create, and the way we create it. In this sense, then, it is about factoring ourselves as players into the situations we practice in.' From a theoretical point of view, 'For both critical realists and reflexive modernisation theorists, reflexivity describes active self-reflection, and personal biographical management on the basis of an active engagement with a complex and changing social world' (Farrugia 2013: 294). In essence, reflexivity combines self-reflection and action or practice. So reflective practice is reflexivity. But the term 'reflexive practice' appears incorrect to us as practice (i.e. action) is embedded in reflexivity.

In summary, one simplistic way of clarifying the meaning discussed above is that reflection involves deeply and critically thinking about the past practice event in order to improve and/or replicate good practice. Reflective practice involves using those critical reflections for better practice and generating practice-based knowledge. A reflexive practitioner is one who has become proficient in using reflective practice.

REFLECTIVE EXERCISE 2.1

Discuss the main difference between reflective practice, critical reflective practice and reflexivity.

Significance and the use of reflective practice

Reflective practice is important and useful from the perspectives of self-learning and education, practice and creating knowledge. It is a powerful method of learning and improving oneself; and of changing oneself and others. It leads to better ways of professional practice to bring change. It contributes to generating practice-based knowledge. Reflective practice is close to the nature of social work education and practice. Long before reflective practice emerged as a new approach to professional practice, social work had some of its elements from the very beginning. As part of their preparation for professional social work, social workers are trained to raise their self- and social awareness so as to improve the quality of their practice. Awareness-raising as part of social workers' being is a continuous process. That is why the process of reflective practice sits very well with social work, which has openly embraced it. Continuous learning and self-improvement is needed in any professional practice. The AASW Code of Ethics, as part of professional integrity, clearly states that it values reflective self-awareness. One of the indicators in the practice standards requires social workers to demonstrate the ability to engage in critical reflective practice in supervision and practice. Similarly, in the education accreditation standards, reflective thinking and analysis is one of the important skills listed. It gives primacy to reflective practice and expects social work graduates to be critically reflective (see chapter 1).

Social workers deal with difficult, complex and unpredictable situations in their practice on a day-to-day basis. There is a danger of routinisation and habitual decision-making. Reflective practice helps to guard against such dangers, and reflections often provide insights for self-learning from practice and improving practice. Reflective practice also helps to challenge and change oppressive and discriminatory practices. Most importantly, it helps to examine dilemmas in practice and take appropriate decisions. It creates opportunities for emancipatory practice in some situations where practitioners feel limited to practice in critical ways (Fook 2004). For example, organisational cultures dominated by managerialism and procedural forms of practice might not encourage a reflective approach (Baldwin 2004). Sharing critical reflections helps to prevent mistakes and replicate good practices. Ongoing reflective practice helps social workers to remain competent and confident in their practice (Bruce 2013).

Finally, reflective practice can be consciously used to create practice-based knowledge. Under the evidence-based, practice-dominated culture, some social work practice contexts are disadvantaged as it is difficult to create evidence from the positivist research framework. Documentation of critical reflections and their use in practice provides alternative evidence for practice. It also helps to question or break the theory–practice linear linkage as sometimes some theories may not make any sense in practice. Alternatively, it helps to create practice-led knowledge and theories.

It may be noted that the significance and usefulness of reflective practice may be lost if it is not practised the way it should be. It is good to be aware that sometimes for some practitioners engaging in reflection can be an anxiety-provoking and not always constructive experience (Rossiter 2005; Litvack, Bogo & Mishna 2010). Overly prescriptive and 'routinised' approaches to reflection may inhibit learning (Wilson 2013: 168).

REFLECTIVE EXERCISE 2.2
What is the significance of reflective practice? How does reflective practice help you as a social worker?

▨ Theoretical bases of reflective practice

Although reflective practice has highly influenced many professional practices, including social work and other helping professions, its theoretical foundations are not well established and are poorly developed and recently contemplated (Bruce 2013; Rolfe et al. 2011; Thomson & Pascal 2012). In a way, the theoretical underpinnings of reflective practice are limited by what we have read and understood, and our ability to theorise it, for which there is enough scope. The notion of reflection has been traced to Socrates' assertion that the 'unexamined life is not worth living', about 2500 years ago (Rolfe, Jasper & Freshwater 2011). Acharya (Basava International Foundation 2009: xi) notes that Indian philosophy and religion has constantly been reflective, analytical and reformative. In the twelfth century, Basavanna, a revolutionary social reformer, considered a universal guru, had introduced reflective practice known as 'Hall of Experience' (Anubhava Mantapa), where people from all walks of life regularly came together to share and deliberate their experiences and implemented great human values such as care for others, equality, freedom and democracy, participation of women, much before the European Reformation in the sixteenth century and the Enlightenment in the eighteenth century. Hence the idea of reflecting on and learning from experiences and using the same for individual and societal benefit is not new.

John Dewey's reflective learning

John Dewey was one of the early proponents of reflective learning. His model of reflective learning focused on experience, which is doing, observation and reflection on it by raising critical questions. Reflections through questioning the experience will result in new learning and knowledge, and brings together knower and knowledge. To Dewey, experience–reflection–knowledge is a continuous process and not a one-off event. Table 2.1 shows principles, focus and the limitations of this model. Gibbs (1988), drawing on Dewey's reflective learning model, has suggested six questions for reflection. In a circular sequence form, these questions are:

- What happened? (description)
- What were you thinking and feeling? (feelings)
- What was good and bad about the experience? (evaluation)
- What sense can you make of the situation? (analysis)
- What else could you have done? (conclusion)
- If it arose again, what would you do? (action plan)

Although the model is useful, its main limitation is that it focuses more on learning and education than on practice.

Donald Schon's reflective practice

Building on John Dewey's work, Donald Schon's thoughts on reflective practice focused on improving professional practice that was dominated by theoretical or technical knowledge. However, professionals were finding the gap between what they do and the theoretical knowledge they have with them. That is why they were not able to effectively address changing needs of modern life. Schon's reflective theory suggested that practitioners' reflections on and in practice will enable them to generate knowledge from practice and integrate such knowledge with theory. That is, instead of applying technical and theoretical knowledge to practice, practice-knowledge and theory have to be integrated. Schon believed that his model of knowing-in-action helps to synthesise doing and thinking and leads to new understanding and change that is needed to meet the demands of the context. Schon (1983) states that, when the practitioner reflects in action, her/his experimenting is at once exploratory (trial and error, get the feel of things), move testing (deliberate action to see intended change) and hypothesis testing (based on practice theories). Reflection in action is progressive and developmental for many practitioners. Some of the major criticisms on Schon's reflective theory are: it focuses only on individuals, does not include practitioners' personal and professional values and excludes daily routine experiences. Importantly, some aspects of knowing in action cannot be communicated and hence cannot be transferred to others (see table 2.2, p. 61).

David Boud's reflective learning from experiences

David Boud, professor of adult education, has made an important contribution to the model of reflective process (Boud, Keogh & Walker 1985). Like Dewy and Schon, Boud et al. focused on learning from experiences from the reflective process, but their analysis importantly brought out the role of emotions and the individual's socio-cultural context (personal journey) in the reflective process and learning. Their framework included revisiting experiences in terms of thoughts, feelings and actions; identifying and attending to positive and negative feelings and analysing how they influenced thoughts and actions; and re-evaluation of experiences (see Pawar, Hanna & Sheridan 2004). Boud et al.'s contribution is very close to what social workers practice as they are trained to look into their own feelings, emotions, values (conflicts) as part of their self-awareness. Boud et al.'s model has four main limitations: it is more focused on individual's self than on others' (Bolton 2010); recollection of memories can fail and may not be accurate (Sparrow 2009); there is an overemphasis on learning; and there is a risk of ritualising the reflective process (Boud & Walker 1998) (see table 2.2).

David Kolb's experiential learning theory

David Kolb's experiential learning theory (1984) is closely linked to reflective practice. Kolb's cycle of experiential learning includes concrete experience, reflective observation of experience, conceptualising or theorising the experience and experimenting or testing the new learning. It has some elements of Schon's reflection in action. It emphasises knowledge arising from practice and integrates practice and theory; that is, doing and thinking. Several frameworks have been developed (e.g. Borton 1970; Rolfe et al. 2001) to apply Kolb's theory to enhance learning and practice. Some of the major criticisms of Kolb's learning theory are that it focuses on management learning, it does not include a range of other influential factors and it concentrates only on individual learning.

Jurgen Habermas' critical reflective practice

The thoughts of Jurgen Habermas (1974) on ways of generating knowledge show how critical reflection leads to emancipation. To Habermas, knowledge can be generated through technical domain (positivistic, scientific), practical domain (social interaction and understanding of meaning, humanities and social sciences) and the emancipatory domain (see Rolfe, Jasper & Freshwater 2011). Although critical reflection can be undertaken under each domain (see Taylor 2006), for Habermas it is in the emancipatory domain of critical reflection on and self-knowledge about social and institutional forces of control and the consequent oppression that leads to social action and transformation. It draws on Marxist philosophy and related theories. That is why, perhaps, it is closely connected to critical reflective practice in social work. Compared to the other reflection theories discussed above, although Habermas' theory of critical reflection provides entirely a different perspective, it is based on subjective self-knowledge, it focuses only on social practice and all contexts may not require transformation. However, social work's social change agenda can learn from this theory.

Other contributors to reflective practice theories

In addition to the above, there are many writers who have contributed to reflective practice theories in terms of additions or slight refinements (Bruce 2013). For example, to Boud et al.'s (1985) model Bolton (2010) adds that negative or obstructive feeling may be related to a person's ethical values or values conflicts. Further, in addition to focusing on self, it is important focus on feelings and emotions of others and to use a supervisor or facilitator for the reflective process in a conducive environment. Thompson and Thompson (2008) have added reflection for action to Schon's reflection on and in action to include anticipation, planning and preparation. Drawing on the reflective theories, Seidel and Blythe (1996, cited in Bruce 2013) have expanded the reflective practice by including backward (past event), inward (feelings/emotions), outward (social culture and others) and forward (action/practice) reflective processes. Irrespective of the models of reflection, level of the ability and skills of a person is important to undertake the reflective process (Moon 1999, 2004). To match the ability and skills of a person who reflects, Ruch (2000) has suggested three levels of reflection with increasing complexity. These are technical (beginning), practical (middle) and critical (higher-level) reflection. In social work, critical reflective practice is highly valued and needed, but some make the distinction between reflective practice and critical reflective practice (see Fook & Askeland 2006; Fook 2007). Such additions and refinements, although important, do not make new theories of reflective practice.

Table 2.1 The theoretical underpinnings of reflective practice

Models and proponents	Principles	Focus	Limitations
Reflective learning model of John Dewey, psychologist and educational philosopher	– learning by doing – knower and the knowledge need to be brought together – knowledge can be constructed by reflecting on current and past experiences – reflective learning is a continuous process	– reflecting on challenging experiences – enquiry/questioning – learning – knowledge-building – wholeheartedness, open-mindedness – awareness of self-beliefs	– only limited to thinking and learning – no focus on practice/action – no focus on positive experiences
Reflective practice theory of Donald Schon, educational philosopher	– changing modern life – need to modify their practice to respond to changes – reflection will lead to modified practice to meet the changing needs – gap between theory and practice – reflective practice provides insights to deal with complexity, uncertainty, instability, values conflicts, unique cases	– reflections on practice knowledge – reflection on and in practice – knowing-in-action – practice-theory integration – improving practice and decision-making	– does not include personal or professional values in practice – limited to individual level practice – everyday practice routines are excluded – transfer or communication of knowing-in-action is problematic
Experiential learning theory of David Kolb, professor of organisational behaviour specialising in learning and development	– experiential learning stages – reflecting on experiences – conceptualising and testing – continuous process	– reflections on experience – knowing/concept/theory – integration of knowing and doing – testing – knowledge creation	– more focused on management and individual learning – decontextualises the learning process – does not include other factors that influence learning
Reflection process in context model of David Boud, professor of adult education	– learning and development is a personal journey – learning from experience – emotions affect the reflective process	– learning – revisit experiences and delineate thoughts, feelings and actions – positive and negative feelings and emotions – analysis of the impact of emotions on actions – re-evaluation of experience	– limited to individual internal processes; does not cover others – often memories may change or fail – overemphasis on learning – risk of ritualising the reflective process
Critical theory of Jurgen Habermas, sociologist and philosopher	– self-knowledge – emancipation – critical reflection – critical self-awareness – draws on Marxist philosophy	– critical reflection – meaning of self in relation to self and social structures – liberation from oppressive, discriminatory and exploitative structures – change transformation	– based on subjective self-experience – all contexts may not call for transformation – emphasis on social practice, societal level

Table 2.1 (cont.)

Models and proponents	Principles	Focus	Limitations
Reflective social work practice model of Manohar Pawar and Bill Anscombe, social work educators	– adherence to social work values and principles – priority on participants and collaboration – open for all sources of diverse knowledge – conscious use of the being – cognisance of the context	– explicit role of the being along with thinking and doing – self- and social awareness – both individual and structural levels – participants – process and outcome – social work practice methods	– some aspects are not verifiable – assumes engagement of participants, who may refuse – virtue development is a long-term process – to be fully tested

---

REFLECTIVE EXERCISE 2.3

What is your understanding of theoretical underpinnings of reflective practice?
   Review the content of table 2.1. Discuss the difference between Jurgen Habermas' critical reflective practice and the others' reflective practice theories or models.

▪ A reflective social work practice model: blending being, thinking and doing with PEOPLE

Irrespective of the theoretical orientations of reflective practice models discussed above, they mostly focus on reflection for doing (practice and action) and knowing (practice knowledge or theory) or knowing and doing. They have missed a vital aspect of the critical and reflective process; that is, the 'knower'. Although some reference has been made to self, feelings and emotions, ability to reflect and skill levels, 'knower' – that is, being of a practitioner – has been almost ignored in the reflective process. The reflective social work practice model presented here brings the 'being' of practitioners into the prime spot in the reflective process and shows how being plays a crucial role in reflective doing and thinking, and thinking and doing. A merely critical and reflective process of thinking and doing and doing and thinking is not adequate in social work practice and education. Equal importance needs to be placed on the being of a practitioner. The stronger the 'being', the better the thinking and doing and doing and thinking.

   We acknowledge that being is complex to comprehend, to operationalise many of its dimensions (see the concept of being discussed in chapter 1) and to subject to scientific verification. Although all dimensions of being are important and have a role, as clarified earlier, we focus on the virtue dimension of the being of a practitioner. Our core principle and assumption is that building the being – that is, developing virtues of practitioners and integrating that with doing and thinking in the critical reflective process – helps to enhance practice. If the practitioner her/himself lacks confidence, courage, motivation, awareness of self and others, judgement or right attitude, no amount of reflection will help, and the practitioner may remain far from critical reflection. Humanistic belief in the basic ability of persons is not enough for critical and reflective practice. Human capacity and qualities need to be strengthened.

The reflective social work practice model explicitly includes being along with doing and thinking and thinking and doing, and applies it across five critical progressive phases of the reflective social work practice model. These are:

- **P**articipants
- **E**nvironmental scan
- **O**bjectives
- **P**rocess and **L**abour
- **E**valuation.

We abbreviate these terms as the PEOPLE model. The PEOPLE model can be reflectively applied across any practice contexts. In chapters 3, 4, 5, 6 and 7, the reflective social work practice model has been applied in the context of work with individuals, groups, communities, organisational management or administration and research issues, respectively as an example. Further, a reflective framework has been used to analyse the practice of the PEOPLE phases within the model. The model stems from reflections on practice, and therefore it is a practice-based theory. For the details of this model, see figure 2.1. The model combines elements of ontological (nature of being in terms of virtues) and epistemological (methods of generating knowledge) perspectives for better reflective practice. The main limitations of the model are that some aspects of it are not verifiable in a positivist sense, some participants may refuse to engage, it is challenging to develop virtues in a short time and the model has yet to be fully tested.

Understanding the model

As discussed above, figure 2.1 shows that the reflective social work practice model, blending being, thinking and doing with PEOPLE, has three main components: first, thinking, doing and being; second, five progressive phases: participants, environmental

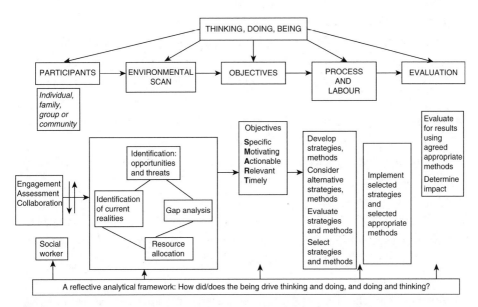

Figure 2.1 A reflective social work practice model: blending being, thinking and doing with PEOPLE

scan, objectives, process and labour and evaluation; and third, a reflective analytical framework. Before discussing each one of them, it is important to look at eight principles on which the model is based.

Principles of the model

In recognition of the fundamental nature of social work and the values espoused by the profession in its codes and definitions (e.g. social justice, human rights, participant self-determination, liberation – see chapter 1), the model:

1 Places a priority on participants (at the individual and/or family, group and community levels) and ensures power-sharing through dialogue or conversation. It is bounded by the 'being' of the social worker and the participants. It counters the imposed and oppressive nature of some social work interventions and solutions.

2 Includes both social worker and the participant to carefully and jointly consider and assess the environment of the participant (whether individual, group, community). Their assessment may or may not immediately show possibilities and resources. These first two principles enable the processes of engagement, collaboration and assessment to have a concrete expression. The first two principles allow for the development of an enabling and empowering relationship, which is not legal or contractual (see Sack 2002: 151).

3 Is open to all sources of diverse knowledge (interdisciplinary theories for practice and practice theories), thinking approaches and practice skills that help to address the situation most efficaciously. It includes and values the participant's worldview and knowledge. It is not committed or limited to one theory or practice perspective.

4 Focuses on the outcome and impact as determined by the participant and social worker in a joint process rather than theoretically or programmatically determined. Such a focus counters the view that social work is ineffective and directionless.

5 Is applicable across most of the social work practice methods and settings. With the model, the practitioner can move across any social work methods and settings to enhance the well-being of the participant and the development of social work. It is important to ensure that the social work profession is not fractured according practice methods and setting.

6 Assumes that reflective social work practice is a continuous process: with the conscious development and use of being, reflective practice continues before, during and after practice.

7 Assumes that social work practice follows the PEOPLE sequence. But depending upon the practice context, social workers can begin at any stage of the model with prior and proper knowledge of what has already occurred, and should be able to move back and ahead, if need be.

8 Is mindful of economic, environmental, political, social and spiritual factors, and is accountable for its actions and interventions.

Thinking, doing and being

Thinking, doing and being on the top of figure 2.1 and its linkages to the PEOPLE model suggests that the social worker's integrated and reflective process of thinking, doing and being occurs at each of the phases from participants to evaluation. You may like to revisit the concept of thinking, doing and being discussed in chapter 1. Thinking includes both content of thinking and the process of thinking (see table 1.1). Doing includes roles and skills of social workers (see table 1.2). Being focuses on the virtues of social workers, although it includes the other dimensions (see figure 1.1), and as far as possible of participants.

The participants: individual, family, group or community and a social worker and/or her/his agency

In the reflective social work practice model, participants include individual, family, group or community and a social worker and/or her/his agency. The choice of the term 'participant' is favoured against such terms as 'client' or 'customer' as they connote an unequal power relationship. The participant may be understood in the light of various dimensions of being (see figure 1.1 in chapter 1): physical/organic; mental/emotional; social relational; and spiritual/existential.

Physical/organic characteristics

The participant (whether individual, community or group or society) has a range of physical/organic characteristics. These include appearances (including, but not limited to) physical appearances, territoriality, haptics (the study of touch), kinesics (the interpretation of body language), proxemics (the measurement of distance between interacting people), chronemics (the study of the use of time), artefactual and olfactory cues, which are communicated verbally and non-verbally and actively and/or passively. The physical considerations of the model may include considerations of biological, physiological and biosocial theories. Consideration of the physical may include research and understandings about chromosomes, the central nervous system, endorphins, the role of neurotransmitters, the role and function of DNA and the setting (as with a group or community). The physical component also includes health and developmental stages (for individuals, groups, communities and society). The consideration of only physical characteristics without consideration of other factors leads to a position that is hard determinism and opens the way for the devaluation of human beings to the point where the spectre of eugenics (the idea that society can be improved by allowing people to become parents only if they are likely to produce healthy and intelligent children) and/or discriminatory practices is open.

Emotional/mental characteristics

The participant has a range of emotional/mental characteristics that include, but are not limited to, intelligence, the capacity to think and to reflect, the capacity to express and control emotion, their past experiences, mood, willingness and motivation. The participant (whether individual, group or community) may have a range of limiting and/or enhancing self-talk. The participant will often have theories for describing and/or analysing and/or explaining behaviour and attitudes. These may or may not be articulated and may or may not be well developed.

Social/relational characteristics

The participant will have an understanding of the social/relational and will have an appreciation of the extent and depth of connectedness to family, school, employment, recreational and other facets of life. They may have an appreciation of art, music and culture. They may or may not have well-considered and articulated values and ethics. They may have well-established patterns of social interactions and may or may not understand the impact of relationships and activities that are shared with others. They may or may not be connected to community, social or political processes and may or may not have views in relation to the acceptance of differences, cultural and ethnic factors. The participant may or may not be able to critique his, her or their 'place in the world' and the influence of the world upon him, her or them.

Spiritual/existential characteristics

The spiritual/existential factors will involve the notions of identity and the sense of being. There will be consideration of hope and optimism, consideration of the sense of aesthetics, consideration of the sense of purpose, understanding of religion and consideration of ontological (nature of being) and existential issues. The participant may or may not have a well-articulated position on these issues. Groups and communities have a sense of the spiritual and existential. Lean (1995) evidences the importance of the spirit in community work.

Social worker as a participant

The social worker is also construed as one of the main participants in the reflective practice process. Thus the social worker's physical/organic; mental/emotional; social relational; and spiritual/existential aspects are important and do play a role in verbal and non-verbal communication. The social worker will have a wide range of emotional/mental characteristics, which include, but are not limited to, intelligence, the capacity to think and to reflect, the capacity to express and control emotion, past experiences, mood, willingness and motivation. The social worker will also have a wide range of formal theories upon which to draw that may prove helpful.

Emotional/mental theories will include, but are not limited to, psychoanalytic approaches (e.g. Freud, Jung and so on), trait-based theories (e.g. Allport 1964; Cleckley 1941; Eysenck 1977 and Sutherland & Shepherd 2002); behavioural learning theories (e.g. Pavlov 1906; Skinner 1971); social learning and modelling theories (Bandura 1977); cognitive theories (e.g. Piaget cited in Mussen 1983; Kohlberg 1969; Clark, Beck & Alford 1999) and the ecological psychological theory expounded by Levine and Perkins (1987).

Social process theories can arguably sit in the overlap between emotional/mental and social/relational. Sutherland's Differential Association Theory (1947) involves both learning (mind/emotional) and the social environment (social/relational). Akers (1998), a social process theorist , is a good example of how the operant conditioning of Skinner is combined with Sutherland's differential association and someone who perceives an intimate connection between the complexity of the emotional/mental and the social environment.

The social/relational aspect of human beings may include understanding of theories for practice, including control theory (Hirschi 1969; Akers 1994) with its emphasis on bonding, and labelling theory (e.g. Lemert 1967; Becker 1973; Goffman 1961; Young 1971; Braithewaite 1989). Also included in the social/relational is social ecology (including the Chicago School), with its emphasis on design ecology (i.e. designing societies and communities to avoid social and relational problems – Jeffery 1971; Newman 1973; Taylor & Harrell 1996), critical ecology (with an emphasis on local institutions and organisations – Gill 1977; Markowitz et al. 2001) and integrated and systemic ecology (which attempts to integrate ecological, biological, social learning, and cultural theories – Vila 1994).

The social/relational must also include a consideration of society. Here the social worker may draw on the insights of Durkheim (1950) or Merton (1968) in relation to anomie or Agnew and White's (1992) General Strain Theory. They may draw more widely upon the approaches of Marx in his critique of capitalism, or from feminism (which may be subcategorised into liberal, radical, Marxist or socialist feminism). The social/relational may also include theories for practice from a very wide range of sources that may help in discerning and understanding the practical situation.

Consideration of the social/relational will involve the social worker making some assessments as to the participant's connectedness to and within society, the breadth and depth of the connections, the helpfulness or otherwise of the connections, the participant's (and social worker's) acceptance of difference, the satisfaction of the connectedness, cultural and ethnic values, living conditions, political and community features.

The spiritual factors for the social worker will involve the notions of identity and the sense of being. There will be consideration of hope and optimism, consideration of the sense of aesthetics, consideration of the sense of purpose, understandings of religion and consideration of ontological and existential issues. The social worker ought to have a well-considered position on these issues.

The social worker's agency or organisation is also an indirect participant in the practice as that often sets policies and procedures and provides the platform for the social workers to practice and sometimes influences the nature of practice.

The interaction of the participants

The individual/family/group/community participant and the social worker participant bring different perspectives to the interaction. The individual/family/group/community participant brings the lived experience and the unique characteristics of their situation. The social worker participant brings a range of different experiences, theoretical training, practical wisdom and reflective approaches to the situation. The worker attempts not to overpower any of the participants, nor necessarily to construct a single view of reality, but to accept the diverse views that each brings. Rather than being client-centred, this approach is relationship-centred, with each of the participants bringing particular aspects of being, thinking and doing to the relationship and establishing a dialogue towards a purpose. The interaction is not dependent upon co-equal contributions (for that is not often possible) but recognises the dignity of differential contributions and the fundamental humanity of the participants.

The participant and the social worker are in a process of engagement, collaboration and assessment (Poulter 2005). These operate at all stages of the model but are particularly relevant here. The participants, having established a relationship based on their human experience of thinking, doing and being, move to consider the environment and the objectives that are desired.

REFLECTIVE EXERCISE 2.4

Is it possible to engage the participant in the way it is suggested in the model? If yes, how do you go about engaging the participant? If not, why?

The environmental scan

Building on the participant's relationship and engagement, it is important to collaboratively undertake the environmental scan as part of the assessment. A key component of social work is considering the person (participant)-in-the-environment, both social and physical. In the model, the participant and the social worker jointly scan the environment. That includes the consideration of the current realities (the presenting issue, other issues, geographic considerations, willingness of others and capacity of others); of resources that are available (this will include the current state of knowledge, the social worker's and participant's skill base, legitimate

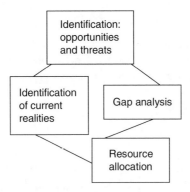

Figure 2.2 The environmental scan box

activities of the social worker and participant, finance, sources of referral, supervision and support, time, technological aids); and the opportunities and threats that the environment poses.

Both the participant and the social worker carefully note the gaps and inconsistencies that exist in knowledge, understanding and resources and whether these gaps will render involvement and solutions impossible.

In scanning the environment, critical thinking/critical reflection, systemic/logical and creative/lateral thinking need to be applied. Lateral thinking is required in relation to considering the alternatives that may be present. Many of the theories for practice that are applicable to the participant and social worker also apply to the environmental scan, particularly the social learning theories, theories of state and community theories. Social workers may use a range of frameworks (e.g. Cheers, Darracott & Lonne 2005 – eight domains of practice) to undertake the environmental scan depending upon the context of practice. From a critical reflective practice perspective, the social worker with the participant (individual/family/groups/communities) may analyse the following questions:

- What is the presenting situation?
- Why is the present situation?
- What causes the present situation?
- What can be done to address the situation at various levels?
- What resources are needed, and how could they be mobilised?

Collaborative critical analyses of such questions should help to bring out unequal structural power relationships within the environment at various levels: individual, family, groups, community, society, culture and gender and socioeconomic, political and/or legal institutions. Most importantly, the ways of addressing them should be considered, too.

The objective(s)

The participants' assessment and environmental scan need to appropriately focus on setting objectives. Recognising the priority on human objectives and activity, any social work objective must be specific, motivating, have a priority of action, be relevant (and, by implication, realistic) and be timely. This usage of the acronym SMART objectives allows for the continuing change that is part of being human (whether developmental or degenerative change). An objective in one situation may be to develop greater insight or, in another, to retard or postpone degeneration. The objective will be situation specific in the light of the participants' contributions and the environmental scan. For example, the mutually agreed objective for one alcoholic may be complete abstinence while for another it may be a reduction of usage to still hazardous levels. For one community, the objective may be growth and development of infrastructure while for another community the objective may be to assist adjustment to a reality of loss of services and infrastructure due to population decline with a degree of dignity and understanding of the related grief and loss.

The participant and the social worker jointly decide the objectives. It is here that the issues of client self-determination and the social worker's responsibility and even the social control focus are clearly articulated. There may be conflict over goals that require creative approaches that offer enabling and empowering solutions within the environmental parameters or the dictates of the agency or society. There may be subobjectives or milestones or steps to the objectives. The objectives may be tangible outcomes; they may be process-oriented; or they may be a simple reframing of the issue that allows for a different conceptualisation.

Process(es) and labour/doing

The process(es) and labour/doing elements of the model arise from the participant and social worker's being, thinking and doing, from the environmental scan and from the objectives that have been jointly agreed. Both process and labour, as terms, have been deliberately chosen. They should not be misunderstood and maliciously reinterpreted. Social work is not entirely process-oriented nor is it simply labour-oriented but rather a thoughtful use of different processes adhering to social work values and principles, and an appropriate use of effort by both participant and social worker. It essentially includes a lot of roles and doings of social workers (see table 1.1 in chapter 1). This is to counter the critique that social work is ineffective and relies upon talk. Interviewing, providing support, mobilising resourcing, going with a participant to a job interview, going to a barricade, motivating, teaching a skill, initiating a fresh approach or reframing a problem (and many other examples) are significant social work labour/doing.

This phase of the model involves two steps that require all forms of thinking and a consideration of the 'doing' of social work. It requires the development of strategies and methods and the consideration of alternative strategies and methods with the consideration of the likely utility and probability of the methods and strategies being useful in achieving the desired outcomes. Preferred strategies and methods are decided upon, then the allocation of responsibility for implementation occurs. This element involves critical thinking and reflection and systemic or logical thinking as well as lateral and creative thinking that can generate possibilities and alternatives. It requires the input of both the participant and the social worker.

The selected strategy and the selected methods are then implemented. Some strategies will be appropriate in some situations and others will not be possible, given the limitations of the participant, the social worker, the environment or the objectives. But creative and unusual approaches will also be possible. The model is not prescriptive about the methods and strategies but allows for them to be implemented as the circumstances determine.

Having thoroughly engaged, collaborated and assessed the participants and social worker and the environment, and having decided upon the agreed objectives, the process and labour/doing element of the model involves both the social worker and the participant implementing the agreed strategies chosen and labouring separately and together on items in order to achieve the objectives. The model is not prescriptive about the 'doings' that the social worker undertakes. Nor is it prescriptive of the labour and process undertaken by the participants. It will vary from situation to situation – with some participants being able to (say) advocate for him/

herself while others will not. Some participants will need the social worker to enable or initiate while others will require different 'doing' skills from the social worker. What is important in the whole process is reflective doing on the part of the worker.

REFLECTIVE EXERCISE 2.7
Select a case from any of the social work practice methods you are working with and reflectively analyse the process you have followed in terms of your roles and skills (doings) and the participant's doings.

Evaluation

The very nature of reflective social work practice has an element of evaluation. Reflective evaluation questions are raised at every stage of the practice to guide further appropriate steps. It is also important to undertake specific evaluation at the end for a range of reasons such as learning, improvement, funding, agency, professional, accountability and so on. Basic reflective questions for evaluation would be:

- What was the whole practice experience?
- What were the process and outcome?
- What objectives have been achieved and not achieved, and why?
- Were there any better ways of doing?
- What are the lessons for the future?

It is important include participants in the process of evaluation. Key considerations in all evaluations are: appropriateness (the extent to which the objectives and priorities match the needs of the participants and the goals of the organisation); effectiveness (the extent to which the intervention outcomes match stated objectives); and efficiency (objectives are achieved at reasonable cost and in a reasonable time).

Evaluation is sometimes seen as the end of a linear process – conceptualised in the following way:

$$assessment \rightarrow intervention \rightarrow evaluation$$

This linear conceptualisation is unhelpful. Evaluation needs to be built in at each point of the process. Goals need to be framed with evaluative impact as a factor. Inputs, processes and outputs (sometimes called outcomes) ought to be subject to evaluation. A more helpful model modified and used is presented in figure 2.3.

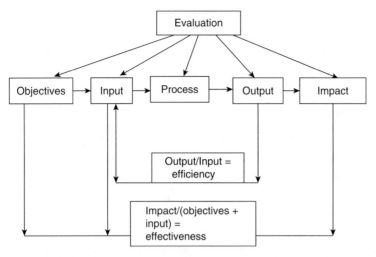

Figure 2.3 Evaluation diagram

Evaluation can be considered from a range of views related to purpose, context and time horizons. Evaluation, as the name implies, involves judgements and valuations about different facts or perspectives. Owen (2003) says that the purposes of an evaluation include: enlightenment; accountability; program improvement; program clarification; program development; and symbolic reasons (e.g. a funding or auspicing body requires an evaluation). Evaluations need to take account of the context, design limitations (e.g. budget, ethics, educational levels of respondents and so on), the process undertaken and the anticipated and/or serendipitous outcomes. Legitimate foci of an evaluation are the planning, programs, policies, organisation, individuals and processes. Evaluations and managerial judgements assess the efficiency and effectiveness of practices and processes for achieving improved outcomes in systems for participants. 'Effectiveness' refers to the achievement of some goal, if possible, at minimum cost, but above all successfully. 'Efficiency' refers to an input–output relationship; that is, optimisation – obtaining maximum satisfaction for a given outlay of resources.

The values and forces that shape the social work environment also shape the evaluation of social work. It may be noted that there are difficulties related to calculating the impact of social work practice. These include:

- when individuals, governments and agencies pursue incompatible goals and policies
- the fact that some programs and activities have primarily symbolic value
- that there is a vested interest in 'proving' that programs or actions have a positive effect (i.e. that they work)
- when approaches that solve the problems of one person or group in society may create problems for another group

- that people may adapt themselves in ways which render the impact of social work useless
- the fact that societal problems have multiple causes and a specific social work action may be devised to correct only some causes or may create further problems
- that the solution to some problems may require approaches that are more costly than the problem
- that the political system and individuals do not use completely rational decision-making processes
- that the impact of social work is assessed against standards or criteria promulgated by those in authority rather than by participants, and can be inherently conservative and promote the maintenance of the status quo, which entrenches inherently conservative 'top-down' approaches, and
- that social work is subverted by forces or values opposed to the social work (i.e. it is subject to manipulation).

While these are very real considerations, evaluating for results can be as simple as asking the participant. In individual work, assessment is sometimes done by scaling techniques (1–10), while other measures may be behavioural change or attitudinal change, time out of jail, a new job, a new program, a submission, greater access to children or many other matters related to the objective. Although evidence-based evaluation is important, in some areas of social work practice such as recovery in mental health and a series of counselling sessions without tangible outcome, it may be difficult to show tangible outcomes. In such contexts, reflective evaluation is helpful. The purpose of reflective evaluation need not be to meet the external agency requirement, but for self-learning and improving practice and practice knowledge.

REFLECTIVE EXERCISE 2.8
Do you think you should evaluate your social work practice? Apply the evaluation process suggested in the model to one of your practice cases. What are the difficulties in evaluating some of the social work practice situations?

A reflective analytical framework

At the bottom of figure 2.1: Reflective social work practice model: blending being, thinking and doing with PEOPLE, a reflective analytical framework is included. The framework includes four fundamental questions for reflective analysis. They are

Table 2.2 A reflective analytical framework

	Participants	Environmental scan	Objectives	Process/labour	Evaluation
Social work	How did the being drive thinking and doing and doing and thinking?				
practice	What were the dynamics among being, thinking and doing and being, doing and thinking?				
methods	How does being drive thinking and doing, and doing and thinking?				
	What are the dynamics among being, thinking and doing and being, doing and thinking?				

included in table 2.2. The framework is linked to each phase of the model from participant to evaluation. The first two questions relate to reflections on practice; that is, after the practice experience completed, social workers analyse the role of her/his being at every phase of the model from participants to evaluation. It is also important to look at the dynamics among being, thinking and doing and being, doing and thinking. In chapters 3 to 7, these questions are used for reflective analysis. The last two questions relate to reflections in action. It is suggestive to social workers that while practising itself, they can consciously use their being for thinking and doing and doing and thinking. Strengthening being in terms of virtues is important. But it is also some workers' internal reality that, contrary to such virtues as courage and confidence, they do experience fear, lack of confidence, anxiety, uncertainty and so on. It is important to reflect on what causes them and how they affect thinking and doing and doing and thinking, and how social workers deal with them or overcome in the course of their practice.

> **REFLECTIVE EXERCISE 2.9**
> Reflect on your first interview with a participant in your field placement agency. What was the role of your being in thinking and doing and doing and thinking?

Conclusion

As set out in the introduction, the main objective of this chapter is to discuss the meaning, significance and theoretical bases of reflective practice, and to present the details of the reflective social work model that blends being, thinking and doing with

PEOPLE. It also brings out the role of being in practice. Although there is some confusion about the range of concepts of reflective practice and the way they have been used interchangeably by some writers and practitioners, by systematically analysing their meanings a clear distinction can be drawn among them for enhancing our own understanding and practice. There is some commonality between social work in terms of self and social awareness and reflective practice.

Reflective practice is important as it enhances self-learning, improves practice and professional standards and contributes to building knowledge. Theoretical underpinnings of reflective practice have been analysed by looking at their principles/assumptions, main focus and limitations.

The reflective social work practice model consists of thinking, doing and being, PEOPLE and the reflective analytical framework, and it has tried to blend all the three together. It begins with the participant and the social worker–participant rather than beginning with abstract theory or inappropriate actions. It puts the priority on the relationship between the participant and the social worker. The model utilises the dynamic interplay of participants within their environment and creates the opportunity for a social worker and participant to jointly scan the environment, determine goals, decide upon strategies from a competing array, jointly action the preferred strategy and consider impact and outcomes. There is agreement upon process, and there is a jointly allocated responsibility for implementation and the responsibility for outcomes. At each point of the model the various components of thinking and doing and being are used. Particularly, the role of being in driving thinking and doing and doing and thinking pointed to the reflective analytical framework. The model is not prescriptive as to content and allows both participant and social worker participant to bring their varying being, thinking and doing to the issues at hand. The model is flexible and allows content and theories to be implemented at various points. Chapters 3 to 7 show how social work/welfare or human services students, practitioners and educators can use reflective practice knowledge, the reflective social work practice model and reflective analytical framework in their settings and across a range of social work practice methods.

▓ Questions and exercises

1   Discuss the meaning of reflection, reflective practice, critical reflective practice and reflexivity.
2   What is your experience of using the reflective practice approach? Does it help you to improve your practice? Discuss in what ways it has helped and not helped you.

3   Write a reflective note on your first placement interview or your first day at the placement or your first interview with a client.
4   Review the theoretical underpinnings of reflective practice.
5   What do you think about the reflective social work practice model discussed in this chapter? For a quick summary of it, look at figure 2.1.
6   Identify one of your social work practice experiences and analyse it by applying the reflective social work practice model.
7   Why do you think it is important to focus on the being of a social worker? Reflect on your own being and identify strengths and aspects of your being that need strengthening.

3

Being in the context of reflective practice with individuals and families

T HIS CHAPTER CONSIDERS aspects of working with individuals and families. It demonstrates the reflective practice of being, thinking and doing as an individual and/or family worker. This chapter will begin with a case study provided by the author, Bill Anscombe. This case study will be used as a means of exploring the central ideas and practice elements of individual and family work.

As a social worker, the author worked with individuals and families as a direct service provider predominantly in the areas of corrections and child protection. His experiences include dealing with individuals, families, drug and alcohol issues, mental health issues (psychosis, compulsions, depression and so on), poverty issues, sexual issues, matters of violence, issues of aged care, physical and intellectual disabilities, violence, child protection issues, Indigenous issues and others. He has worked in many communities in both metropolitan and rural and regional areas and with more than 10 000 individuals and their families. He has used approaches including crisis intervention (for short-term work), long-term casework and case management, existential approaches, behavioural approaches and psychoanalytic approaches.

◼ Chapter objectives

After reading this chapter you should:
- appreciate, through one example, the nature and characteristics of individual and family work
- reflect upon your own personal and theoretical orientations and approaches
- consider the constraints and attributes of working with individuals and families
- consider and apply aspects of being while working with individuals and families.

▨ Main themes and concepts used

This chapter is focused upon reflective practice in individual and family work through a single case study. In this chapter, the social worker demonstrates how he worked with an individual and family and with the wider system. To understand this chapter, some familiarity with the approaches of crisis intervention, psychotherapies, cognitive-behavioural therapies, solution-focused approaches or others will be beneficial and while these will not be detailed, the discerning reader may identify elements from each of these in the case study.

Crisis intervention

By way of summary, crisis intervention aims to assist individuals in a crisis situation and to restore equilibrium in their biopsychosocial functioning (homeostasis). Roberts & Ottens (2005) identify seven stages in their model: planning and assessing, establishing rapport and collaborative relationships; identifying the dimensions of presenting problems; exploring feelings and emotions; generating and exploring alternatives; developing and formulating an action plan; and follow-up planning and agreement. It is of course important to reflect upon whether the events in the case studies are crises (and for whom) and whether restoration to the pre-crisis functioning, which had significant elements of dysfunction, was appropriate.

Psychotherapies

Psychotherapies encompasses a very wide range of approaches including psychoananlytic, behavioural therapies, cognitive behavioural, psychodrama, existential, humanistic, brief, systemic and solution-focused, among others.

Cognitive–behavioural approaches

The reader will observe some cognitive–behavioural approaches that address dysfunctional emotions, behaviours and distorted cognitive processes by systematic and explicit goal-oriented behaviour change. While there are many forms of CBT, the key components used here related to (re)orientation, skills development and relapse prevention.

Systemic approaches

Systemic approaches seek to consider the individual in their relationships to other systems and subsystems and consider the interactions, including the patterns and dynamics.

Solution-focused approaches

Solution-focused approaches focus upon what clients want to achieve by typically focusing upon the present and the future. In the case study, these were important – but the past could not be ignored (nor returned to).

REFLECTIVE EXERCISE 3.1

'Who is the client?' is a commonly asked question where there are competing interests in a family. What if the question was framed differently as 'who are the clients'? Does that offer more possibilities?

Aquinas said, 'Beware the man of one book', and Maslow said, 'If your only tool is a hammer – everything looks like a nail.' To what extent does an individual or family worker need to have a range of different clinical approaches rather than a singular preferred theoretical approach?

Consider your personality. To what extent does it influence your work with individuals and families?

The individual or family case study

Ixx (all names and specific identifying details have been changed) was convicted of multiple indecent assaults on his partner's daughters, each aged under ten years. He was imprisoned for two years and sentenced to bonds with specific conditions relating to supervision, undergoing psychological or psychiatric counselling and was prohibited from seeing his stepdaughters or residing in the family home *except* with the permission of the authorities.

Ixx was mildly intellectually delayed. Until entering the six-year relationship with his partner, he had no sexual experience, no formal sex education and little or no appreciation of psychosexual or psychosocial development. Ixx claimed that his offending behaviour commenced as part of a game, some of which was initiated by the children. He said, 'In my eyes I wasn't doing anything wrong.' He had little insight into the possible consequences of sexual interference on children and a tendency to displace responsibility onto others, including both the victims and his partner.

Ixx was short and overweight and had poor personal hygiene. He had little formal education, no employment history and a propensity for threatening behaviour. Possibly a victim of child abuse in his childhood and adolescence, he was econom-ically poor and socially isolated. He had no parenting skills when he entered, partnered and consequently took significant responsibility for a family for which he seemed ill-equipped.

Vxx was the partner of Ixx. She was physically large, had few communication skills and was emotionally dependent upon Ixx. She had reportedly been the victim of child sexual assault. Her life had been marked by poverty, early cessation of schooling, an early event of child-bearing, a period of sole-parenting, a marriage with further children and subsequent desertion and divorce. Her current relationship offered her the opportunity for mobility, mutual gratification, assistance with her family, an opportunity to express and receive affection and stability.

The offences had caused a crisis for Vxx. Her initial reaction to the disclosure of the offences was of disbelief. She denied any prior knowledge, although she agreed that her daughters had told her of the behaviour and she had dismissed their disclosure as not being true. She denied any ill-effect of her own childhood sexual assault (CSA) and could see no reason to involve any outside authorities. After initially requiring Ixx to leave the relationship upon disclosure of the offences, the couple reunited before Ixx went to prison and the victims of the offences were placed in care in order to protect them from physical, sexual or emotional abuse. Vxx simply wanted Ixx back in her life.

Fxx and Txx were younger than ten at the time of the disclosure of the offences. Fxx had a close relationship with her sister, but the mother–daughter relationship was ambivalent. She cared very much for Ixx and considered him to be the only real father in her life. She wanted the family living together harmoniously, but she did not wish to be assaulted again. She had no friends, was performing very poorly at school and was presenting as a behavioural problem in the school environment. Fxx had originally disclosed Ixx's sexual assaults to the school counsellor.

Txx was small in stature, timid and withdrawn, and had attempted to take her own life. Often depressed, Txx had little regard for Ixx but was in desperate need of the continuing support of her mother. She was performing poorly at school, could not identify a single friend and had few social relationships. She was sad, and her drawings illustrated a sense of hopelessness and fear.

Rxx was the 18-month-old son of Ixx and Vxx who had not reached the stage of verbalising. He appeared to be developmentally delayed in verbal, motor and social skills. He was much loved by all members of the family.

Within weeks of release from prison Ixx (and Vxx) approached me about residing with Vxx and 'his family'. All members of the family wished to have the offender reunited in the family environment. A psychological report was commissioned. It concluded that continued offending behaviour was likely if Ixx was returned to the home as none of the pre-offence conditions had altered. A further report from a family counsellor drew the same conclusion. My assessment was in accord with these views.

Ixx had successfully lied his way through the prison term by maintaining the secrecy of his offence by inventing a more prison-acceptable offence. He convinced himself that by comparison to others he was not a criminal.

Ixx and Vxx indicated that they were going to live together. They indicated that if I would not give them permission under the terms of the bond and the parole order to reside together as a family, then Vxx would surrender the children to the authorities in order to cohabit with Ixx. He would therefore not be in breach of any legal orders. This had been the situation when Ixx was on bail. Ixx and Vxx had carefully thought through their legal situation.

PERSONAL REFLECTION

My involvement with the family extended over a five-year period. While I was involved in the initial sentencing hearing, this reflective analysis is primarily directed at the post-release supervision period.

I have long believed that no single approach to individual and family work can be applied to the very great multiplicity and diversity of humanity that is the daily experience of social workers. Knowledge (be it empirical, cultural or practice wisdom) needs to be drawn from many sources, and it seemed to me that a singular social work approach or one dominating theory would be insufficient in dealing with such issues as violence, physical or mental impairment, drugs and alcohol, depression, marital conflict or sexual aberrations.

REFLECTIVE EXERCISE 3.2

What are your immediate reactions to the above case? Read it again, and identify issues and needs in the case.

Thinking and reflecting on individual and family work

Research has found that virtually all therapeutic approaches are equally effective (Smith, Glass & Miller 1980). The essence of therapeutic success, at least in the clinical setting, is a good working relationship between clinician and client (Frank 1982; Marziali & Alexander 1991; Camilleri 1996; Garvin 1997; Brown 1992). Integral to establishing and maintaining such a relationship is the use of self in the application of any specific approach or technique (McConnaughy 1987). Marshall (2005: 115), writing about programs for sex offenders, argues for less detailed treatment manuals, which reduce treatment programs to psychoeducational processes, and for establishing a proper balance between specifying procedures and allowing sufficient flexibility for the therapist to use his/her influence to maximise treatment outcomes.

Strupp (as cited in Edwards & Bess 1998: 91) asserts that 'the person of the therapist is far more important than his theoretical orientation'. Hubble, Miller and Duncan (1999) note that, in the therapeutic setting, outcome variance is related to the strengths and resources the client brings (40 per cent), the therapeutic relationship that is developed (30 per cent), client expectation and capacity for hope (15 per cent) and the technique or model employed (15 per cent). Writing in relation to family therapy, Flaskas (2004: 14) says that 'the therapeutic relationship rated barely a mention in the first thirty years of family therapy theory'.

PERSONAL REFLECTION

Systemic thinking is always about content and processes. In thinking about this case, I was informed by the current state of knowledge and theories for practice. I was informed by attachment theory and particularly the classifications of attachment (Crittenden & Ainsworth 1989: 437). The female victims bore many of the characteristics of neglect attributable to primary-aged children (growth retardation, enuresis, lethergy, depression, below-average intellectual functioning, cooperative, compliant and less able to seek emotional support). I was consciously informed by developmental theories (Piaget 1983 on developmental stages; Bandura 1977 on social learning theory; Vygotsky 1978 on social and cultural learning; and Kohlberg 1973, 1981 on moral development).

Corrections had been deeply influenced by the Martinson paper (1974), which asserts that 'nothing works'. I have never accepted that approach – being too optimistic and seeing too much 'evidence' of real and sustained change in offenders. Nevertheless, it was the prevailing contextual paradigm.

Specialised services for sex offenders, especially in rural areas, were unknown. Material from Canada (John Howard Society of Alberta 2002) addresses the needs and approaches that work with clients who are sexual offenders of limited intelligence. The recidivism rates for incest offenders are quite low (8.4 per cent) when compared to non-incest child molesters who recidivate (19.5 per cent). The literature does not clearly delineate whether stepfathers (as in this case) are consistently classified as incest or non-incest child molesters. The dominant community counselling intervention approach for sex offenders was based on Jenkins's *Invitation to Responsibility* (1990). This was used as a framework for thinking about Ixx and the situation. Theoretically, the discount hierarchy (Flandreau West 1989) was also thought through and used.

It would have been possible to think in a limited way and define Ixx as the client (and the corrections mandate certainly would have supported that view). It would have been possible to enforce the condition of the parole order and the recognisance and keep Ixx and the victims separated. That would have meant that the girls were placed in foster care and would face an uncertain future as it is likely that Vxx would choose Ixx rather than her daughters. Critical/reflective/systemic thinking allowed for an analysis of the wider family and social system and the redefinition of the client as the family rather than the individual. This meant considering other alternatives to the binary 'either/or' proposed by Ixx and Vxxx and working through a range of possibilities that might achieve good outcomes for all concerned.

The theories for practice included understandings of power and control (e.g. Hagan 1989, who studies social structure in terms of vertical, hierarchical power relations between individuals and groups as part of structural criminology), interactional theories (e.g. Thornberry, who developed a model of control theory which posited that 'the fundamental cause of delinquency lies in the weakening of social constraints over the conduct of the individual' (1987: 865), the use by Groth, Hobson & Gary (1982) of the concepts of fixated and regressed child sex offenders and recognition of the developmental needs of the victims (including safety and certainty).

PERSONAL REFLECTION

My thinking considered the current values and beliefs of Western society directed at protection of children from sexual assault. Dominant conventions included pathologising the offender and separating him/her from the family. Current laws and protocols favoured isolating the victims from the source of harm, usually by the removal of the offender or the removal of the children from harm.

I also used a modified US Risk/Need/Responsivity assessment tool, knowledge related to parole and probation law and the relevant administrative procedures. I brought knowledge acquired in relation to deviance (e.g. Sutherland & Cressey 1978, Becker 1963, Matza 1960), understanding of the nature and dynamics of why and under what circumstances people ceased offending behaviour, and desistance theory (see Grove 1985, Loeber & LeBlanc 1990), relapse prevention theory (Marlatt & Gordon 1985), criminology theory (Gottfredson & Hirschi 1990), sex offender patterns of behaviour, and intervention and general casework and case management theory.

Knowledge drew on child protection, mental health, sexual assault and developmental disability. In a multidimensional and interdisciplinary approach, there will be different thinking and knowledge. The application of the appropriate social worker's knowledge and skills through a reflective process enables each unique situation to be acted upon in an individualised and appropriate way. 'Practice wisdom' included that appropriate foster care for the victims would be difficult given their damage, age and circumstances (Cashmore & Paxman 1996); that outcomes for older aged children placed in foster care are very poor (Cashmore & Paxman 1996); that sex offenders who are stepparents have difficulty changing patterns of behaviour but less difficulty in changing families and developing new victims; that external resources in an isolated community were unlikely; that stigmatisation of the victims occurs; that double victimisation (being a victim of an offence, then being victimised by removal from home) was frequent; that developmental disability influences outcomes; and that risk is being borne by those who are already victims.

PERSONAL REFLECTION

Systemic/critical thinking about the practice reality involved recognising that there could be multiple objectives and multiple outcomes. The objective of safety for the children could involve removing the children to a very uncertain future or working within an informed risky set of parameters. The rural locality and the low intelligence levels of Ixx and Vxx made intensive family-based therapies both impractical and unsuitable. The significant interpersonal, intra-personal and resource gaps were noted and strategies devised to minimise the gaps. In thinking about evaluation in the human services, it became clear to me that multiple types of evaluation were needed. I began thinking about process evaluation, impact evaluation and unobtrusive observation as a means of evaluating (Owen 1993). Some of the evaluation methods for this case would be quite formal (e.g. testing) while others would include unobtrusive observation, and others may include self-evaluation (including myself) with triangulation from other sources. No one tool or method would be relied upon but rather a range of methods and tools was employed.

▨ Doing: What the individual/family worker did

When confronted with the ultimatum regarding the couple, my immediate thinking was to delay a decision while I gave myself time and space to think of alternatives. I wanted to assess the attitudes of other professionals in the situation and decided to call a workers' gathering to think of the possibilities for the future. I initially thought through my own assessment of the situation. I then involved a range of other agencies to determine their view of the ultimatum. There was predictable anger and concern.

The role of the social worker operating as a direct service provider can involve individual problem-solving, marital or family counselling, group service work and as educator or disseminator of information (Hepworth, Rooney & Larsen 1997). Hepworth, Rooney and Larsen (1997) have a distinctive category that they call systems linkage roles, which include broker, case manager/coordinator and mediator/arbitrator/advocate. These roles were evident at different times.

I involved Ixx and Vxx, who wished to be a 'family'. We explored their meaning of 'family' and their desired outcomes. They saw their analysis as being directed at Ixx being able to live in the 'home', simplistically defined as the physical entity with a street address rather than the more difficult and inclusive concept of home as a set of relationships built upon a series of principles and virtues and with an ongoing commitment. Through the process of collaboration, assessment and engagement over three one-hour sessions, they were able to see that the present reality was that they would not be a 'family' living together in the near future and that the notions of 'home' and 'family' were developmental and would require work and change. I asked them to place themselves in my agency's position in the light of the evidence of Ixx's offences against the girls, his lies in prison and his lack of any real change since the disclosure of the offences. If their ultimatum was acted upon, the girls would be removed immediately and the 'family' – as they conceptualised it – would not occur. If the situation was a contest (as constructed by Ixx) between the professionals and the 'family', no one would achieve their goals. Constructing the situation as 'either/or' would mean that the family did not cohabit at all, that the girls would be removed and that destructive consequences would occur for all. The post-removal family may consist of Ixx and Vxx. This brought a hostile reaction and called for considerable fortitude and prudence.

After dealing with their anger and hostility, we revisited their thinking around the concept of 'family'. Their concept was a nuclear family cohabiting together immediately. They gradually came to understand that families had many different structures and many different ways of being 'family'. Vxx's need for 'family' was acute, and it may have been significant in her overlooking the disclosure of sexual assault from her daughters. We considered how other families operated (e.g. a family that they knew where the man worked away for weeks at a time) and considered how each person could be safe and happy in the complex family matrix.

I drafted and presented a complex plan and a two-year timeline for change that was carefully sequenced and logically structured, considered the needs of all the parties and could be the basis of a long-term cohabiting 'family'. This was put to the workers from different agencies and the two girls in separate forums. With all parties agreeing, I then chaired a family and workers' meeting. The first meeting was abandoned after thirty minutes. Ixx was determined to have a guarantee that if he did 'his bit' then we (the professionals) had to promise that the family could all live together. Others (including myself) were determined that the program be implemented successfully and that the objective (family safely living together) be motivating and conditional upon successful implementation. In this I was guided by some practice wisdom whereby participants consider that mere attendance rather than performance or insight is all that is required.

After a further four weeks of working with Ixx, including reviewing his behaviour at the meeting, a second meeting was successful, with agency staff remarking on the change that had occurred in Ixx.

The detailed plan of action

The partialised detailed plan is shown in tables 3.1, 3.2, 3.3, 3.4 and 3.5.

Table 3.1 Overall case plan for the family

Objective	Methodology	Method of evaluation	Outcome	Impact
Family happily reconciled such that the victims are not at risk of sexual assault from their stepfather	As per case management plan	Various: • self-reporting • question and answer • unobtrusive observation • school performance	Desired: 1 A well-adjusted Ixx 2 A well-adjusted Vxxx 3 A well-adjusted Txx and Fxx 4 Effects of the offending behaviour minimised 5 Happy agencies Actual: 1 Major changes in Ixx 2 Vxx has enhanced self-esteem but remains damaged and uncooperative 3 Txx and Fxx remain with Vxxx	Desired: A happy reconciled family at no risk of further offending

Table 3.2 Case plan for Ixx

Objective	Methodology	Method of evaluation	Outcome	Impact
To have client develop a knowledge of female sexuality	Six weeks with male Health Dept worker with a program of information giving	Tests knowledge by verbal question and answer quiz	Client has knowledge of terms and functions in female sexuality	Client appreciates the physical and psychological damage he has inflicted
To gain a knowledge of psychosocial development	Six weeks with male health worker on information giving	Tests knowledge by verbal questions and answer quiz	Client has knowledge of age-appropriate social sexual behaviour	Client appreciates the inappropriateness of his behaviour
To have client accept the 'wrongness' of his behaviour	Counselling with me focusing on breach of trust, force and power issues Written article on incest victims read to and discussed with Ixx	1 Does client blame victims? 2 Can he focus on his own actions? 3 Can he state why he was wrong? 4 Does his affect demonstrate any change (observation)? 5 Four and 16 weeks later – does he still see the 'wrongness'?	Client says he has 'done wrong' Affect supports claim Resolve and plans support change	Client takes responsibility for behaviour Acceptance of that responsibility persists Guilt develops Asks for forgiveness from stepdaughters
To have client develop strategies of impulse control	Discussions with probation and parole officer suggestions of ways to brainstorm ideas with client and de facto	1 What strategies can client think of? 2 What does he do about them?	Locks on doors and shower Not alone with girls No discipline of girls Temper control by counting, going for a walk, outside ventilation	Impulse control significantly improved
To have client use no alcohol	Probation and parole officer direction to client	1 Self-reporting 2 Vxx's report 3 Home visits checking re alcohol 4 Visit hotels on pension day by myself 5 Financial method	Direction obeyed	No use of alcohol

Table 3.3 Case plan for Vxx

Objective	Methodology	Method of evaluation	Outcome	Impact
Have Vxx see the need for counselling for the girls	Six weekly sessions with child protection worker (female)	Will she allow the girls to have counselling?	No. Failed to attend more than twice Agreed to the girls having counselling – but not supportive of it	Vxx is strongly resistant to counselling
Have Vxx express her love for the girls	Weekly information sessions with child protection worker Have Vxx and girls done things together, e.g. shopping?	1 Observation of relationship 2 Diary of activities done together 3 Feedback from girls	Activities done jointly Diary kept Girls seen	Have expressed love but girls want more
Have Vxx see the need of child sexual assault counselling for herself	Two sessions with Sexual Assault Service	1 Did she attend? 2 Will she accept help?	Did not attend the second time	Did not come to terms with her own child sexual assault. This objective was not achievable (my judgement)
Build Vxx's self-esteem	Involve her in pottery classes and social activities	1 Attendance recorded 2 Self-reporting	Nice pottery; new group of friends; first female friend in many years	Vxx achieved and felt good. Program to continue
Have Vxx become more assertive	Counselling with child protection workers and health workers	Will she: 1 express an opinion? 2 take control of issues? 3 recognise capabilities?	More outspoken and claimed 'I'm not stupid' in a disagreement with me	Vxx has developed more assertion

Table 3.4 Case plan for family

Objective	Methodology	Method of evaluation	Outcome	Impact
To have the family build trust in each other	Family outings – initially supervised – becoming progressively more frequent and less supervised. Must be in a public place with itinerary given to me one week ahead	Self-reporting by family. Supervising families report. Assessment by probation and parole officer	1. More frequent family outings 2. Less supervision going to nil supervision	Family trust develops. Girls more relaxed with stepfather Boundaries established

Table 3.4 (cont.)

Objective	Methodology	Method of evaluation	Outcome	Impact
Have the family adapt 'Family Rules'	Negotiation of rules with the family	Is there a tangible, achievable set of rules with enforceable consequences for all parties?	Tangible achievable set of rules	Privacy of girls guaranteed. Discipline code that does not include corporal punishment is in effect
To develop a safety net; that is, action to be taken if offending behaviour commences	1 Discussion 2 Locks that ensure privacy 3 Significant-other list 4 Safety plan	Does the safety net exist? Judgement as to whether it would be used	Significant-others list exists. Locks in place	Some confidence that authorities would be notified by Txx and Fxx. No confidence that Vxx would notify offending behaviour

Table 3.5 Case plan for Txx and Fxx

Objective	Methodology	Method of evaluation	Outcome	Impact
Have Txx & Fxx improve their self-esteem	Involve in sewing, dancing, basketball and children/youth group; counselling sessions	Do they go? Diary	Regular at activities	Feel good they can achieve Diary of feelings and success kept
Have Txx & Fxx improved scholastically	Regular study time More structured maternal involvement	Have school counsellor report progress	Vast improvement in grades; circle of friends developed; book of school achievements developed	Girls feel positive about school
Have Txx & Fxx learn protective behaviour	Use a Protective Behaviour Training Program	Do they understand their needs?	Program completed	Confident they could say 'no'
Have Txx & Fxx experience a more complete family life	Fortnightly weekend foster care placements in a home with a disabled child	Experiential foster carer reports	Fortnightly weekend foster care	Positive experience; likes the family

The 'doing' in this case also involved negotiations, undertaking advocacy, brokering services, mediating, speaking in public (the case conferences), educating (on the nature of families, the impact of offending and so on), initiating (future possibilities) and group facilitating (the case conferences were a complex group with a wide spread of ages, interests, agendas, decision-making processes, communication styles, educational backgrounds and agency requirements).

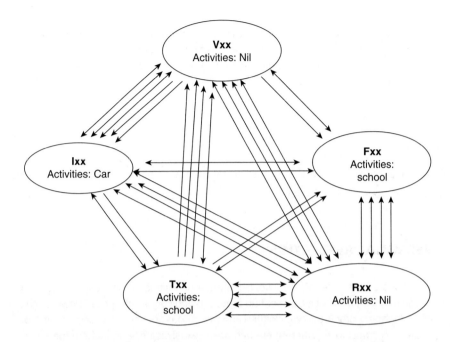

The strength of the association is designated by the number of lines and the direction of the arrows, as assessed by the professionals involved after a systematic ranking.

Figure 3.1 Ecomap

Ecomapping

An ecomap is a graphical representation that shows all the systems that interact in the life of an individual or family. An ecogram is a combination of an ecomap and a genogram, but the terms 'ecogram' and 'ecomap' are often used interchangeably in practice.

PERSONAL REFLECTION

Following input from the other professionals involved in the situation, an ecomap of the family was constructed. We used it to develop an estimate that showed differential associations and attachments (as would be expected in most families) but which highlighted the very close attachment of the youngest daughter to the mother. The association with the strongest attachment was the mother to her partner. The ecogram was a practical way to visually describe the relationships and to show the very restricted relationships and interests that existed outside the immediate family. The very nature of these relationships and the social situation (poverty, housing location and social skill set) reinforced the social isolation and created the conditions that allowed Ixx to construct the family as 'different' and 'against' the rest of society ('different' and 'against' were his terms).

Shuttle negotiations

Shuttle negotiation involves acting as an intermediary between the various parties, rather than have direct contacts between them.

PERSONAL REFLECTION

The doing of the case initially involved 'shuttle negotiations' whereby I acted as a liaison between the parties, presenting proposals and counter-proposals between the offender, the mother, the two children and the various agencies. This seemed appropriate in circumstances where there had been sexual violence and where there was still a significant power differential. I was aware that some theoretical positions in relation to negotiating recommend that negotiation and mediation are not appropriate in situations of violence and where the power imbalance is pronounced. It was inappropriate to bring all parties together (especially the girls) on some issues where hostility and anger may have had a debilitating effect. The children participated in their own forum (away from Ixx's early intimidation) and then their views were represented by others or myself in the role of advocate. Although not in a legal sense, the concept was that of guardian *ad litem*.

The overall objective of attempting to change the family dynamics so that the whole family could reside together at a specified time in the future and subject to specified changes within individuals and within the family was reached following 'shuttle negotiations' in the sessions between the first and second meetings. The plan extended over a two-year period, and Ixx would continue to reside outside the home while progressive positive changes were developed. Rather than rely upon one approach (casework for example), multiple approaches were used (casework, family group conferences, activity-based approaches, advocacy, educational approaches, partner counselling, developing social and relational contacts external to the family) and a variety of theories were used as indicated above. Each approach and theory had something to contribute both to the understanding of the problems and issues and to their solutions.

Building a relationship

Establishing a working relationship is critical. Working intensively with Ixx and Vxx, it was important to explore whether there were other options. The environmental scan led to working with them to explore the situation. The ecomap/ecogram was a visual help. Using and reading research literature to them highlighted the impact of sexual assault on girls. It had an impact on Ixx but not on Vxx. Together, the elements of a two-year plan was devised that would allow the girls to remain at home in a safe environment while each member of the family worked on specific objectives. Ixx agreed to remain away from the home except for every second weekend, when the girls would go into temporary respite and Ixx would move 'home'. This allowed Ixx and Vxx to see themselves as a couple. The planned approach was worked out using such methods as mapping and time-lining. The plan was highly structured and was kept simple, comprehensible and visual. The objectives were specific, motivating, clearly actionable and relevant and had time parameters.

PERSONAL REFLECTION

My 'doing' involved evaluation and was necessary to protect the victims and the agencies who were taking significant risks. Evaluation occurred at all parts of the process, including an evaluation of the objectives, the inputs (i.e. the resources available), the processes adopted, the actual outcomes and the impact (if any) upon the family and community.

The education of Ixx was instructive. He developed a knowledge and awareness of his assault behaviour that he had not previously had, and he seemed to feel genuine remorse for the behaviour. He needed to ask for and accept forgiveness and to re-evaluate himself in the light of his abusive behaviour. It was important that this 'forgiveness' for wronging the girls did not become part of the pattern of discounting the offences. The danger was in 'cheap' forgiveness, and here it was important to read the body language, the tears, the resolve and the insights he developed in order to 'be' different.

The progress of Fxx and Txx was monitored, in part, through their school perform-ance. While Ixx was in prison the school performance of the girls had improved sub-stantially. Upon his release, the school performance of the two victims plummeted to the pre-imprisonment level as measured by school testing, and Txx redeveloped an enuresis problem at school. Once the intervention plan was approved and agreed to by all parties, the school performance returned to the improved levels and the enuresis problem did not occur again. This was taken as evidence from the physical/organic and mental/emotional areas as a good indicator of the existence of abuse and/or stress. Both girls cooperated to develop a safety plan, did a 'Right to Say No' and 'Your Body is

Your Own' program and, importantly, developed a much wider circle of interests and associates. The social isolation that had left them vulnerable was ameliorated. Their social/relational and emotional/mental capacities were substantially built and the networks and trust relationships (in part through the Out-of-Home Care family to whom they went each second weekend to enable Ixx and Vxx to have time in her home together) were developed.

Vxx remained resistant to dealing with her own issues of childhood sexual assault (CSA). While she made substantial changes in her social life, appearance, parenting skills and general ability to care for the girls, her ability to protect them from further harm was questionable; hence the emphasis on building the girls' own capacity.

The inability of Vxx to achieve the objective (regarding her own CSA) that had been mutually set and agreed was a serious concern. The issue became whether the inability to achieve this objective rendered the whole family objective and the whole direction of the case as being unachievable. Thinking was around whether she was deliberately sabotaging the family goal (including consideration of whether she really did not want to be a reconciled and safe family; or whether it was simply too painful to consider her own CSA experience; or whether she wanted to remain personally powerful by negating the efforts of those around her; or whether her own sense of 'being' genuinely found no difficulty with her childhood experiences of CSA). A further environmental scan and some enhanced safety modifications, which were agreed to by all, enabled the plan to continue despite this particular element of it not being achieved.

Outcomes

After two and a half years, the family reunited. A further year of monitoring indicated that the school performance of the girls remained high. No further attempts at self-harm occurred; there was no reoccurrence of the enuresis problem; the outside social activities (which for the girls now included access to a town youth group and singing in a local choir) occurred; these young women's level of assertiveness and confidence continued to develop and grow in age-appropriate ways; the respite care foster family continued to be a source of advice and inspiration for the young women; the safety plans and 'family rules' remained in place; the nomenclature deliberately changed from 'girls' to 'young women' as a way of differentiating the past from the present; Ixx gained employment for the first time; and there was no indication of any offending behaviour. Whether the cycle of intergenerational abuse (which had occurred with Vxx, then her children) will have been interrupted in Vxx's grandchildren is a matter for some years into the future. In any evaluation, the time horizon is important – but the time horizon here was determined by the bond and the post-release period of imprisonment. This is a challenge to the 'being' of workers. While I could plan for the time when no services would be formally involved in the life of this family, the parameters are not dictated by the needs and circumstances of those involved but by legislation.

Reflecting on being as an individual and family worker

Understanding the self or 'being' of the social worker is important. Cournoyer (2000: 35) says, 'because social work practice involves the conscious and deliberate use of oneself, you become the medium through which knowledge, attitudes and skills are conveyed'. The social worker's self acts as a filter. Yan and Wong (2005), drawing on Kondrat (1999), use the social construction principles and assert that the social worker's self can be understood only in relation to others. Social work then becomes a site where the social worker and others negotiate and co-create new meanings and relationships.

The being or virtues are most important in areas of child sexual abuse, where it is easy to see people as the 'label' (i.e. an offender, child molester) to the exclusion of other characteristics (partner, driver) and consider children under the label of 'victim' (rather than the context of his/her whole life). Equally, it is important not to depreciate and discount the impact of offending behaviour or its consequences. The inter-relationship of the virtues (particularly of charity, hope and faith) needs to be carefully balanced with temperance and fortitude.

PERSONAL REFLECTION

At a personal level, CSA offenders show emotional reactions that are negative, and this was compounded by Ixx's failure to be truthful and by his avoidance of responsibility for his crimes. My way of dealing with this need for balance was twofold. First, I recognised that the balance was not like a set of scales where one weighs the various virtues to reach an equilibrium. Rather the virtues are required simultaneously. They reinforce each other in order to contribute to a positive and whole outcome. I re-examined the notion of charity (love) and reminded myself that charity (love) is not a weak or inconsequential notion but one of strength that requires fortitude to continue in difficult times and through very difficult circumstances over a long period. I had to hold charity and fortitude, hope and temperance, faith and prudence as well as justice simultaneously. In theological terms, I went back to my theological studies and recognised that the Christian Gospel (at least in the Protestant tradition) does not have a hierarchy of evil but acknowledges that all people stand in need of grace. Most of the religions do convey similar message. I needed to recognise that there was a measure of hopelessness that had also been appropriated by some of the agencies involved. Equally, the participants had a measure of hopelessness.

A particular challenge to my being was when Ixx made comments about offending against the girls not being important because they had been sexually assaulted before. I struggled with his lack of compassion, lack of insight, lack of understanding, apparent callous disregard for other human beings and the complete self-centredness. In this, I had to go back to my own sense of being and within my own Christian tradition and understanding recognise that 'all people have fallen short of the glory of God' and that 'we are all beggars – some may know where to find bread'. This reflection and reframing was helpful to me. I am sure other social workers from different faiths may be able to reflect and reframe depending upon their work contexts.

It was also initially difficult to exercise justice towards Vxx, who wanted others to maintain their commitments but was unable (or unwilling) to keep some of the commitments that she made. I recognised that my approach to justice was a 'recip-rocal justice', whereby you treated someone justly if they treated you justly and honoured their commitments. When Vxx was unable or unwilling to take responsi-bility at that time for her development and her commitments, I had to reconsider very carefully the assumption of reciprocity. I realised that faith involves recognising the things that your reason has accepted in spite of changing emotions and feelings. I had long recognised the need to practice in a way that promotes pro-social change. In practice, it was important to be temperate and make commitments only to the level that they could be kept and monitored. It was important that Ixx and Vxx (in different ways) did not extract concessions or directions that they would want kept but which could prove injurious or have counter-productive outcomes, especially for those who were most vulnerable (i.e. Txx and Fxx). I developed a technique of saying that I would like a couple of days to consider any request that was made and that I would not be responding to the immediate demands. This pattern was set at the first meeting and gave the impression that I had a long-term (hopeful) perspective rather than a short-term perspective.

Fortitude was critical. Ixx was aggressive to professionals and others. He had constructed a world of 'them and us' ('us' being the family) and had constructed himself as the guardian of 'us'. He was powerless in many areas of his life (work, education, friendships) but was dominating within 'his family'. Fortitude was required in challenging his dominion but in a way that allowed for positive change rather than resulting in adversarial and oppositional outcomes (reinforcing 'them and us') or complete withdrawal from the situation ('see what they have done to us').

Part of the case plan was to assist Ixx to 'be' someone different. This was achieved by removing the excuses that had developed and had been maintained throughout the period of imprisonment. This involved confrontation. Using the discount hierarchy as a guide and examining Ixx's statements in an hermeneutic way, Ixx progressed. At the level of existence, he initially and throughout his imprisonment denied his involvement ('I did not do anything at all – it's lies'). He moved to a stage of significance by admitting offending, but by denying the severity of the offending ('I only touched them through their clothes') and by discounting the significance (as the girls had been assaulted before, his offences were 'like a slice off a cut loaf'). At the level of solvability, Ixx admitted the impact of his behaviour but asserted that 'it has happened and I can't do anything about it now'. Although the classic discount hierarchy involves the level of self, I prefer the term 'level of responsibility' (using the concept from Jenkins 1990). Here, Ixx acknowledges that his behaviour was wrong, hurtful and criminal and that he could personally change a range of actions, behaviours and attitudes that could ameliorate or remediate some of the effects of his behaviour. It was also acknowledged that some of the effects were irreparable. To achieve these changes involved education on psycho-social and psycho-sexual issues and on the nature of families, 'home' and being a 'man'. It involved developing real empathy for the victims and understanding the nature of his offending actions. It then involved redeveloping an alternative narrative with an understanding of responsibility.

A most important part of the case plan was to assist the girls to 'be' different and to reframe the deficit stories and hopelessness with positive experiences and a sense of value and personal worth. The plan involved the girls in positive experiences of their choice, including sport, ballet and music. The fortnightly respite care for the girls (which allowed Ixx and Vxxx to have time together in her home) had the effect of providing an alternative family for the girls, an alternative role model of family, stability and access to other avenues of help in their future and provided one piece in the safety plan that was developed. The plan meant that the girls had a guaranteed two years of remaining with their mother and the opportunity to develop other skills and attributes as well as two years of developmental maturation. Programs such as the 'Right to Say No' program enabled the girls to reflect upon their worth and their self-esteem and to develop self-protection strategies.

Vxx was also offered the opportunity to 'be'. This was offered through activities and programs of her choice. She laboured fully in the activities and developed a range of additional skills (including pottery, parenting skills and learning to drive a car).

PERSONAL REFLECTION

I am conscious that in the Western tradition, thinking leads to doing. There are other traditions in which 'doing' (or praxis) comes first and reflective thinking occurs later as part of the cycle of thinking about the action. I am part of the Western tradition, and I wondered what might have occurred had I followed a different and less structured tradition. Having collected a range of information and assessed the possible uses of the information, I spent time thinking about the possibilities (whole family, divided family, family in progress, no family) and used de Bono's six-hat thinking as a way of bringing order, structure and creativity to the situation. Thinking also dominated theories for practice that could be used in the situation. Among the plethora of theories for practice, some seemed appropriate to the environmental and participant context, and others that required intensive or specialist resources or high intellect and high capacity for insight or high levels of literacy on the part of the participants were dismissed.

Better thinking and assessment may have prevented the first whole-of-family conference from being abandoned. On reflection, I think that I simply assessed the situation wrongly, and in that regard I behaved intemperately (I went too far, too quickly). I thought that the shuttle negotiations and individual work with Ixx had led to a point where the whole family could discuss their future in a sensible way. However, Ixx had not changed to the extent that I had thought, and the case conference was abandoned. I think that I underestimated the strength of his past learned behaviour and his understandings as 'head' of the family (Ixx's phrase). His perception of 'headship' needed to be thought through and work then done on the nature of 'headship' in families. This had particular gender implications in that a female worker may have more quickly and accurately assessed the situation. My own maleness and understanding of the concept of 'headship' in the Christian tradition (the concept of relational mutuality as based around Ephesians 5:21) may have blinded me to Ixx's different understanding for which he used the same terminology. As we explored his and my understandings of 'headship', it became clear that there were significant differences and that these needed to be resolved before any further meetings.

One of the difficulties here was that Vxx had appropriated a passive female role and reinforced Ixx's perception that the man was the head and defender of the family. Ixx had appropriated a conservative male approach that fitted well within the rural community but became distorted and had the corollary of being in part responsible for his justification for his offending and his considering 'the family' as his personal fiefdom. This was supported by the comments and views of Vxx. Over time, Ixx came to see that headship meant responsibility rather than power. Despite the rise of feminist ideology and practices, Ixx's view (and that of Vxx) of a man's function in a family was not particularly atypical of rural, conservative, single-income families. However, he used that perception to distort and justify his behaviour. My own being as a Christian person was sometimes helpful in challenging this pervading ideology as many, including Ixx, considered that male headship was somehow 'the right way' even if they could not articulate the premises upon which they based the behaviour and their being. Their concept of 'headship' was poorly considered and was more a reflection of Victorian values than theological or well-thought-out considerations.

Formal and informal theory

Payne (2005: 6) following Sibeon (1990) uses the terms 'formal' and 'informal' theory, although it may be argued that 'explicit' and 'implicit' theory are more appropriate terms. Payne identifies 'formal theory' as that which is written down and debated within the profession and academia whereas 'informal theory' consists of the moral, political and cultural values that exist in society and constructions from practical experiences.

PERSONAL REFLECTION

There were many times when I was involved in 'doing' (action) without that 'doing' being tied to a formal or explicit theory. But guiding any action ought to be the implicit or informal theory derived from moral, political, cultural and social (and I would argue spiritual and existential) values and/or from practical experience.

Informal or implicit theory becomes part of the way the social worker practices and becomes part of his/her being. This allows for formal and informal (explicit and implicit) theory to be valued and used. The real question to be reflected upon involves the relationship between the formal and informal (explicit and implicit) theory and when the formal and informal theory needs to be challenged and changed so that it is not an agent of oppression or incorrectly based on bias and/or prejudice. Client confidentiality will serve as a good example. Formally, a client has a right to confidentiality in most circumstances (e.g. in the AASW's *Code of Ethics*). Formal and informal theory notes that confidentiality in sexual assault matters can become part of the culture of secrecy, which is a feature of the grooming process and the offending behaviour.

We argue that confidentiality is not an absolute, nor that it is between the participant and the participant's worker but rather have accepted that confidentiality is between the participant and the agency. The challenge in working in a family environment with multiple agencies is determining who is entitled to know certain information and at what point (if at all) is confidentiality overridden.

PERSONAL REFLECTION

Confidentiality is a real issue in multiagency case conferences, and I had to challenge my acceptance that confidentiality was a matter between the individual and the mandated agency. I read extensively on privacy and confidentiality but found that it was highly principled and philosophical but not very useful in everyday practice. Confidentiality became an issue, for example, when school personnel were at the workers' conference and the discussion moved to the current relationships of Ixx and Vxx. As chair of the case conference, I considered to what extent individual privacy could be infringed in the interest of the family. I suggested that the discussion we were about to have was not really relevant to the school and that it may be an opportune time for the school representatives to have coffee or tea. I could not have explicitly aligned the action to a formal theory of privacy and confidentiality, and it may have infringed family confer- encing protocol and endangered agency relationships. It was a function of my 'being' that it was not prudent, and perhaps unjust, to allow the conference to discuss these issues with a membership that included some people who did not need to know this information. Confidentiality will include considerations of the principle of 'need to know', which generally refers to telling people only as much as they need to know at the time. It will also be influenced by legislation regarding privacy.

Habitual and heuristic practices

Experienced practitioners may act habitually (in the sense of practising what has worked previously) or heuristically (in the sense of *discovery learning* through trial and error). Clinical practice can be dominated by particular theoretical positions, the influence of past cases and the dominance of one approach. It is important to recognise the unique-ness of every situation. While involved in this case, I was working on other longitudinal sexual assault matters. One involved a long-term, single, ageing predatory paedophile with a history of sexual assault on pre-pubescent boys who fitted the description of a fixated sex offender (see Groth et al. 1982). My approach was to limit his access to pre-pubescent boys and to monitor his social relationships. Another matter involved intra-familial sexual assault of daughters over a sustained period in a situation of acute social isolation. While the offender was in prison, the family moved to a large town, made excellent progress and had decided not to resume any relationship with him upon his release. My chief concerns were in protecting the family members from threatening and/ or ingratiating behaviour by the offender and ensuring that he did not form other relationships with other women who had young daughters.

These matters required different approaches. In the first case, the offender was prepared to acknowledge his disposition (nature) towards pre-pubescent boys and had rationalised his behaviour as 'teaching them how to love' and called upon the examples of history (Roman and Greek) as indicating that 'man–boy love' had been socially acceptable in the past and that it was only quite recently constructed as a crime. In the other example, there were features similar to those of Ixx (similar views of family relationships, a view of the proprietorial rights of a man with respect to his family) and some similar family features (social isolation of the family, restricted insight), but the essential difference was that the period in which the offender was in prison allowed the female family members to develop 'new' and different lives (in my terms, to *be* different and liberated from oppression).

As an experienced practitioner, in dealing with Ixx and Vxx and their situation, I was acting on their individual and particular circumstances. I was seeking to bring my practice experience to their unique situation. Past and current experience is part of a social worker's 'being' and can be a frame for action and a lens for viewing a situation – but it is only one of the elements that are applied.

▥ The nature of evil

Sexual assault matters (and many others in the experience of social workers) raise issues about the nature of evil, the capacity of people to change and about remediation of the effects of evil. Views on evil come from many sources (for example, Tolkien's *Lord of the Rings* trilogy; —Peck 1982). I considered the nature of evil in classical, philosophical terms with evil being either natural (earthquakes, famine and so on) or moral (wilful human acts) with each being able to be subdivided into physical (pain in the body or mind) and metaphysical (injustices, random chance and pain of the soul) evil. I have had to reflect on these issues in relation to Ixx and Vxx (and others). Initially, in my own being, I considered that evil was the antithesis of good. It was an easy, simple classification to allocate people to an either/or category. With experience, advancing age and more profound consideration of Christian theology and Western philosophical reading, I consider that evil is neither a natural or necessary element of human existence nor simply the negation of good, but rather a parasite state that perpetuates itself by misusing God's good resources and by following wrong directions. It is the consequence of human beings who are self-centred and self-absorbed. Human evil has a moral dimension that occurs when individuals fail to develop and live by appropriate virtues (temperance, prudence, justice, fortitude, charity, hope and faith) that manifest themselves in many ways, including excessive drinking, excessive speeding, drug use and the failure to consider the rights of others. For me, this allows a framework for considering gross acts of evil while maintaining hope for the future.

▥ The influence of the personal and the professional

Personal experience affects one's professional being. This is a profound factor that is frequently overlooked. 'Being' involves the personal and the professional, although some helping professions in the positivist tradition attempt to draw a sharp distinction between the personal and the professional. Whether it is a failure on my part to be able to separate the personal and professional is a matter for others to judge. The reality is, however, that the nature of being human requires bringing together disparate knowledge from many sources – some of which might lay outside professional or academic training.

The influence of external conditions and circumstances

I have used the Ixx and Vxx example as a social work training exercise for social work students – some of whom are mature-aged and current employees in child protection (CP) authorities. The case frequently receives a hostile reaction from students as they struggle with the nature of the offences and the attitude of Ixx and their perceived dislike of Vxx for her preparedness to surrender the children to care in order to be with Ixx. These reactions may arise as the example challenges their own sense of 'being'. The reaction of current CP staff is to apply actuarial risk management models and determine that the children would be removed immediately and placed in care. Others have indicated that the type of individual and family work done here would not be possible as managers would not be prepared to take the risk or allocate the time involved in the longitudinal nature of individual and family work of this type in the resource-deprived environment. They cite the public scrutiny, the climate of risk-aversion and the media as combining to ensure that any practice is conservative, evidenced-based (evidence being primarily empirical evidence) and defensible and with a focus on physical safety.

If the criticisms made by students and staff are accurate, then individual and family work needs to return the focus to the centrality of humanity rather than a mechanical application of a risk-assessment tool. Thinking, doing and being offers the opportunity for participants to be heard and valued; for interventions to be appropriate and longitudinal; and for individual and family work to place people as the co-participants in an emancipatory and empowering approach rather than a defensive and regulatory approach.

REFLECTIVE EXERCISE 3.4

While working with the individual and family case discussed above, the social worker used his being in terms of virtues. Critically discuss the following questions.

1 Did the social worker use common sense to act with due consideration of consequences (prudence)?

2 Did the social worker go to the right length with the participant family (temperance)?

3 Did the social worker maintain fairness, honesty and truthfulness, and keep promises (justice)?

4 Did the social worker work with the case with courage and confidence (fortitude)?

5 Did the social worker love and forgive the participant and his family (charity)?

6 Did the social worker give direction and purpose (hope)?

7 Did the social worker hold to reasoned fundamentals irrespective of changing emotions and feelings (faith)?

Conclusion

Individual and family work involves a range of clinical skills and requires careful consideration and thinking. It involves developing collaborative skills with individuals and families but may also involve managing conflict and confronting others. The chapter has not concentrated on techniques for individual and family work (e.g. Milan approaches, brief solution focused, Gestalt, family therapy, psychoanalytic, behavioural, transactional analysis, cognitive-behavioural therapies and many others) but has concentrated on the importance of thinking, doing and being in individual and family work. If the outcome studies are accurate, then 30 per cent of an outcome variance is a result of the relationship that a therapist can form with an individual/family, and a further 15 per cent is determined by the hope and optimism that can be engendered. The being of the therapist and his/her use of self are critical to the outcomes of working with individuals and families. This chapter has demonstrated the use of being in individual and family work where the client contribution was initially hostile and the social and intellectual resources limited.

Questions and exercises

1 What did you learn from this case?
2 Do you react to the use of the term 'case'? What are the implications?
3 What were the main challenges for the worker, and how did he overcome them?
4 Did the social worker jump into action without any explicit theory?
5 What was the thinking, doing and being of the social worker?
6 Did the social worker bring his thinking, doing and being together in a balanced way, or any one was more dominant than the other? Critically discuss.
7 Do you think a social worker can meaningfully use her/his thinking, doing and being together while working with individuals and families?
8 With hindsight, how could difficulties be overcome to practise the conscious use of being along with thinking and doing? Discuss.
9 What do you believe about evil? Why?
10 By applying your own thinking, doing and being assess this individual and family case and prepare a work plan.

4

Being in the context of reflective practice with groups

'HEY, BILL. WE have got a challenge for you! We have a bunch of long-term prisoners that are getting near the end of their sentence, and we need them to be ready for release. There's about 20–30 of them and the average time in prison is about 10 years – some are repeat offenders. They are all institutionalised and function well in prison – but there is not much chance on the outside. We have funding for 20 hours – in 20 hours can you get these guys ready to get out of gaol and stay out? We thought of you because we cannot do it with our workload and because you have a background in corrections. It's urgent.' That was the phone call.

This chapter will consider key aspects of groups and demonstrate the reflective practice of being along with thinking and doing as a group worker in an institutional setting that provides particular challenges including a highly controlled context, rigid top-down bureaucracy and long-term dependency.

▦ Chapter objectives

After reading this chapter you should:

- appreciate the fundamentals of group work and its nature and characteristics
- understand your own personal and theoretical orientations and leadership approaches
- consider the constraints and attributes of working with a specific groups
- consider and apply aspects of being that are relevant to working as a group worker.

PERSONAL REFLECTION

I like group work practice, and I am committed to the notions of service, to the ideology and hope of reformation and rehabilitation. I have a sense of doing something worthwhile for individuals and communities if I contribute to the smooth transition of inmates from the institutional life to law-abiding community life.

Main themes and concepts used

In this chapter, I share my reflections on thinking about group work in terms of the prison context, stages and phases of group development, educational and therapeutic group work in prisons. I consider what I did with group work members in terms of formation of the group and preparing group members for release. I reflect on my being throughout the group work process.

There are extensive and well-developed texts on group work that consider the overall nature of group work (Zastrow 2006, O'Hara & Pockett 2011, Preston-Shoot 2007).

Purpose of group work

Groups can include therapeutic, educational and instructional, supportive and self-help (mutual) groups. They can be didactic, open or closed, voluntary or involuntary, task-focused, psycho-educational, open-ended or time-limited, project-oriented, goal-oriented, supportive, empowering or disempowering, led or leaderless, inclusive or exclusive membership. Although there might be more than one purpose, clarity of *group purpose* is important for all participants. Groups have three levels of purpose: the individual, the group, and the external environment. The relative emphasis on each of these varies depending on the type of group.

Preparation and planning

The importance of preparation and planning cannot be overemphasised, and thorough pre-group planning will result in fewer difficulties in the group itself. This group was set in a prison.

Group design and activity

The activity of this group was to (design and) deliver ten two-hour educational and experiential group sessions for up to ten inmates who had the possibility of release to parole supervision within one year. The sessions were intended to equip participants for successful community living upon their release – the objective set by prison authorities. The group was run for a state department within a private prison. The program was developed and designed with the literature in mind but modified in the light of interviews with prisoners. Excluding participants from setting objectives is a poor process and antithetical to a good reflective, empowering practice. The program was run on three occasions over a two-year period. In all, thirty inmates commenced the program and twenty-nine completed it.

Group membership

The criteria for group membership was that participants had to be long-term prisoners and/or with a record of failure on parole and within one year of the expected earliest date of release. The department wanted to 'require people to attend'. This was resisted, and people 'self-nominated' (although it was recognised that there was pressure on prisoners from staff to 'avail themselves of this opportunity'). All 'self-nominated' prisoners were accepted to the program as an important consideration was to empower prisoners to choose to participate rather than being coerced. Choice is limited within a setting that operates from a paradigm of control and command. This first group of ten long-term prisoners had an average age of 32 years (the range was 23 years to 54 years) with the average time in prison on the current sentence being more than ten years (range 5–22 years). While subject to the normal legal and procedural restraints of a prison, any reporting obligation to the department was refused. Negotiations were conducted with prison authorities to ensure that the group was not under video surveillance. Kendall (1993) found some key therapeutic considerations identified by prisoners as:

1 a space to be themselves
2 a respite from the sense of constant surveillance
3 to be in control of their own lives, and
4 an opportunity to value and be valued by others.

Emphasis was placed on the independence of the program from the prison, the interdependence of group members and the discouraging of attendance simply as a means of impressing for parole purposes. Participants were challenged to commit to new ways of thinking and doing and being and to personal change. In order to pro-socially model change and growth as normal for all people, the group leader committed to some personal goals of change. This limited the power differential between the participants and the leader while recognising that there was mutual respect in spite of substantial differences in power, freedom, education and backgrounds.

Size and composition

The group size and composition will affect what happens in groups. An ideal size for therapeutic groups is quite small. The smaller the group is, the higher the level of intimacy and participation (Wheelan 2005). The leader insisted upon a maximum of ten per group.

Open or closed groups

Open groups tend to be ongoing groups that allow members to join at will. To counter the debilitating effects of imprisonment, this group was *closed and time limited*. Trust and group cohesion are likely to be stronger in closed groups.

Establishing group rules

Establishing a group agreement was critical in this setting. Potential members needed to know that the group would be a safe and respectful place. Agreements on confidentiality, equal space and opportunity, non-violence, non-racism, non-sexism and attendance, gave the potential member the underpinning values of the group and provided a clear basis for members to intervene if unacceptable behaviour occurred.

Potential members needed to know the possible group activities and whether it would be a didactic group that mainly listened to the presenters, or a discussion and/or activity group, and whether there would be experiential exercises or role-plays. These were communicated in the pre-group interview. Members developed more involvement in group activity as group trust grew.

Group development

In group development, a 'linear' model suggests that groups go through a succession of predictable stages often referred to in group work literature as forming, storming, norming, performing and mourning/adjourning (Tuckman 1965). This group showed these features but also showed circular or spiralling tendencies. Storming featured prominently as this was a total institution and it was difficult to separate issues that happened to group members from the institution. The group development was affected by outside factors (cell searches, loss of privileges), which were external to the group itself but were part of the group's lived environment.

Group dynamics and structures

'Group dynamics and structure' refers to the creation and maintenance of relationship patterns, formation of subgroups and cliques, participation, feelings, leadership, leadership struggles, conflict, competition, cooperation, morale, influence and atmosphere. For the social worker, understanding the dynamics and process or the sense of 'being' of the group is important.

Participation expectations

'Participation' refers to the individual's contribution within the group. It is a complex entity that is not to be judged on the quantity of interaction (although this can be a guide) but includes the benefit derived from the group, non-verbal communication within the group and the degree of commitment to the group. In this group, one of the 'high influencers' said little – but their contributions were well timed and insightful, and helped the individuals and the group to achieve its therapeutic work.

Different members exhibited *influence* and had different *styles of influence*. One member was quite autocratic (a directive style attempting to impose his will, values and views by passing judgement on other group members). Another influenced through peacemaking by supporting other group members' decisions, and trying to prevent conflict or the expression of unpleasant feelings. One participant adopted a laissez-faire style of influence. This was exhibited by a lack of involvement in the group and by supporting group decisions without commitment. Being uninvolved may reflect an approach to surviving in prison. As the group developed, this style of influencing declined and a more democratic style developed that allowed for the expression of feelings and ideas without judging and attempted to confront conflict in a constructive, problem-solving way.

Zastrow (2006: 177–81) describes six formal *decision-making approaches*:

1 consensus (where all participants agreed)
2 simple majority vote (where more than 50 per cent agreed)
3 two-thirds or three-quarters majority vote (to be agreed more than two-thirds or three-quarters was required
4 delegated decisions (the decision was left to one person or a small group – often on the basis of the group's perception of expertise or capacity)
5 multiple voting (where the decision is arrived at by a series of votes that progressively eliminates the option with the least votes)
6 averaging individual opinions (seeking a decision based on finding a middle course that is the average of opinions).

In this group, decision-making tended to be far more complex and random. Significant variables included influence, the strength of the opinion and the importance of the decision to different members.

Functions

Task functions include initiating activities, suggesting ideas, clarifying, reflecting on ideas, opinion-seeking, seeking feedback, diagnosing, planning interventions, information-giving, summarising, evaluating.

Maintenance functions of groups are the processes that maintain the group. They facilitate harmonious, cooperative relationships among group members, create an atmosphere that enables each member to contribute maximally, ensure smooth and effective teamwork within the group and include encouraging, being friendly, gatekeeping, facilitating others' participation, expressing feelings, cooperative participation, compromising, mediating, setting and applying standards.

'Norms' refer to standards of behaviour that develop in a group, usually in order to control the behaviour of members. Norms may be stated or implied (e.g. certain topics are avoided; only positive comments are expressed; emotional displays are unacceptable) and may facilitate group progress or hinder it. One of the challenges of this group was to establish norms in the group that were different from the norms of the wider prison. Being referred to by my first name rather than 'sir' was pro-social modelling of a community standard – but it was difficult when, for the remainder of the week, the institutional norm reinforced power and status differentials.

Belbin Team roles – related to managing teams

Meredith Belbin (1981) identified the team roles of Shaper, Plant, Monitor–Evaluator, Resource–Investigator, Coordinator, Teamworker, Implementer, Finisher and Specialist. This is one of a number of approaches that have identified the different roles played in teams and groups.

Harvard One-Minute Evaluation

Note that this type of evaluation may also be called Post-it Note Evaluation or Minute Evaluation. It is a widely used classroom evaluation that asks short questions and takes one minute. The questions can include: what was the most important point? What was the most surprising idea or concept? What questions remain unanswered? What action will you take as a result of the class or activity? (Chizmar & Ostrosky 1998).

Pro-social modelling

Pro-social modelling is an integrated intervention model of working with involuntary clients that involves identifying and reinforcing pro-social things that clients say and do while appropriately challenging antisocial attitudes and behaviour in the context of a collaborative and respectful client–worker relationship (see Trotter 2006).

Tuckman's Model of Group Development

Formed in the 1960s, the original model had four stages. The initial stage of *forming* is often characterised by a member's desire for acceptance, the avoidance of controversy and conflict, establishing expectations, agreement on common goals, identifying and similarities. *Storming* – the next stage – is often about power and control, expressing differences in ideas, personalities and opinions, challenging leadership and other members and identifying issues and resources as well as establishing communication patterns. *Norming* is a further stage where members agree (implicitly or explicitly) on roles and processes and how decisions will be made. In the *performing* stage, members work collaboratively and independently and with care for each other to achieve results and to find solutions or approaches that work. The model now includes a stage of adjourning, where the group members complete their work and disengage both from the task and from other group members.

Please note that the stages model does not necessarily imply a smooth transition from one stage to another – but circumstances or events may force a performing group back to the storming or norming stage.

■ Things that you need to know

It is assumed that you will have a basic knowledge of group work and group work models. Working with groups in a correctional setting has particular features that influence the application of group work models to that setting.

Criminological theories

Criminological theories are extensive and variously classified (e.g. Schmalleger 2008: 21). Criminals, like all human beings, are physical/organic, mental/emotional, social/relational and spiritual/existential beings who live within an environment. Social work is about the person-in-their-environment. Multidimensional approaches from diverse perspectives offer the best opportunity to avoid dangerous practice. 'Scientific' or biological criminologists who emphasise only the physical/organic aspect have a dangerous history. Aristotle was condemned to death partly on the evidence of a physiognomist while medieval imperfections (warts, moles or a third nipple) were used as physical 'evidence' of demonic possession. Della Porte (1535–1615), Beccaria (1764) and the physiognomist Lavater (1775) attributed characteristics such as 'shifty eyes' or 'weak chins' to criminals while phrenologist Gall (1758–1828) related criminal behaviour to bumps on the skull. Lombroso (1876) used the Darwinian theory of evolution to classify criminals as biological throwbacks. The eugenics movement of the early twentieth century has commonality with later work of Jacobs, Brunton and Melville (1965 on XYY Supermale), Wilson (1975 on the survival of the gene pool) and Thornhill and Palmer (2000) on rape in their appeal to biology. Some criminological biophysical theories are reductionist, materialist and determinist.

PERSONAL REFLECTION

I have been influenced by 'labelling theory', and the later developments of other symbolic interactionists who see crime and criminality as people acting, choosing and making sense of the world as best they can rather than crime and criminality being objective facts with an innate causality. I recognise the shifting paradigms in criminology (see Fattah 1997). The paradigm shifts include an interest in scientific criminology through the ecological explanations of the Chicago School (see Shaw & McKay 1969), sceptical criminology (see Sutherland 1947), the synthesising of criminology and sociology by Merton (1968), and the so-called new criminologists or radical criminologists (see Young 1971, Cohen 1983). Martinson's (1974) 'nothing works' was followed by a period of the 'post-social criminologists' (see O'Malley 1996) and symbolic interactionalist, postmodernist theories (see Harvey 1990; Bauman 1991) have given way to a more modern concentration on reconciliation, victimology and reintegrative shaming (see Braithwaite 1989). Each has value and brings a way of looking at the world of crime and criminality.

▮ Systemic/critical thinking

The group worker reflectively applied systemic/critical thinking to the (re)habilitation program logic of prisons. Schematically it operates in the following manner:

Σ (Joe + 500 Joes) × (prison environment) × (time)= ☺ well-adjusted community member

'Joe' represents prisoners, who will be (statistically) male, young, undereducated, unemployed at the time of the offence. Most (74–82 per cent) will self-report a drug and/or alcohol problem. About 30 per cent will have psychiatric disabilities and/or developmental delay and more with learning difficulties, and will be disproportionately Indigenous and have disrupted or destructive parental and family ties.

Joe is then added to (say) 500 others who exhibit Joe's statistical characteristics to a greater or lesser degree.

This group of 501 Joes is placed in a large group environment that is controlling and oppressive and has bizarre norms and a culture of fear, intimidation and dependency. It removes the vast majority of decision-making from Joe, including actual money, the opportunity to meet people unlike oneself, almost any legitimate expression of sexuality, some civil rights, and practical life skills (when to get up, when and what to eat, with whom you will cohabit) and a myriad of small but significant decisions.

These factors are then multiplied by a factor of time, which is based on the offence, the politics of legislators and the exercise of judicial discretion rather than a carefully planned program of reintegration for Joe.

The presumed outcome of this process is a well-adjusted, rehabilitated Joe ready to resume his place in the community.

Prisons serve a multiplicity of functions, including as places of punishment, as a means of specific deterrence, a focus for general deterrence and a place of incapacitation (by restraining freedom and access to others in the 'normal' community). There is separate program logic for incapacitation, punishment and deterrence. The Prison (Re)habilitation Program logic is not well reasoned to promote positive change. The evidence of recidivism rates is 64 per cent within two years.

Reflecting on therapeutic group work within prisons

Surprisingly little has been written on therapeutic groups specifically within prisons. As a knowledge base for prison group work, it was important to reflect upon a number of features from different models. Such features create a 'mental map' that can compare what is actually occurring in the group to the 'mental map' (what generally should be occurring).

PERSONAL REFLECTION

In relation to leadership, I used a number of approaches. The behaviour-oriented criteria of Krech, Crutchfield and Ballachey (1962) recognises that a leader is a member of the group that s/he is leading; embodies the norms and values that are central to the group; and fits the expectations of the members about how a leader for this particular group should behave. Other leadership criteria are 'trait-based' (see Johnson & Johnson 2000: 189) and functional or performance-based with leadership tasks being distributed among group members. Having undertaken the Belbin (1981) Group/Team Questionnaire on a number of occasions, I operate most effectively in the role of Shaper and Coordinator. I anticipated that I would need to provide behaviour and trait-based leadership and progressively lessen the reliance of the members on my leadership and develop in the members 'functional and distributional' leadership.

Power and control in this group was central. French and Raven (1968) recognise five types of power. It was my intention not to use coercive power at all and to progressively pass expert, referent and legitimate power to group members. Reward power was limited – with rewards intrinsic to a member's being.

This group was time-limited, person-centred, mildly psychotherapeutic, guided, problem-solving and social skills oriented.

The work of Howells and Day (1999) showed that prison groups needed to unpack the cognitive processes that allow offenders to justify their offending. The most successful approaches were behavioural, cognitive behavioural and social cognitive. McGuire and Rowson (1996: 84; 2013) state that social, cognitive behavioural and cognitive self-instruction appeared to have efficacy. In the context of this case study, the existential/spiritual dimension was considered a necessary addition.

Most group programs operating in correctional settings are instructional or educational rather than therapeutic. Howells and Day (1999: 4) recommended that programs should run for at least 100 hours and take place over three to four months in order to establish new behaviour and to ensure that they are embedded and practised. Participants of this group did exercises as practice. The imposed parameter of ten weeks (20 hours in all per group) was directly contrary to the research findings.

Unique features of prisons might not be conducive to group work theory applied from other settings. Prison groups have particular environmental features. These include:

- power vested in the prison authorities
- destructive institutional norms
- restrictive rules
- a formal and informal hierarchy
- goals and objectives set by the institution
- limited capacity or willingness to accommodate individual differences
- clear standards of unacceptable behaviour
- strong formal and informal institutional sanctions
- competing subgroups
- varying commitment of prisoners to institutional goals
- limited or non-existent participant involvement in the decision-making of the institution
- an oppressive institutional ethos.

With these environmental factors and the existing research, expectations of the group were modest. The environment involved significant social exclusion not generally conducive to developing positive attitudes and behaviour change. Participants had the opportunity to be involved with a mildly therapeutic program that acknowledged the static reoffending risk factors but aimed at the dynamic risk factors that have been identified as the high-risk factors for parole failure (Gendreau, Little & Coggin 1996, Hanson & Thornton 1999). The static risk factors are: socioeconomic deprivation; poor parenting; family deviance; school problems; hyperactivity–impulsivity–attention deficit; early antisocial behaviour; the age of first conviction; and the number of previous convictions. The dynamic risk factors relevant to this group were:

- accommodation
- employment
- alcohol and other drug use
- relationships
- relapse prevention
- leisure
- attitude and motivation, and
- thinking and beliefs.

In this case, it was important to target the *dynamic risk factors* while acknowledging the presence of the static factors.

▧ Doing: what the group worker did

This group used experiential and didactic approaches that focused on awareness and behaviour change, knowledge acquisition, transferring learning to risk situations via games and role plays, developing skills with an emphasis on practice, and challenging and changing attitudes via group processes and individual reflections by creating the space for 'aha' experiences through inductive and deductive reasoning. Using phrases like 'holding in tension' or 'separate ways of seeing things that together give you a fuller picture and more opportunities', the program was designed to assist participants to explore new and different ways of thinking, doing and being. It was structured around three core living skills (see figure 4.1) that were considered necessary for successful integration into the community. These core skills were applied to the dynamic risk factors.

The anticipated outcomes included:

- knowledge of key risk factors
- skills in creative thinking
- strengths-focused problem reframing
- skills in communicating

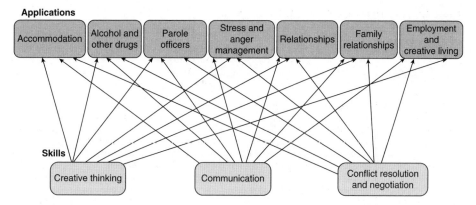

Figure 4.1 Successful parole program

- strategies to address expected problem situations
- realistic expectations of relationships and accommodation options
- useful strategies for drugs and alcohol avoidance or control
- first day or first week release planning
- exploring the relationship with previous parole or release experiences
- skills in negotiating and conflict resolution.

Non-compulsory process evaluations were encouraged. The sessions were evaluated on a scale of 1 to 10 on meeting session objectives and participant satisfaction and learning. The sessions are detailed in table 4.1.

Qualitative comments

Written and drawn qualitative anonymous comments were also sought. Based on the 'Harvard One-Minute Evaluation' approach and modified for this group, comments included:

- This session has given me food for thought
- It's not too late to follow dreams
- I truly feel positive after leaving this group
- It was fun
- I start to motivate myself more
- I learned what's going on outside so you can interact and not feel left out
- Excellent communication … friendly and relaxed … no one is treated any differently from another
- I do not feel pressured in any way
- Changing my personal irritating behaviour and I will shower more

Table 4.1 Activities and program evaluation

Session and topic	Objective(s)	Content	My doing as a group worker (roles as per Zastrow 2003)	Participants' doing	Session evaluation
1 Introduction and new ways of thinking	Introduce the facilitator and participants; outline the rationale and sessions or program; discuss dynamic and static risk factors; review the program logic of imprisonment	Discussion; getting to know you exercises; systemic and creative thinking exercises; team-building exercise; de Bono's six-hat thinking exercises; discuss the ethical and practical limitations of groups in prison	Consider 'forming' stages of a group **Role:** initiator, public speaker, educator, coordinator	Determine post-release goals; self-identify current patterns of thinking; covenant with the group	Returned: 10/10 Satisfaction Rating (SR): 7.8/10 Meeting objectives (MO): 7.3/10 My evaluation (ME): fun, safe and participatory
2 Communication	Give a theoretical overview of communicating and develop new skills	Communication skills (non-verbal, paralinguistic, meta-communication); 'I statements'; active listening games; reflecting skills; role plays	Teach/instruct; elicit contextual examples extended to community settings; explain role plays as rehearsals with flexibility; Consider conflict; ensure differentiation **Role:** educator, enabler, empowerer	Discussion; role plays; analyse pieces of communication; develop skills	Returned: 10/10 SR: 7.5/10 MO: 8/10 ME: participatory, well received
3 Negotiating and conflict resolution	Consider ways to negotiate and resolve conflict and develop personal strategies for conflict resolution	Conflict resolution material; creating win–win situations; Kennedy's model of negotiating; the 'new truck problem'	Normalise conflict; develop conflict resolution skills; direct role plays; reinforce 'I messages' **Role:** mediator/ activist/ coordinator/ educator	Analyse previous means of resolving conflict; identify conflict personal 'triggers'; role play 'at risk' situations; do the 'new truck problem'	Returned: 10/10 SR: 9.5/10 MO: 8.5/10 ME: outstanding; excellent participation
4 Accommodation	To apply new ways of thinking, by using and applying the three core skills to post-release accommodation	Values clarification exercise based around accommodation; identified affordable accommodation possibilities	Develop the clarification exercise; challenge irrational or shallow thinking; consider group norms; consider issues of closeness;	Proposed post-release accommodation plans; values clarification exercise; identify personal irritating behaviour; assess and identify dangers	Returned: 10/10 SR: 7/10 MO: 8/10 ME: Excellent participation; new learning; ability to apply core concepts to an application

Table 4.1 (cont.)

Session and topic	Objective(s)	Content	My doing as a group worker (roles as per Zastrow 2003)	Participants' doing	Session evaluation
			power, control, intimacy, differentiation **Role:** researcher, enabler, advocate, negotiator	in the plans; undertake a preliminary post-release budget	
5 Alcohol and other drugs	Applying the core skills to alcohol and other drugs	Brief purpose-designed questionnaire about knowledge and attitudes to drugs and alcohol; purpose designed AOD personal inventory	Designed AOD questionnaire; suggest ways to manage AOD issues; manage conflict; self-check on my use of power – sought participant feedback **Role:** initiator, empowerer, educator, researcher	Undertake a personal drinking/drug history; engaged in a brief alcohol education package based on cartoons; develop a drink/drug covenant; role-play difficult scenarios in sobriety	Returned: 9/9 SR: 7/10 MO: 8/10 ME: excellent participation; new learning; ability to apply core concepts to an application
6 Managing stress and anger	Applying the core skills to stress management	A purpose-designed stress inventory; identified physiological, psychological and behavioural responses to stress; identified methods of stress release; identified precipitators of anger; identified anger management techniques; taught relaxation and anger management techniques; a video on anger in relationships	Develop the stress inventory; lead the relaxation exercises; self-disclose personal stressors; suggest a range of management of stress plans that deal with the bio, psycho, socio and existential elements **Role:** initiator, educator, empowerer, researcher, coordinator	Identify personal stressors, risk factors or situations in relapse; do stress management exercises; rehearse relaxation techniques; identified personal stress management plan; identified 'nice' things will manage stress in the first day and first week of release	Returned: 9/9 SR: 7.5/10 MO: 6.5/10 ME: too much content so teaching relaxation and identifying relapse prevention strategies was rushed. There was a need for the reinforcement of concepts
7 Parole and parole officers	Applying the core skills to the development of a relationship with parole officers	Outlined the expectations of parole; discussed the prior experiences of parole; discussed the expectations that parole	The session was conducted by a parole officer. I attempted to change the instructional (telling) approach but	Listeners and limited interaction. Specific questions but little engagement	Returned: 4/9 SR: 5/10 MO: 8/10 ME: Low response rate; low participation of members

Table 4.1 (cont.)

Session and topic	Objective(s)	Content	My doing as a group worker (roles as per Zastrow 2003)	Participants' doing	Session evaluation
		officers can have of participants; discussed the use and relationship of authority to participants; clarified roles and role differentiation; and used role plays of differing post-release situations	with limited success. I developed a picture version of gambits (games) used to obtain parole **Role:** coordinator		
8 Relationships	Applying the core skills to positive relationships	Identified roles and responsibilities in relationships; used a value clarification game; developed skills in forming and maintaining positive relationships	Develop a values clarification game regarding relationships; challenged notions and conceptions of 'love' (using the four loves identified as sexual love, friendship, affection and unconditional love) **Role:** enabler, educator, activist	Discuss resolving difficulties in relating; identify the contextual features of relating; learn skills in 'letting go' of relationships; focus on being the right person rather than finding the right person	Returned: 9/9 SR: 8/10 MO: 8/10 ME: positive session; too much content, too little time; processing material needed to be done outside group
9 Family relationships	Applying the core skills family relationships	Develop and use a questionnaire; identify key issues expected regarding partners, siblings, other family members; identify and develop skills in concern to participants in the post-release plans; use family therapy concepts focusing on strengths, miracle questioning,	Develop questionnaire; use Love/Hate video; reconsider issues of closeness; power and control, intimacy, differentiation and separation; Reapply the Belbin Team role assessment; assess leadership on autonomous/ allonomous scale **Role:** researcher, advocate,	Discuss individual circumstances of family; consider concepts of manhood; consider the person that each would like to be; identifying issues of concern into the future; group critique of each individual's plan	Returned: 9/9 SR: 9/10 MO: 8.5/10 ME: excellent, supportive group with a number of members changing plans for release. Leadership was autonomous rather than allonomous

Table 4.1 (cont.)

Session and topic	Objective(s)	Content	My doing as a group worker (roles as per Zastrow 2003)	Participants' doing	Session evaluation
		exceptionality to enhance coping and life skills; identify relapse triggers and plan appropriate responses	enabler, empowerer		
10 Creatively living in the community	Applying the core skills to barriers to successful community living; identifying resources available upon release; identifying strategies for first day and the first week of release; identifying time management strategies for full occupation of time; identifying 'nice things' to do immediately and in the medium term upon release	Create and use cue cards to brainstorm barriers; hand-out of community resources; develop day planner; bring food etc into the prison for the celebration lunch	Create and use cue cards; develop handout, first day and first week planner; review dynamic risk factors; plan for termination of group through group lunch; develop post-group commitments and establish a weekly time for personal revision and reflection; review; attend to issues of 'adjourning' rather than termination. **Role:** all roles as per Zastrow 2003	Rehearsed a range of topics on which participants can talk; review issues that have changed since being in prison (e.g. music, cars); reviewed review skills and applications; receive graduation certificates and commit to lifelong learning	Returned: 9/9 SR: 10/10 MO: 10/10 ME: excellent finish to the group but may have been influenced by food

Source: Anscombe 2009

- I will drink less coffee and more water
- Good group
- [I will] give up smoking
- Abstinence when released
- Adopting abstinence is the only way for me
- Techniques for stress release – they work
- Other ways to release anger – I'm going to try it
- How to control my feelings when people annoy me

Participants were asked to prepare a non-prison-related topic of interest as a conversation starter. Generally drawn from a paper, book, television show or from their own thinking about an issue, on two occasions, the group worker set the topic (fashion, race relations) in order that participants had to think and research the topic, then report to the group on a conversation they had held on the topic with a non-group member.

Group dynamics were positive as evidenced by the evaluations and the group worker's observations. Participants maintained a focus upon tasks but also considered maintenance roles; personal goals and group goals were highlighted in week 2 with the modified game 'Hidden Agenda'. Members began to see themselves in different roles within the group (the group members had been introduced to Belbin's team roles), and they began to appreciate the diversity and interconnectedness of members. There were appropriate challenges both to other group members and to the content of the sessions, which ensured that the group did not have destructive or negative norms that simply demanded conformity and compliance.

PERSONAL REFLECTION

On one occasion, I used a commercial overhead that stated that *'every mistake is simply a step to the next success'*. Led by a participant who was in his fifteenth year of a sentence for a double murder – he responded with: *Bull—t – I made one mistake and it doesn't feel like a step to success.*

He received wide support. The overhead was inappropriate to the setting, and I apologised for the trite sentiment it contained. One participant retorted: 'That's OK . . . don't beat yourself up over that crap – some people think like that – but they've never been to prison.'

The group communication was initially problematic in that it passed through the group leader. Setting up the room in a way that was not a classroom with all the focus upon the front and the 'teacher' was challenging. Participants were comfortable with a classroom format and a table separating them from the teacher and with little eye contact with any other members. Setting the room up in a U-shape enabled the barrier of the desk to remain, but allowed eye contact between members. By week 4, the seating structure involved the removal of the desks and the development of a circle in which I was one member. This was related historically to 'King Arthur and the Round Table' as a reflection of the way the physical/organic can determine social/relational aspects of living. It was an excellent exercise in reflection. The change in communication patterns and seating relationships reflected the therapeutic nature of the group, which had initially replicated the prison communication, which passes through perceived authorities with a great degree of deference to power and status. Gratifyingly, this changed over the course of the group as it moved from allonomous leadership to autonomous leadership and as the deference moved from the group worker to the expertise of the whole group.

The dyads, triads and scenarios developed for role plays enabled different participants to work together and encouraged reflection and creativity. The triads meant that some participants were observers who had to be able to assist in developing creative and helpful approaches when others were 'stuck'. This developed a group climate of 'helpfulness and support'. There was initial high anxiety about the role plays as it was thought that there was a 'right' way to do role plays.

The immediate measure for this first group was that there were 94 of 100 possible attendances. At the end of week 4 one group member was sent to a different prison by a judicial decision.

Cost–benefit evaluations use a variety of assumptions. This program cost $400 per participant. Costs are easily quantified. Real benefits to participants are known only upon release. Measured against imprisonment costs, $400 represents about two to five days of imprisonment. Other benefits include lower incidence of crime, reduced victimisation, taxation paid and enhanced social functioning. There may also be second- and third-generation effects that are not quantifiable.

▨ Reflecting on being and the group

Prison groups pose a challenge to our sense of being, with an environment focused upon control and oppression that is not generally conducive to change. The current approach is towards using cognitive behavioural therapy (CBT), which focuses on the mental/emotional, rather than holistic or social/relational or spiritual/existential approaches. This encourages conservative ideologies that pathologise prisoners and seeks individual change. Social workers may unreflectively appropriate the prevailing conventions and exclude consideration of the whole human being. We are not immune from the oppressive and controlling influences and, as the group worker, I was concerned to avoid promulgating oppressive and controlling approaches. This is especially the case where the objectives are unilaterally set by the controlling organisation.

Emancipatory practices within a prison pose problems for the being of prisoners as they conflict with the control ideology of the institution. Prisoners develop means of defending themselves in a hostile, abnormal environment. In this group, members took time to build trust as the prison's environmental features were not conducive to trust. Some adopted approaches that were designed to be exclusionary from the group by emphasising negativity and hopelessness – Zastrow's 'catastrophier' and 'paranoiac' (2006: 104). For others, the notion of changing behavioural–attitudinal approaches was initially quite alien to their own self-perceptions. For some, their whole being was defined by their offence or prison classification/label ('I am 843675'; 'I am a murderer'; 'I am a junkie'; 'I am a C2'; 'I'm a sweeper'). Defining one's being was in relation to the prison. Creating a sense of being that was different from the prison was a challenge.

Apart from self-definition (being), other barriers to community social inclusiveness included the lack of experience in managing 'normal' social behaviour. Conditioned to certain narrow responses to situations, participants found that enlarging their range of responses was not difficult but challenged their previously learned habitual behaviour and sense of themselves. A brainstorming, creative thinking exercise served as a good example of expanding options. Participants were posed the problem: 'It is Wednesday and your $200 rent is due on Friday – what will you do?'

Initially, participants responded with anticipated responses including 'pull a job', 'snatch a bag', 'do over a house' and 'put my sister on the street'. After exposure to different techniques of brainstorming, this group developed sixty-three legal approaches to resolving the problem that had a high likelihood of success. They were amazed at the solutions. They partialised the $200 into smaller monetary units. They cooperated to develop ideas and refine possibilities. They perceived that they were creative and capable of thinking expansively, and the value of working together. It profoundly challenged their concept of being and their perception of capacity and worth.

Feeling different was common. Some felt that everyone knew you had been in prison and that everyone was watching. One participant identified that his return to prison was as a result of being treated suspiciously by everyone else saying: 'If you are being wrongly accused you might as well do the thing that you are being accused of.'

Another barrier to social inclusion was the expectations of society and their sense of being ill-equipped to meet those expectations. There was a view of their return to the community that included high expectations of the level of support and assistance. Others exhibited fear and irrationality. These matters were often addressed by other group participants rather than by the group worker, and there was a level of genuine support for each other.

PERSONAL REFLECTION

My sense of being was challenged. I hoped prison privatisation offered innovative approaches. I hoped for paradigms that were prisoner-centric or relationship-centred, flexible and solution-focused rather than being prison-centric, problem-saturated and control-dominated. Private providers have become subcontractors of people in a system that offers only marginal differences. The opportunity to introduce prisoner choice (e.g. the choice of control regimes from the state or the choice of personal growth and development in a private system) that provides something essentially different to prisoners has been lost. From a basis of human rights and social justice and with a framework that involved a focus upon the whole individual, I hoped for private prisons as small (say, ten-bed), dual-sex hostels operating as a therapeutic group or community with different clothing and different social and authority relationships, and surrounded by music, literature, art and opportunity, with a focus upon the individual, staffed by social workers, educators and health professionals who bring a variety of approaches so that detained 'participants' had positive 'aha' experiences and learned new ways of 'being'.

Sexuality and love are part of being. Using C.S. Lewis's book, *The Four Loves* (1960), was useful as a framework. The composition of the group included participants whose life situations were a litany of broken trust, broken relationships and questions about why they were 'unloved' and 'unwanted', and such questions as 'what is wrong with me?' Preparing for a two-gendered world was a significant issue. For one participant (assented to by at least three others) there was a sharp dichotomy relating to his perception of women who were either like his mother (warm and affectionate and protective) or 'sluts'. Given the very limited recent exposure of a number of the participants to female role models (other than some prison staff), it was a dichotomy that was difficult to change.

For three participants, their only experiences of love (in the brotherly sense) were from prison where they could identify shared interests and a sense of brotherhood that was not replicated in their experience in the community.

PERSONAL REFLECTION

I was challenged around questions including to what extent I should cooperate with the dominant oppressive paradigm that can be considered as the antithesis of emancipatory social work and which continues to fail prisoners. How do social workers maintain optimism in the face of daily injustice and violence? How do we balance the virtues, including the need for fortitude (courage) and the exercise of appropriate prudence? These required temperance and justice. There were some issues that were simply too entrenched in the environment to be amenable to change in the short term and would require a systemic commitment to change.

Appropriate self-disclosure is an example of the use of self in social work. I have suffered panic attacks and claustrophobic reactions to confined environments for many years. Locked into the confined and unmonitored education room with neither fresh air nor means of access or escape, I could feel the anxiety and panic attacks developing. Physical/organic, mental/emotional, social/relational and spiritual/existential responses were used to meet the challenge posed. Other participants – for whom being confined was no challenge at all (and for some represented a sense of security and their chief fear was in release) – found it useful to see my experience and the way I used stress management techniques holistically. Other members appreciated the diversity of stressors, and it assisted them in disclosing their own stressors and in developing their own coping strategies.

Being integrates with thinking and doing. Social workers are shapers of the environment and are shaped by it. For example, my being is shaped by the thinking of the correctional paradigms from scientific criminology, symbolic interactionism, labelling theory, structural criminology and reconciliation as well as others that have a significant insight to offer (poetry, music, art, theology). The thoughtful use of knowledge may assist group members. It is not a matter or 'either/or' but reflecting on 'all/and' or 'most/and'. Dealing with the complexity of human beings and the complexity of human systems means reflectively drawing from the insights that are most useful and sensible.

REFLECTIVE EXERCISE 4.2

Consider how your being is shaped by your environment.

The group worker must take account of the environment and the sociopolitical and structural issues. The group worker insisted that the group be in one of three areas of the prison that was not under constant video surveillance and monitoring. One session had to be moved to an area that is under video surveillance and monitoring, drawing such comments as:

- Can't we go somewhere else?
- *I hate that thing* (pointing to the surveillance equipment)
- This is going to change things
- I'll wave to the screws
- Can they hear what we talk about?

The group worker reflected upon Kendall's (1993) observation about the importance of personal space and used that as an incentive for successful parole.

Another session started late as authorities had locked down the prison for a cell search. The group worker was able to politely demand that the members of the group be released from the lock-down in order to participate in the group. This was done. Wanting to know how this was achieved, surprised group members reflected upon how resolving conflict is both an attitude and a behaviour.

Group workers make considered decisions about how much members' information they need and want. Information can mean accepting the prevailing standard and prejudging the contribution. While there is much to be gained by a thorough understanding of the group members, the group worker chose not to seek any details of the group members. It was decided to take a here-and-now approach and consider the past only as it was revealed by participants and was relevant to creating a new 'story'. Some of the physical characteristics of the group members were instantly identifiable (physique, tattoos, haircuts, prison green clothes) and some of the social/relational matters became quickly evident (seating arrangements, prison nicknames, general affect, wariness). Some of the mental/emotional was evident (capacity to assimilate information capacity to think in different ways; the timing of the group relevant to the methadone dosage; limited experience in reflecting and assimilating emotions). The spiritual/existential was evident in belonging and identity, self-esteem, purpose of life, guilt and restitution, the role of fathers as models, nightmares and sweats as indicators of anxiety and the capacity for realistic hope for a different life.

PERSONAL REFLECTION

I reflected on the capacity to transfer learning to unfamiliar circumstances. At the eighth week, members were asked to decide upon an end-of-program celebration. A meal was decided upon, and members had to determine the type of food, design the menu and the activities and the attendance list. I provided a Chinese meal (ordered by the participants from a menu) from the 'outside' (I kept reframing this language as 'community'). Fruits that are unavailable in prison (kiwi fruit, pineapple, peaches, cherries) had to be consumed at the celebration dinner (as any fruit substance is a potential brew in prisons). The participants had a notional budget, which made participants appreciate the costs and variety of choices available. They had to make the decision as a group within the budget, which practised their negotiating skills. For some participants, there were items on the menu that were not known to them. We used this new and unknown situation to practise the strategies that they could use in a social setting when confronted by information that they did not understand. We rehearsed the kind of 'self-talk' that they could use to counter the immediate feelings of inadequacy and 'different-ness' that situations like this created for their sense of being and worth.

Getting non-prison-prepared food into the prison involved considerable negotiations with prison authorities but also served to model the way negotiation skills can be used and have beneficial outcomes, and involved pro-social modelling. For a short period, some invited prison authorities joined the celebration. Participants spoke with them on a range of issues not associated with the prison or prison life. My unobtrusive observations were that participants were speaking with prison authorities on prepared topics (usually starting with comments about the excellent food) that were not prison-related and used recently acquired communication skills by asking open questions that encouraged dialogue. After lunch, the participants reflected on food as a natural 'leveller of people' and that they could meet prison authorities as 'men'. While authorities were respected, there was a change in that the deference towards authorities was realistic and more equitable. One commented: 'They're not that bad really – when you know them – they are just like us.' Another commented: 'Mr ... I almost felt sorry for the bloke ... he is really sick, poor b –.'

The focus in the group was upon the future and the successful reintegration into the community through thinking, visualising the participant's response and with an emphasis on rehearsing and practising responses to community situations. Participants recognised a number of barriers to reintegration and social inclusion. As participants thought and acted reflectively, they began to change. While all underwent a transfor-mation, some recognised the need to change dominant thinking patterns, others the need to change their actions and behaviour (doing) and some recognised that they needed to change how they thought of themselves and how they identified themselves (being).

Being encompasses the physical/organic. The folk saying is that 'clothes maketh the man'. Prison clothing is designed to identify 'them' and 'us'. For one member close to release, receiving comfortably fitting modern clothes made a significant difference to his sense of being.

Nine of the ten participants had very poor experiences of being fathered (five indicated lengthy foster-care experiences or orphanages, and four described their father as 'drunk and violent'). Six of the ten men were fathers themselves, although four had no contact with their children. A number of the participants wanted to explore the impact of their childhood on their own sense of being and its impact on their lives. The group explored the concept of 'fatherhood', 'manhood' and 'being a man', includ-ing looking at male role models available to them as boys, the characteristics of being a man and the men they now admired. For all but two, Nelson Mandela was the most inspirational as he reflected strength in adversity, courage, an ability to love (the participants' word) without bitterness and always remain positive and hopeful. The group discussed the man that each participant would like to *be*. Reflecting on the classic virtues and the theological virtues, we considered the areas that each needed to con-tinue to develop. We considered ourselves as a 'work in progress'. For each participant there was a commitment to think, act and be different. For one participant, it was to 'forgive his father'; for another it was to write to his former wife regarding contacting his daughter; and for another it was to reframe his adoption as an act of love rather than an act of surrender and betrayal.

PERSONAL REFLECTION

I was uneasy with managing the after-group emotions and the reactions of the participants when they returned to the prison wings. I was not confident in the ability of the prison regime to respond empathically and appropriately to emotion. The group spoke about the dangers of being different and committed to care for each other. Considering existential issues in this environment was a matter of concern. It reinforced why many prison groups are educational rather than mildly therapeutic.

The social/relational barriers also rested upon the lack of social and occupational skills necessary to be part of the society that they were re-entering. For many, the attainment of vocational skills that enhanced their sense of worth and their hope for the future was tempered by the fact that the skills were obtained (and publicly named as having occurred) while in prison. The participants perceived that there was a social stigma in having obtained qualifications (a forklift licence) while serving a lengthy prison sentence, and they believed this created a barrier to inclusion in the non-prison world.

Long-serving prisoners have little recent and relevant experience of community life, which reinforces their exclusion. The conversations and interests are limited and restricted. As a form of self-protection while in prison, participants expressed that they do not think about the 'outside world'. 'To think about outside things makes jail time harder', one prisoner commented, and you do only those things appropriate to being a prisoner. While there is a certain fatalism and lack of hope, it may also be prudent and sensible in a difficult environment. So a practical feature of this program was that participants read articles or books and newspapers and listened to radio and watched television with a view to rehearsing conversations about issues unrelated to prison. Participants recognised that being ill-equipped for 'normal community living' enhanced their exclusion and reinforced their opportunity for continuing in behaviour and attitudes that continued their exclusion.

Visualising and developing a being that was *other-than-a-prisoner* required participants to develop experiences and interests that assisted them to reintegrate in the community. Being involves how one sees oneself, how one projects oneself and how one is seen by others (possibly including how one is seen by God). Participants were asked to think, act and be different. One participant believed that everyone in the community would be looking at him and could tell that he had been in prison. The group asserted that most people were interested in themselves and he was not important to them. Other group members agreed and kindly asserted that the only thing people in the community would notice 'was his big head'.

> ## PERSONAL REFLECTION
>
> I had safety concerns at certain points as group participants appropriated new ways of thinking, new actions and began to *be* different. They were demonstrating these changes in an environment of control and violence (verbal more than physical) where difference and diversity was not readily accommodated, where thinking for oneself was not a high priority and where particular virtues were misunderstood or dangerous.

Conclusion

In this chapter you will have gained an appreciation of the fundamentals of group work as applied to a specific group in an institutional context. You will have reflected upon your own personal and theoretical orientations and leadership approaches. We trust that you will have reflected upon the issues of context, purpose, group size, group composition, decision-making styles, leadership, theoretical and philosophical influences relevant to your context and setting. We trust that you will engage in group work with consideration of thinking, doing and being.

The group offered the opportunity to think, act and be a social worker within a correctional environment. There is little theoretical guidance on the operation of social work groups contextualised specifically for correctional settings. There is little written in Australia on the specific social work contribution to corrections. There is little social work guidance with respect to enacting virtues and human rights within a setting of oppression and control. The insights of prisoners and their knowledge are rarely sought. Prisoners are largely shunned, and frequently voiceless. These are serious issues for social workers and group workers and for Australian social work. Will social work listen to and engage with prisoners and be an advocate for human rights and virtue-building, or will Australian social workers continue to be voiceless with respect to making real and sustained changes in corrections?

Questions and exercises

1   Consider whether a group worker in an institutional setting (such as a prison, hospital, nursing home, mental health facility, family group home and so on) is

better being part of the institution or apart from the institution and contracted to the organisation. Consider the advantages and disadvantages of each situation.

2 Can a social worker functioning as a group worker function in an ethical and empowering way in an environment that does not encourage an empowerment approach?

3 To what extent is the operation of a therapeutic group premised upon an idea of what a 'good or whole person' is as it is conceived by those outside the group?

4 List the differences between a therapeutic group, an education group and a social group in terms of purpose, power, communication, norms, leadership and decision-making.

5 Consider your own sense of being and to what extent it influences the types of groups in which you participate and in the approach that you take. Which features of your own sense of being inhibit or promote your involvement?

Exercise 1: Your experience

List the groups you have belonged to, including family, sporting, school, church and other religious, social, political and other groups. Identify the strengths and weaknesses of each group and those that contributed meaningfully to your development. How were they led? Who were the members? What were the membership characteristics? Were they open or closed groups? How were decisions made? Who had influence? Was power based on position, authority, money, charisma, knowledge, commitment, intelligence?

Exercise 2: Leadership

What characteristics do you expect in a group leader? What essential knowledge does a group leader need? In what ways will a group leader's style vary according to the client group? What steps does a group leader need to take if their ethical base is not similar to that of members of the group? In a therapeutic group, to what extent is the nature and leadership of the group established by the philosophical or treatment orientation of the leader? Do group leaders have a preferred style based significantly on their personality and/or their group work philosophical orientation? What are the advantages and disadvantages of equal and unequal co-leadership?

Exercise 3

Consider reflectively the following groups:

- a group of eight children aged six to eight years who had been victims of or witnesses to serious domestic violence
- a group of 16–25-year-old community-based young people with extensive mental health issues, including depression, anxiety, psychosis and self-harm

- a reminiscing group of frail aged people in a nursing home who have varying degrees of dementia
- a group of men and women whose partners are serving overseas in a military deployment to a war zone or peacekeeping zone
- a project group of high achievers who have come together for a service club venture
- a group of five people tasked with developing business activity in a small rural community of declining population and influence
- a group of mothers in a local school parents' club
- a stroke awareness support group established by a local hospital to help families managing a stroke victim.

As you reflect on the above groups, what are the qualities of being that you bring? What are the likely purposes for each group? What would be appropriate activities and methods? What are the likely characteristics of members of the group? What function does the group play, both formally and informally? What might a program look like? What would be the likely duration of meetings? In the children's group, what is the place of parents or legal guardians? Are there special legal considerations for any of the groups?

5

Being in the context of reflective practice with communities

THIS CHAPTER WILL consider key practical aspects of community work and demonstrate the reflective practice of being along with thinking and doing as a community worker.

The community development and work presented in this chapter relates to awareness-raising and capacity-building of communities to support families affected by drug and alcohol usage. It explores three communities, all of which are small rural towns in western New South Wales: Community A, Community B and Community C. The case study was chosen from a range of possibilities owing to its longitudinal nature and its capacity to highlight important concepts of being.

Other examples of community work could include the Community Optimist Program for a church in an area of poverty; refugee resettlement programs, including development of a Dinka Sudanese congregation; para-church movements (e.g. Scripture Union with camps for disadvantaged children, family camping); programs and services to community events and community film nights; sporting clubs (e.g. forming a cricket and football team from juvenile justice and correctional clients); developing Aboriginal work collectives; developing online communities of practice; and community organisations (e.g. school programs of integration for children with disabilities). The opportunities for community work are extensive.

▤ Chapter objectives

After reading this chapter, you should be able to:
- appreciate the fundamentals of community work and its nature and characteristics
- understand your own personal and theoretical orientations
- consider the constraints and attributes of working as a community worker
- consider and apply aspects of being that are relevant to working as a community worker.

▥ Main themes and concepts used

Ife (2002: 1) states 'there is no clear agreement on the nature of the activity described as
community work'. The terms 'community work', 'community development', 'community organisation', 'community action', 'community practice' and 'community change'
are all commonly used, often interchangeably, and although many would claim that
there are important differences between some or all of the terms, there is no agreement
as to what these differences are, and no clear consensus as to the different shades of
meaning that each implies.

'Community', as a term, is used in different ways. Some use the term to mean
a geographic entity defined by physical or other boundaries such as a neighbourhood or locality (e.g. Community C). Others use the term to refer to common
attributes, which are used to identify membership (e.g. Christian community, gay
and lesbian community, Aboriginal community, Facebook community). The term
is sometimes used to describe both attributes and locality (e.g. Community B
Aboriginal community).

Warren (1963) writes of communities as historically having five functions: production, socialisation, social control, social participation and mutual support. Kenny (1994)
emphasises that community is essentially a subjective notion, and defines community
as what we experience as community. Ife (2013: 112–13) writes of community as 'a form
of social organisation' with: human scale (where interactions are readily accessible to
all); identity and belonging (a sense of identity from belonging to a community);
obligation (a sense of rights and responsibilities); 'gemeinschaft' (people can interact
with each other in a variety of roles and as whole people); and culture (local culture
expressing the unique characteristics of that community).

Writers on community work are also explicit about the range of frameworks and
tools used. Rothman and Tropman's (1987: 5–6) three models of community work
suggest that community work can be considered in terms of locality development,

social action or social planning. Payne (2005: 49) summarises models of community and macro work, and subsequently (p. 223) considers Henderson and Thomas's (2002) concepts of social capital, civil society, capacity-building and social inclusion as key contemporary concepts in community work.

Definitions of community work make assumptions about the capacities and interests of community members and the value and necessity of including community members in decision-making about community issues. McArdle (1993: 20), for example, sees community development as 'the development and utilisation of a set of ongoing structures which allow the community to meet its own needs'. Community development is therefore concerned with bringing about change through the community. Kenny (1994) sees that notions of transformation are implicit in the term 'development'.

PERSONAL REFLECTION

My thinking was that, in practice, communities can be understood as organic rather than mechanistic; dynamic and interrelated with the environment, rather than constant in structure and form. Each community has its own being, depending on local, physical, social, economic, political, cultural, environmental and existential or spiritual characteristics. 'Community organisation' refers to strengthening social interactions *within* a community by bringing people together and helping them to communicate in ways that build genuine dialogue, understanding and potential for social change.

REFLECTIVE EXERCISE 5.2
What would you think are the critical elements or matters that define a community?

Case study

Setting and origin

The Commonwealth Government had provided funding through the State of New South Wales for community capacity-building projects. A proposal had to be developed including a clear budget, auspicing to a non-government organisation

(NGO) and a clear methodology. The time frame for development was six hours or the funding would be lost. The state government department had a clear strategy to develop the community capabilities of its western New South Wales communities. The development and implementation of the project called for the rapid application of the thinking, doing and being framework for a social worker acting in the capacity of a community worker and organiser. The case study describes and analyses some features of a fixed-term project in which funding was provided by the Commonwealth through a state department to an NGO in order to develop the community capacities of families in coping with illicit drug use and licit drug misuse in three communities. The project had a maximum fixed term of twenty-four months and funding of about $100,000 per year. The project funding was not recurrent, and it could not develop services that required funding beyond the expiry date. The project guidelines were aimed at illicit drug use. The priority and the major drug issues in the identified communities were alcohol, marijuana and tobacco consumption. As the developer of the project, I provided the intellectual and some physical resources, and offered some over-sight of the work. I also developed the project implementation plan and eval-uated the project. The funded project was handed to an NGO, which implemented the project and undertook the actual fieldwork. The genesis of the program indicated a 'top-down' approach to communities. The project out-comes were defined by the Council of Australian Governments (COAG) and the National Illicit Drug Strategy and were overseen at the local level by a project reference group.

The objectives were modified to include 'licit drug misuse' as statistical mapping (using freely available public data drawn from health status reports and court figures) had indicated that misuse of alcohol, tobacco and marijuana were the most serious contributors to poor health outcomes, child protection reports and a host of other health and welfare outcomes. However, the approach did not involve actually meeting with the communities at the development stage. Although a good knowledge of the communities might have existed, this was not a substitute for living in the commun-ities or first-hand consultation with the communities.

The specific objectives for the project had to be consistent with national objec-tives. The specific national objectives were to map existing services available to families whose members were using illicit drugs; identify the options available to support families in the community; assess the appropriateness and availability of existing community resources; deliver programs of education and intervention in response to identified needs; provide information to services in order to link and coordinate pathways to health-related counselling, community and preventative services; and to develop programs at primary, secondary and tertiary intervention levels that used creative media and innovative approaches to address the issues and illicit drug use. These media were to include (possibly) music, art, dance and narrative approaches.

There were three groups of participants: the whole community (primary intervention); at-risk groups (secondary intervention); and confirmed drug users and their families (tertiary intervention). The programs were to focus upon engagement with the community and creating pathways to services (where those services existed). In analysing the objectives, there seemed to be a progression of program logic from the knowable, empirical and scientific (the mapping stages) to the creative and innovative.

◼ On Community A, Community B and Community C

Communities have a sense of being that includes physical/organic, social/relational, mental/emotional, spiritual/existential and virtue features. Community A, Community B and Community C are rural and/or remote communities. The definition of the term 'rural' has had little consensus. Notwithstanding technical definitions, in practice, these communities have common features, including:

- isolation (the communities are separated by about 250 kilometres with no regular public bus or train service)
- high Aboriginal populations
- high youth populations
- educational disadvantage
- employment issues.

From local and anecdotal sources, the communities also feature high adolescent pregnancy rates, issues of petrol sniffing, use of marijuana and other illicit drugs and excessive alcohol use. The communities have high levels of violence and long court lists.

These are disadvantaged communities. Disadvantage in New South Wales is well established and has been visually mapped (see Vinson 1999, 2004). Additionally, the SEIFA (Socio-Economic Index for Advantage) uses four indexes (Index of Relative Socioeconomic Advantage; Index of Relative Socioeconomic Advantage/Disadvantage; Index of Economic Resources; and Index of Education and Occupation) as a summary obtained from using the technique of principal component analysis. High scores on the SEIFA scale indicate relative advantage and low scores indicate relative disadvantage. This is shown in table 5.1.

Table 5.1 Relative socioeconomic disadvantage

Name	Index of relative socioeconomic advantage/disadvantage
Sydney	1051.3
Far West (includes Community A, Community C, Community B)	908.7
New South Wales	1015.3

Source: Australian Bureau of Statistics 2001

While these are three difficult communities (as physically evidenced by the shops and stores being encased in wire mesh or having roller shutter doors that are pulled to shut at 5.30pm and the presence of closed circuit television in the main streets), they are not without strengths. There is a long Indigenous history, culture and association with the land, and one community has the oldest structure in the world. These are rich and vibrant agricultural communities with a sound economic base. There is community infrastructure, including many services, education through schools and TAFE, police, churches, local government, a strong commitment to Indigenous Community Working Parties and a strong alliance between local government and Indigenous groups. There are future economic opportunities related to natural and cultural assets. There is an awareness of the issues of ecological sustainability. Many of the people are resilient, and the communities

PERSONAL REFLECTION

In thinking about Community A, Community B and Community C as diverse rural communities, I applied a classification of regional and rural communities developed in the western New South Wales region of a government department. This was built from the collective lived experience rather than statistical or theoretical approaches. The four-stage classification was not to be seen as prescriptive and immutable but rather as diagnostic and a benchmark against which action could be taken. The system was a basis for analysing the community and takes account of the physical/organic, mental/emotional, social/relational and the spiritual/existential. It sought to bring together information and assessments from a variety of sources. This fits also with the social work emphasis on thinking, doing and being. As a useful 'first-cut' tool, communities can be located upon a continuum from impoverished through to mature. It is possible for communities to develop towards maturity as well as move towards impoverishment. Decisions taken outside the community have the potential to move communities in either direction. Taking this approach means that there is recognition of the dynamic interplay between community- and outside-community forces.

have continued despite racial riots (see Cowlishaw 2004), droughts and other natural events and economic restructuring.

Table 5.2 lists a series of characteristics that, taken together, may indicate the health of a community as defined in the locality sense. The characteristics are points to consider and seek to provide a sensible way to consider communities especially where funding and service decisions need to be made.

Table 5.2 An heuristic categorisation of communities

Community category and characteristics			
Impoverished	**Emerging**	**Maturing**	**Mature**
• Having few opinion-makers • power vested in few people • few services and/or fragmented services • little information, or the information is held by a few • a lack of social cohesion • a lack of acknow-ledgement or respect for diversity • vandalism, violence, lawlessness • visible drug and alcohol issues • social isolation, disempowerment, low employment or high unemployment • cultural and spiritual quality of life experienced as lack of connectedness • inertia and expectation of external solutions • a lack of mechanisms for 'belonging'	• Mechanisms to stimulate leaders or catalysts and opinion-makers • small scale/practice • few services – emerging coordination – gap identification • information access points clearly identified and information broadly available • responsive to community; increased tension • developing mechanisms for and exercising of community voice; groups and communities of shared values, beliefs and expectations that are articulated in behaviour • a focus on shared community	• Dynamic and diverse range of catalysts, champions, opinion-makers and ambassadors • advocates; mixed service systems • coordinated collaborative reinvigorating, regenerative responses to need • creative and challenging outcomes focused on clients and the community; information readily accessible in multiple formats; community profile to which the community is responding; community participation mechanisms and visioning processes integrated into general community life • organisational and social constructs that support effective use of community resources,	• Formal processes for community representation • participation from all sectors of the community • service systems that are operative, including funding and service provision • a healthy market economy free of monopolies and oligopolies • charity models formalised into fundraising • sophisticated community and social constructs • tolerance of diversity • inclusion of difference • information available that is current, targeted or responsive;

Table 5.2 (cont.)

Community category and characteristics			
Impoverished	**Emerging**	**Maturing**	**Mature**
• a lack of shared community visioning • dependency	responsibility and recognition of community members contribution to well-being and health of the community • community action strategies; alternative employment and training • community participation with diversification of opportunities emerging • community identification and belonging with confidence and pride, and • emerging cultural and spiritual connectedness	harnesses energy, builds diversity and solution-building based on inclusion • formal and informal community organisation for well-being and health of all members • organised and spontaneous community solution-building; relationships and interrelationships emerge that are celebrated and strengthened • a dynamic economic and social interface • preventative and diversionary processes prominent in the law and order and tertiary systems; independence moving to interdependence	accessibility of information to all • community expectation for increased government visibility and action in a partnership with the community responsibility and care • enhanced informal care systems • community reconciliation approaches and alternative dispute resolution mechanisms • interdependence and cooperation; and community confidence and shared vision of the future

■ Doing: What did the community worker do?

The doing included being an initiator, enabler, broker, advocate, negotiator, educator, coordinator, researcher and group facilitator with public speaking duties. The originally planned project had four phases: orientation and mapping; development; implementation; and reporting.

The 'orientation and mapping' phase developed familiarity with the community using the physical/organic, mental/emotional, social/relational and existential/spiritual schemata. This involved mapping the physical conditions and the 'mental and emotional health' of the community by transect walks, interviews and participatory diagramming, and required engagement skills and collaboration skills to gain access to the communities. It involved the doings described by Henderson and Thomas (2002), including entering the neighbourhood, knowing the neighbourhood, identifying needs, goals and roles, making contacts and bringing people together. It required mapping the existing relationships and organisations, their ethos or being, an environmental scan, and identifying the problem situations and potential solutions.

The 'development' phase was designed to enlist community and agency support by conducting community development and education training sessions with community residents and with partner agencies. Critical to this phase was the development of trusting relationships that would enable access to the more marginalised secondary and tertiary groups.

'Doings' in the implementation phase included obtaining and reviewing resources related to supporting families and individuals with drug and alcohol issues that had been helpful in other communities, then modifying them or developing local and appropriate resources using music, art, dance and culture, and narrative approaches. Some resources could be utilised or modified for primary prevention (community education). Other resources and approaches were selected for secondary intervention groups (e.g. young people at risk of alcohol or marijuana use) and tertiary intervention groups (e.g. young people actively using illicit drugs or misusing legal drugs: amphetamines users, petrol-sniffing groups, riverbank alcoholics, smokers, alcohol binge-drinkers).

The 'evaluation and reporting' phase used techniques that included participatory research approaches, stakeholder analysis and beneficiary assessment (see Narayan & Rietbergen-McCracken 1998).

Services mapping

While it could be argued that the primary doing skills used here were research skills, it also required negotiating skills (to gain access to schools and communities), coordinating and mediating skills, group facilitation and public speaking skills. I had considered that the major issues in the community were licit drug misuse and probably marijuana use. The services mapping was undertaken as an early part of this project to ensure that my perception was the same as the community perception. Service-mapping included meeting with all service providers (drug and alcohol workers, doctors, hospitals, police and so on) to seek their input on the issues. Community members were also contacted. A directory of services available both locally and within the region, which would assist families who were dealing with members who had a drug or alcohol problem, was developed at this time. Service-mapping in these communities needs to be undertaken at least annually, given the instability and unavailability of some services through their inability to attract appropriately qualified employees. Current service directories – a tangible outcome of this project – were free, appropriately simple in format, short and colourful, widely distributed and available to service providers and service users in

Table 5.3 Most serious AOD ratings by high school students

Issue/school	No.	Alcohol (%)	Marijuana (%)	Cigarettes (%)	Speed (%)	Heroin (%)	Petrol (%)
Community A (Years 7–12)	39	30	30	15	7	5	13
Community B (Years 7–10)	8	27	33	20	0	7	13
Community C (Years 7–12)	41	31	28	22	3	3	13

Source: author

places where members of the community gathered (hotels, schools, churches, the police station, Council, Indigenous housing corporations and so on).

While service providers and community members provided insight into problems related to alcohol and other drugs (AOD), it was important to seek the 'voice' of young people and to triangulate information. Accordingly, a number of pair-wise rankings were undertaken with young people of high school age. The results showed differences and similarities across communities (see table 5.3).

The mapping of the services and drug issues was also supplemented by focus groups and conversation with young people who were not represented in the schools. The mapping of the existing services had also identified options available for families in the community to support members who were having a drug or alcohol problem.

Participatory diagramming as awareness-raising

The project envisaged mapping the physical location of places within Community A, Community B and Community C that were the sources of, or had the highest likelihood of, people addicted to alcohol or other drugs being present. Very large physical maps of the towns were made and laminated and taken to different groups of people within each of the three communities. This process was undertaken in Community C and Community A but met significant community resistance at Community B. This high-lighted the diversity of communities that, on the basis of socioeconomic factors, had many similarities. It may also highlight the possible flaws in engagement of the workers with the community. The original intention was to map the AOD users and their patterns, associations and involvement. However, some community members at Community B refused to identify locations, which indicated a basic level of mistrust between community members and the 'professionals'.

Where the community mapping was undertaken, the outcomes from Community C included identification of the sources of problems that were predominantly around a particular hotel and a local public reserve. This locality-specific result came as a surprise to the participants and was an example of the 'conscientisation' (Freire 1975). It also led to the community considering possible solutions. The outcome included making changes to the lighting in the reserve. This social mapping or participatory diagramming was intended primarily to identify locations at which services could be delivered in the community. Discussion with services in Community C, Community B and Community A indicated that services needed to go out into the public places rather than wait for clients to access services at the service provider's address. Services that waited for the community to access them were frequently underutilised. Taking the services out to the places where the community naturally congregated (e.g. parks, the homes of informal community leaders, to the local schools and at the Indigenous community organisations) proved to be far more effective.

Doing as an educator in response to identified needs

One social work activity is as an educator. The outstanding needs of these three communities on all the available evidence was a reduction of alcohol use, the substantial reduction in use of marijuana and the significant reduction of cigarette-smoking within the community. In this case, the community worker was guided by Bradshaw's (1972) taxonomy of need, whereby need can be felt, comparative, normative or expressed. In community organising in these communities, the need was certainly comparative, expressed by some, normative and felt by some members of the communities. Alcohol, marijuana and cigarettes were the three most prevalent drugs used in these communities (as assessed on a range of figures and supported by the school analysis). Each is known to have significant health effects and significant effects on the community as a whole. Indications from a variety of sources were that petrol-sniffing can be problematic – but it was episodic in nature. While extreme indications were given (e.g. a three-year-old who was petrol sniffing), it was not generally seen to be the most significant issue.

The work done in the schools confirmed the three major significant drug usages. It needs to be noted that one particular group (a mother's group at Community A) maintained that heroin was a very significant problem, and it was identified as being more significant than any other. This may have been a reflection of reality, or it may be an acceptance of the widespread use of alcohol, nicotine and marijuana within the communities, or it may be wrong. Triangulation involves seeking evidence from a variety of sources to support a comment or view, and in this instance the official reports (police and court records), others with a possible avenue to knowledge (e.g. inquiries made of garbage collectors and street sweepers who may have been seeing discarded needles) and statements from others did not support that view. A number of service providers did not see nicotine as a drug until it was specifically raised. One service provider in the health sector commented: 'You know, it's so widespread that I don't even think about that now – but I should.'

One of the results of this project was to bring information and knowledge in an accessible form to service providers. The Commonwealth had produced an excellent 'glossy' document on illicit drug use. However, by showing it to community focus groups, it was clear that its language and close print meant that it was unusable with a poorly educated and orally based community. The document was rewritten and shortened with culturally appropriate pictures and local illustrations. Family workers were trained in its use. They could then deposit appropriate knowledge in the three communities. The community worker undertook the training and performed the role of educator.

Initiating and brokering creative and innovative approaches for primary, secondary and tertiary interventions

The heart of this project was to think laterally and creatively and to find ways of reaching people with creative and innovative approaches that may have a significant influence on their drug and alcohol usage. The intention of the project was not to create dependencies on a service that would not exist beyond the funding period but rather to deposit capacity within the community for addressing some of the community's drug and alcohol issues.

Within Community C, young people took part in a mural and photographic approach, which created links to the learning program for ten young people (particularly young women) through the Department of Education. This was precisely in line with the project outcomes, which attempted to link current AOD users to other services and, in this particular instance, to educational services. The situation in Community C was made more difficult by the loss of the Youth Development Officer, and plans needed to be revised to link young people with a newly appointed Sports and Recreation Officer.

Community A developed a number of significant and innovative programs. An outstanding video was produced which relates to the drinking behaviour of young men and young women in Community A. The video depicted a well-known young Aboriginal man from Community A being a responsible driver while his four friends are intoxicated. The driver is stopped by police and breath-tested by local police (the police officers were part of the Indigenous youth mentoring program), passing the breath test and subsequently going on to a party where he is consuming water. At the party, he is surrounded by young Aboriginal women who value the fact that he does not drink whereas his intoxicated mates fail to make any impression on the girls. The messages of the video are clear and highly applicable to this group. Members of a group are early school-leavers and do not receive appropriate formal drug and alcohol education as part of their normal educational development. The community organiser worked with this group of about fifty young men, who were often reputed to be excessive consumers of alcohol and were significant troublemakers within the community. The organiser brokered other services and expertise and the involvement of police. The five young men in the group on the video are reputed to be among the informal leaders. Comments indicated that their participation in the video caused at least some of the young people to reconsider their alcohol consumption, had changed some attitudes towards the police and law enforcement, and has encouraged the development of new video programs. The video was originally made for the 'Getting Smashed' program, and there was keen interest in a new program. The community organiser had roles that included initiator (of the program, involved in obtaining the funding, making contact with the groups of young people), broker (e.g. obtaining police involvement, obtaining the skills required for the technical editing of the project), educator (on the role of alcohol and cannabis in health) and coordinator.

PERSONAL REFLECTION

At Community A, a group of young men who would generally fit the categorisation of 'social exclusion' developed and produced a rap CD. This group developed out of the video project (as above) and developed independently of the organiser. The dress, accent, gestures and even words conveyed an Afro-American inner-city rap culture. In my critical reflection on this, I struggled with the 'aha' moment of realising that the local Indigenous culture and approaches were being overlaid by a globalised culture. I wondered whether local and poorly resourced communities would be able to resist and/or appropriate globalising influences in a way that contributes to understanding of being or whether these influences would undermine them. Indigenous self-determination has often been held up as a choice; that is, you can choose to be Indigenous or to assimilate into the dominant culture. These young men were accepting and developing an alternative culture that was neither assimilative to the dominant Australian white culture nor specifically Indigenous.

A creative project initiated through the Family Support Service at Community B included young mothers (the incidence of teenage pregnancy in Community B is among the highest in New South Wales) making picture books and encouraging mothers to tell the stories. These books had no words and comprised pictures cut out from the newspapers or magazines. They had themes that included non-use of alcohol during pregnancy, toilet training, nutrition and the effect of smoking during pregnancy and on newborn babies. The nursing mothers 'read' the books to the child(ren). This stimulated auditory and tactile sensations and experiences for the child while allowing the mother to appropriate knowledge that she needed and had been taught – but within an oral tradition. The pages of the books were in plastic Glad Bags and tied together with wool, which ensured a measure of sustainability and longevity that would not be available in the community if they were paper-based. The organiser was the initiator of this activity, provided the resources (magazines, plastic bags and so on), suggested themes, contacted the prospective participants and developed a community group. The books were made in a public park, which enabled others to readily join. Storytelling, narrative and oral traditions were brought together with health and education messages that were acceptable and accepted, whereas literacy-based approaches have not found a ready reception in these communities. The books that were made needed to be simple and culturally appropriate. They were 'owned' by the women who made them, thereby ensuring greater usage and longevity.

Four ethnobiographies were undertaken of four former alcoholics who lived in and were well known within the communities. The community organiser obtained permissions and considered legal and ethical matters before taking oral histories (subsequently transcribed) that narrated the way each person overcame their addiction. These were photocopied and widely circulated (among high school students). Audio-copies were produced for those not able to read. They charted individual narratives in the individual's voice but with the purpose of being instructive to others battling with addiction. They were far more powerful than stories emanating from outside the community and with whom the community had no relationship. The organiser's role here included initiating, brokering, educating and empowering.

The project was time limited and sought to deposit and embed information, knowledge and skills within members of the community. Drug and alcohol training was provided to family support workers in each of the three communities. Two hundred copies of the training resource relating to drugs and alcohol were produced and made available across the three communities in accessible public places. Designed primarily for family support workers – some of whom have limited literacy and education and no qualifications – the resource was designed to be photocopied and used as and when the need arose. The training program gave the information necessary for family support workers working with families affected by drug and alcohol use and in a culturally appropriate format. The community organiser embedded information not only through the training resource but also through her being with the community remembering both the resource document and, equally importantly, the person who delivered the resource.

REFLECTIVE EXERCISE 5.4

Discuss various roles performed by the social worker. If you were to work with these communities in this project, what would you do?

▥ Reflecting on being as a community worker

PERSONAL REFLECTION

Being as it relates to purpose and objectives

My being was challenged by the externally imposed objectives, the limited time frame and the external restraints. Government-directed, centralised programs presumed that they knew what is best for communities. I was also recruited into that 'mindset' by being asked to develop a program with a very short time frame and without significant community consultation. I think that the best community development arises from within the community and has local community champions who may be assisted by external people and programs. Centrally imposed programs are often not equipped to understand the unique and peculiar features of a specific community. I approached an NGO that I knew was working within the community and had the capacity to operationalise this program. But it was not an open or transparent process. It might not have been the best organisation, and an Indigenous organisation might have been more appropriate. The challenge was whether to be involved at all in a less than perfect set of conditions or to let the opportunity for the communities simply disappear. I had to compromise some of the virtue of justice (fairness) in the interests of prudence.

My being was challenged by the issue of changing the objectives. This was an urban-centric program aimed at illicit drug use. The evidence from many sources, both empirical and anecdotal, was that the needs of these communities were predominantly related to legal drug misuse. By 'jumping together' both illicit drug use and licit drug misuse, I was aware that I had to exercise prudence in making this change. This may look like duplicity or even corruption of purpose. Upon reflection I considered that it was worthwhile and empowering, and had the potential to be liberating for these communities. However, I was uncomfortable with making this subtle but substantial change in the program focus (see Maynard-Moody et al. 2000).

As a way of undertaking an environmental scan and assessing the being of communities, I developed a semi-structured approach to determining the characteristics of any particular community that seeks information from many sources. These are used to assist in rapidly understanding the physical/organic, mental/emotional, social/relational and spiritual/existential nature of a community – in short, its being. They call for judgements that are not readily and easily defensible. They are often my judgements. They are disputable. They are made by someone who does not live in the community. Communities are complex and multidimensional and contain within them a range of physical, social and spiritual/existential understandings that my semi-structured approach attempts to uncover. Communities have a sense of being and, more or less, exhibit the cardinal and theological virtues. Some have great fortitude, others lack hope, and still others are beset by racial or social divisions with no acceptance of diversity and lack charity and justice. These matters are often reflected in the town planning and in the local press (see also Cowlishaw 2004 on Community A).

A challenge to my being was to find an appropriate community worker whose own being was complementary to those of the communities. There were times when the project worker needed to engender hope and other times when community enthusiasm was heightened, when prudence and temperance were needed. For example there were distinct youth subgroups with the communities that needed to be carefully and thoughtfully managed and with a degree of balance and fairness. These subgroups can be divided on race, or interest or identity (e.g. which hotel is frequented or school is attended).

Being and evaluation

My being influenced the evaluation that was undertaken. An evaluation of the communities was required by the Commonwealth funding body. It involved criteria that were positivist (e.g. the number of people contacted through the project, size of the problem, links made to existing services and so on). These measures alone would not reflect either the intent or the outcomes of the project. It was important to give due regard to the innovative changes that had been left in the community. The evaluation included comment from participants, ethnobiographies, a copy of the video, newspaper reports and a range of materials that had been developed within these communities. These were supplementary to the requirements – but were designed to humanise the project's outcomes. From my sense of being, they also had the purpose of educating those in decision-making roles, and attempting to ensure that rural communities were appreciated for their individual diversity.

I was struck by the profound poverty of some parts of these communities and the lack of opportunity for many young people. For Indigenous young people, many were committed to the area (by reason of kinship and association with the land) while others were motivated to leave the area but lacked the financial, social or educational means. Their sense of being was confused, and there seemed to be a lack of direction and hope. One young person expressed it thus: 'There is nothing to do here – until you die.' For me, as a non-drinker and non-smoker who holds a physical/organic, mental/emotional, social/relational and spiritual/existential view of people, the damage being done via foetal alcohol spectrum, through smoking and excessive alcohol use, reckless and dangerous behaviour (as evidenced by eighteen deaths of 12–25-year-olds in twelve months), was disturbing and was interpreted by me as evidence of alienation and hopelessness.

I struggled with the approach of some service organisations that, in the face of easily identified needs, waited to be approached. I likened this to the difference between 'outreach' and 'in-drag' that was as applicable to community organising as to the church context from which I had drawn it. Both in myself and in the project worker, the qualities of prudence, temperance, justice, fortitude, faith, charity and hope (all necessary characteristics of 'being') were significant in engaging and working with the communities.

Thinking dominated the initial development of the project. 'Jumping together' different forms of knowledge (ABS statistics, local profiles, Indigenous knowledge, personal knowledge and experience, theories of communities, contextual matters including project objectives and so on). It involved using critical/reflective/systemic/logical thinking and creative/lateral thinking. In the initial phase, local input was entirely absent, and I constructed the community project from a distance of 700km away. This was not consistent with good community organising practice.

The community and its impact on the being of community workers

The project worker lived in one of the three communities. They are difficult communities in which to live, and there are significant pressures and stresses. To ensure the continuing competence of the project worker, it was important to choose an organisation that had good support and supervision structures. The auspicing agency also needed to support and develop staff members and understand the individual communities. There needed to be an apportioning of the worker's time that was prudent and just.

One of the significant problems in rural and remote Australia is attracting and retaining qualified, skilled, creative workers with appropriate virtues. This project's commencement was delayed for eight months primarily through the inability to attract an employee to the communities with the right being, thinking ability and doing skills. The person required engagement, assessment and collaboration skills and the capacity to think both critically/systemically/reflectively and laterally/creatively. Additionally, a wide range of doing skills were required that involved very practical matters (e.g. skills in driving long distances) through the spectrum from interpersonal skills and group skills to highly developed organisation, advocacy and public speaking skills. The person required the cardinal and theological virtues and to be able to apply those in communities beset by physical/organic, social/relational, mental/emotional and spiritual/existential problems. Both required skills in relating to the Indigenous community and an understanding of national and local Indigenous history and oppression, poverty and the importance of country. Bringing a sense of being that respects and appreciates these matters can be developed from a range of sources and in a range of ways including, but not limited to, formal education. The capacities to admit error and to laugh at oneself and seek to correct wrongs are important elements in communicating in Indigenous communities. Each of the communities had specific and individual features that required flexible and creative approaches. Communities are diverse and dynamic, and a change in one area of a community (e.g. job losses or the attraction of a natural leader, transience of participants and service workers, service closures and, in this case, the project funding) may markedly affect the whole community. Communities are flexible and in some instances unstable. The capacity to deal with serious illicit drug use or licit drug misuse can vary depending on the skills and quality of being of the worker and the availability of social and community support.

Being and creative responses to intergenerational disadvantage

In these communities there was an intergenerational and interrelational element that was profoundly disturbing to me. I reflected upon the concepts of social capital and social inclusion/exclusion (see Henderson & Thomas 2002) and the practical implications for these communities. For example, there is no alcohol and other drug worker at Community B and, consequently, there were no alcohol and drug education or prevention programs. Life Education vans (an education program for the prevention of drug and alcohol misuse beginning in primary schools) do not visit any of the three communities, as they require a financial co-contribution from the communities who, on every economic measure, are economically poor. Children are being born to very young mothers (as young as thirteen years) whose alcohol consumption may be resulting in foetal alcohol spectrum with its associated physical/ organic, social/relational, spiritual/existential and mental/emotional consequences. Social exclusion in practice means that low incomes can directly translate into not having money for the co-contribution. As a result, services such as the Life Education vans and drug and alcohol prevention programs do not exist in the communities with arguably the greatest (comparative and normative) need. This serious and significant issue (the development of accurate drug and alcohol knowledge from an early age) is not rectified in children at high-school level as many young people of Aboriginal background are not proceeding to high school on a regular basis, beyond the ages of twelve or thirteen years.

Thinking, doing and being as a community organiser may mean considering local service development (or locality development). This was done with the ethno-biographies and other activities. But other locality development opportunities arise serendipitously. Education and school truancy were clearly identified as a problem. This truancy, in the opinion of key informants, was a result of drug and alcohol use by parents and their inability or unwillingness to prepare their children for the next day at school. However, community-owned innovative responses have developed. One community on an Aboriginal reserve had no school truancy. That particular community placed a high value on education and modified its alcohol intake in such a way as to ensure that its children were going to school. On the regular monthly drinking days, which were related to income support, the women appoint one of their members on a 'rotational' basis as the 'designated mother' who was 'mother' to all the children, remained alcohol-free and was responsible for caring, feeding, housing and getting them all to school. The community being here was positive towards education, child protection and welfare and instilled hope in their children.

Bringing together thinking and doing and being resulted in approaches that used television/video and oral methods as they are more likely to be effective, given the literacy levels and the reading capacity of some in the communities. There was sound thinking behind free community family film nights with short but visual messages targeted appropriately to the Aboriginal communities in relation to alcohol and nicotine. This provided the opportunity for educational and preventative information in the context of a community social activity.

Thinking about underpinning theory, current activity and the sense of being may result in discarding possible alternatives. One key informant suggested that, given the occurrence of teenage pregnancies, there may be opportunity to utilise an urban program (seen on television) that required teenage girls to care for anatomical dolls in order to teach the responsibility of care that parents have for children. The program was reputed to have had success in city schools in lowering teenage pregnancy rates. But on reflection and in the light of community discussion, this approach might not be as successful in these communities as in other areas, for the reality is that many teenage women are already exercising significant responsibility for their younger brothers or sisters. Information from a funded youth group for 12–25-year-olds was that half of their attendees were under ten years old (the youngest being eight months) as the teen-age girls had to bring all their brothers and sisters to the youth group. While this made discussion of teenage issues very difficult (e.g. contraception, cigarettes, dating and so on), it negated the likely influence of the program using anatomical dolls as the suggested experience with the dolls was the already lived experience of most of the teenage women in this community. Thinking, doing and being accepts information from all sources but carefully evaluates all information in the light of the current realities.

PERSONAL REFLECTION

While I had thought that dance and drama would be significant media in which to convey alcohol and drug messages, they were not evident. This might reflect poor thinking on my part in designing the project, or the skills and capacities of the project officer, or it might indicate that dance and drama are not media that would be suitable in these communities.

Community development involves thinking, doing and being. In general, the three communities were serviced by organisations primarily providing a conservative, euro-centric (see Payne 2005: 210) casework model of intervention. There were no group programs and few self-help programs. Approaches to illicit drug misuse included some mezzo-level policy issues such as the licensing of premises for the sale and distribution of alcohol. Community compacts formed between the police, communities and licensed premises have prescribed the times at which alcohol can be purchased. As yet, there has been no desire or demand from whole communities to restrict alcohol to certain days (such as has occurred in other Indigenous communities) or to declare certain areas alcohol-free. While such restrictions have statistically lowered public order offences, there is an argument that the restriction of alcohol in public places simply drives the consumption of alcohol to private homes and thereby increases both the risk and severity of assaultive behaviour towards women and children. Community workers will carefully consider and understand these competing views and be held in tension in order to lead to new and creative approaches that might both lessen the public disorder *and* result in safety for women and children.

Being and communities

Communities can be formed around locality, social activity, social structure and/or a community of sentiment (e.g. shared beliefs). The two fundamental communal elements of any social system (Dempsey 1990) are a sense of solidarity and a sense of significance. These two elements of community are closely linked, and rarely can a person feel a sense of belonging without also gaining a sense of significance.

These communities had a sense of being (shared sentiment) and a sense of the individual's place in that community. In the Indigenous community that sense of being was (for some) identified by skin names or clan association. There were subcommunities of social activity within the geographic locality. These social activity and social structural elements were based around race (Indigenous/non-Indigenous), gender (male/female) and primary allegiances (work, sporting team, churches, schools, hotels and so on). Many community members have their primary solidarity to their colleagues who are part of their primary allegiance rather than to the geographical community. Although knowledge of communities was helpful, the practice situation with these groups drew as heavily from knowledge gained from gang studies including Cohen (1972) and Cloward and Ohlin (1960) and material from the US National Gang Centre (see http://www.nationalgangcenter.gov/). Some members felt alienated from the wider community (having left school early, perceiving that they would never have a job) and were critical of the community of locality. There was an acceptance of hopelessness and a belief that things could never change.

The video project gave the opportunity for new skills, rethinking values and a degree of notoriety in a positive way. Studies of gangs (see for example the National Youth Gang Centre Survey 2004) indicate that members are often looking for ways out of their current identification and affiliation. 'Jumping together' knowledge and approaches and skills from many sources can create a diverse opportunity for action.

PERSONAL REFLECTION

The CD project illustrated the complexity of being. When I had conceived this project, I had assumed that many Indigenous young people would be attracted to Indigenous culture and that identity would be developed through Indigenous music, storytelling and dance and would be centred upon Indigenous culture and history. The CD rap project could have been taken directly from the Afro-American inner-city music scene as conveyed through television programs. Some Indigenous youth of Community A were not dissimilar in dress, language, dance, music, attitudes and physical expression to their television rap idols. There was no evidence of any Indigenous cultural influence in this project. That forced me to reflect on the nature of being – and that being in this instance was adopted from a globalised electronic source that none of the young people had seen in person but had appropriated through an electronic medium. As I thought about the comments from the Indigenous elders that their young people did not respect the elders and their traditions, it became clear that the voices that were heavily influencing the sense of being of these young people were voices external to Community A and which had no intimate connection with it. I was intrigued by the question of why young people were appropriating this new sense of being. Among many possible answers, I considered that they were reacting to the oppressive conditions in the community; that they were simply differentiating themselves as the normal part of the adolescent development process; that they had identified with 'blackness' as a reaction and rebellion to the dominance of 'whiteness'; and that the music and lyrics met an emotional/mental need that no other medium or voice was currently reaching. Reflecting on being allowed for these possible considerations to be 'jumped together' as well as the recognition that each individual may have held these and other explanations in diverse proportions to others of the group.

This project delivered outcomes in terms of building the capacities of communities and in mapping existing service providers and pathways for users of services. Innovative, culturally appropriate, accessible and creative approaches were developed and embedded within the three communities. Significant problems were encountered, including the skill and capacity of the workforce, the transience of skilled workers, suspicion of 'outsiders', entrenched multidimensional and widespread licit drug misuse and illicit drug use. The web of disadvantage was extensive, and most services were provided on an individual casework model rather than on a whole-of-community model. The many positive developments in these three communities were often small scale and dwarfed by the totality of need.

▪ Conclusion

Community organisers who are working in or developing communities will value both local *and* 'outside' knowledge; recognise current realities; promote positive change (hope); use quantitative and qualitative approaches that are community-building rather than community-diminishing; and will empower members of communities to under-stand their situation, then take control of it. In the fluidity of practice, bringing the being of the social worker together with facts and approaches from many sources offers a framework that is inclusive and honours the local community. The capacity of communities is built through thinking, doing and being. The social worker operating as a community worker brings being, thoughts and skills to a community even if it is only for a specified period of time. Those capacities are important assets for the community. Thinking without action is sterile and contrary to social work. Doing without thought is likely to be misguided. Neither thought nor action will be effective without prudence, temperance, justice, fortitude, charity, hope and faith. This community project illus-trated that there was no single 'answer' to the support for families managing drug and alcohol issues – but rather multiple approaches that recognised diversity and creatively reflected opportunities for change. The practice model provided a useful framework for considering the many participants involved and the environment, within a set of objec-tives that had been developed nationally and were modified to fit local requirements.

Questions and exercises

1 What did you learn from this chapter?
2 What kind of qualities did the social worker demonstrate in his community work discussed in this chapter?
3 How does the conscious use of being make a difference in community organisation/development work?

Exercise 1: Self-assessment as a community worker

We invite you to consider the following as a guide to the areas of development that you may need as a community worker. You may care to rate yourself on a 1–10 scale. You may like to ask a trusted colleague who knows you well to also rate you.

Attitudinal and personal attributes

Genuineness; empathy; respect; confidentiality; neutrality with respect to power groups; determination and resilience (courage); vision with respect to the future; willingness to listen; optimism (hope); friendliness/sociability.

Knowledge and skills

An understanding of the nature, background and issues for community work; social research and planning skills related to needs assessment, policy analysis, social impact assessment and evaluation; communication and education skills; organisational skills, including networking skills; management skills, including basic accounting skills; interpersonal skills, including advocacy, negotiation and mediation skills; political skills, including a knowledge of relevant legislation and the capacity to form alliances and lobbying skills; knowledge and skills in public speaking and public representation; knowledge and skills in debates and discourses in sociology, psychology, education and politics; knowledge of sociological and political theories related to the State, class, gender and power, social and developmental movements, race and ethnicity, sexuality and conformity and deviance; an understanding of local history and key community historic and social events.

Exercise 2: Community profiling

Imagine that you are to work in the (mythical) community of Wongabilla. You have not been there before. You know nothing about the community. How would you approach learning about that community? Now, try using the following template to consider a real geographic community that you do not know well.

Community profiling

Stages in the community-profiling process
- Preparing the ground: creating a steering group; initial planning; making contacts; learning from others' experiences; identifying resources; engaging consultants or professional researchers; developing a management structure
- Setting aims and objectives
- Deciding on methods
- Fieldwork: production of information-gathering tools, for example questionnaires; training of staff involved in data collection; collecting 'new' information; recording information; analysing information
- Reporting: writing up fieldwork; production of draft profile; consultants on draft profile; amendments to draft profile; production of final community profile; dissemination of research findings
- Action: consultations over key issues, priorities, actions to be taken; drafting community action plan; consultations over draft plan; production of action plan; dissemination of action plan; implementation; monitoring and evaluation.

Methods
- Review previous community profiles; community consultation; unobtrusive observation; community walks
- Research based an analysis of the local newspaper, local government annual report, school bulletins; other documents
- Meetings with individuals and groups and service providers.

Observe and consider
Housing, infrastructure and community facilities; health of the community; enterprise, employment and training; law and justice; education; heritage and culture.

Community resources
- Land: what is it used for; areas that are unused or derelict
- Environment: condition of public and private spaces; extent of air, water, noise pollution; roads, railways, footpaths
- Population: size; characteristics – age, ethnic composition, employment; status; household composition etc
- Housing: type, size and tenure of property; standard of repair; house prices/rent levels

- Local economy: types of industry and occupation; extent of employment/ unemployment
- Services: statutory (e.g. education, health, welfare, benefits etc); voluntary (e.g. self-help groups, housing, associations, social groups etc); private sector (e.g. banks, shops repair services, pubs, cinemas, cafes, garages etc)
- Transport: buses, trains, community transport, roads etc
- Communications: newspapers, local radio and television, newsletters
- Power structures: elected representatives, key groups or activists.

Services to communities

- Statutory services: social services; housing; police; library; leisure/sports centres; local schools; planning department; health centre; youth services; local government
- Voluntary/community organisations: tenants/residents group; neighbourhood association; parent and toddler group; advocacy groups; service clubs
- Community representatives: ward councillors (parish, district/city, country); MPs; other community 'leaders'.

Issues

Employment; finances; alcohol/drugs; gambling; family or marital; medical; psychiatric; education; legal; accommodation; social network, for example transport, knowledge of history; rates; water/sewerage; garbage; land claims; community consultation; cultural activities; environmental protection; sporting facilities; youth centres; child-minding centres; public toilets; playground equipment.

Community attributes

Cohesion; aspirations/hopes; frustrations; future; leadership; community priorities.

6

Being in the context of social work research for action and change

SOCIAL WORK IS a research-oriented profession. Some consider research as one of the important methods of social work, irrespective of whether you practice with individuals, families, groups or communities, or in government or non-government organisations. Social work research often includes – and should include – evaluation, action and change (action research).

The reflective social work practice model presented in chapter 2 shows that research in terms of evaluation and action is inherent in social work practice. From this perspective, social work research may be somewhat different from conventional research, where research outcomes in terms of knowledge creation and reporting sometimes find a place on the shelf rather than in practice or the field. It is important to think about how research in social work or social workers' research is different in terms of values, the practice orientation or its applied nature, knowledge creation from practice and its approach to research participants.

This chapter first presents a research project conducted in Aboriginal communities, then discusses the thinking of a social work researcher, what the researcher did or how the research project was conducted; that is, the doing and being of the social work researcher and the role it played in the whole research process. It makes an important point that research in social work is action- and change-oriented and attempts to ensure that change occurs and that it occurs with a difference. Merely thinking and doing is not enough; being should have an equal place along with them.

▪ Chapter objectives

The main objective of this chapter is to discuss what role research plays or should play in initiating action and change, and how conscious use of being along with thinking and doing facilitates that process. After reading this chapter, readers should be able to reflect on:

- epistemological issues (relationship between the 'knower' and the 'known'; theory of knowledge), research methodology and research methods
- how research can be employed for emancipatory purposes
- the influence and use of 'being' in research
- how social workers can use their 'being' in research.

REFLECTIVE EXERCISE 6.1

What is your understanding of research in social work? What kind of research would you like to undertake?

■ Main themes and concepts used

This chapter demonstrates how a social work researcher (Bill Anscombe), by consciously using his thinking, doing and being, creatively combined multiple research methods to address the research agenda set by an Aboriginal council. It also shows the use of findings to point out systemic anomalies and to initiate action and change towards empowering and enabling Aboriginal communities by developing and negotiating understanding with local communities and governments.

To understand this chapter some basic knowledge of research methodology is necessary. It uses several concepts related to the research problem, such as regional and local agreements, rates and reconciliation. Some terms related to research methodology are qualitative and quantitative research methods, and objectivist, constructivist and indigenous research approaches. Some of them are defined in the text, but for definitions of some other concepts that are not defined, we suggest you to look at *Sage Encyclopedia of Social Science Research Methods* (http://knowledge.sagepub.com/view/socialscience/n783.xml).

■ A brief description of the research project

The project aimed to facilitate effective service delivery and coordination in Aboriginal communities and reconciliation in local communities. The study area covered western and south-western New South Wales. It was developed in response to a call for tenders. The main focus of the research project was to develop regional and local agreements (which are defined below) by engaging Aboriginal peoples and all other stakeholders.

It is important to understand what these regional and local agreements are. Regional agreements denote broadly land-based agreements between Aboriginal and

Torres Strait Islanders and others, such as local governments and relevant organisations and agencies. The term 'local agreement' connotes a smaller unit than regional agreements and encompasses non-land-based aspects of relationships. The concept of a local agreement was that it was narrower in its geographic span but broader in the issues encompassed. Local agreements may be contracts, covenants or arrangements that give Indigenous interests greater recognition and/or control over services and development. Given that the focus was upon local government and local Indigenous communities, its use was confined to local government boundaries, and local issues such as consultation, rates, local development, local housing, recognition of Indigenous people, access to local government employment, industry development, negotiation processes, dog control and a host of other locally significant issues that occur without necessarily having a land-based agreement.

▦ Research objectives

The Binaal Billa Regional Council (which does not now exist) of the Aboriginal and Torres Strait Islander Commission (ATSIC; no longer in existence) invited tenders to undertake pilot research related to regional agreements. The objective of the research was

> to examine and develop strategies, processes and models for developing protocol regional agreements between the Binaal Billa ATSIC Regional Council, Local Government Regional Groups and other agencies. These agreements should facilitate effective service delivery and coordination in a context of support for self-determination of local Aboriginal communities and reconciliation in local communities. (Tender document)

In announcing the project, the chair of Binaal Billa Regional Council said:

> Aboriginal people have the potential to play a more significant role at the local level to the benefit of all local government's constituents through the development of a range of agreements relating to local government issues. Local and regional agreements offer a positive and constructive approach at the local level for the development of economic, social and community goals to the benefit of both Aboriginal and non-Aboriginal residents. (Press release, 6 May 1996)

Other requirements

In developing the tender brief, the ATSIC Regional Council Steering Committee required the successful tenderer to employ sessional Indigenous staff with local knowledge and access to the community, and they hoped that the project would also develop some research potential in the Indigenous sessional staff employed. The committee recognised that the project required skills in working with Indigenous (communities) and non-Indigenous people (local government) and that a partnership of Indigenous and non-Indigenous researchers was most appropriate. In their selection interviews, the committee recognised that they would like to have Indigenous researchers undertaking the project but that the skills and abilities did not (yet) exist within the Indigenous communities to undertake the research. The committee considered that Indigenous Australians were the most researched people in the world and that they wanted to ensure that this research made a difference and had practical outcomes capable of implementation at the local level. Although they wanted research, they wanted it to involve community development and to deliver directions that could be followed and applied to the benefit of 'their people'.

PERSONAL REFLECTION

The objectives and the steering committee requirements fitted my own values and thinking about social work and the role of a social work researcher and practice. I believe in undertaking research that has practical and tangible outcomes and that acts as a tool of emancipation rather than a tool of oppression. Such values support indigenous research methodology (see Foley 2003; Rigney 1997; Weber-Pillwax 2001; brief details are provided in the next section). It appeared to me that the thinking of the Steering Committee promoted participatory research methods and progressive learning, empowering people rather than extracting data, a visual rather than a verbal approach, and the use of multiple methods rather than a rigorous adherence to one method of research. I decided to make a tender application on the basis of a long-standing interest in Indigenous communities and because I wanted to undertake research that had practical outcomes and that could pro-socially model a research approach that was not inherently 'colonising' and was driven by Indigenous priorities.

■ Research team and research methods

The research team that was co-participant in this research included the ten Indigenous communities, the ten local governments, the Binaal Billa ATSIC Council Steering Committee, Indigenous sessional staff and potentially the non-Indigenous community. The research project was led by a social work researcher (Bill Anscombe) and co-team leader, another senior social work academic as co-team leader, a lawyer and three Indigenous research assistants, although it was initiated and controlled by the Binaal Billa Regional Council. A mixed research methods approach, combining objectivist, constructivist, qualitative, quantitative and indigenous research methods, was adopted. This consisted of literature and legal searches, transect walks, participatory diagramming, ethnobiographies, secondary data (e.g. ABS statistics and local media content analysis), key informant interviews, community meetings with the number of participants ranging from six to seventy-three people. These terms will be explained and explored in the following section.

PERSONAL REFLECTION

As the social work researcher, my thinking was focused on the terms of the tender, the objectives and the steering committee requirements, and accordingly developing the appropriate research design befitting the socioeconomic, political and cultural contexts of Aboriginal communities. Given the terms of the tender and the committee's requirements, I contemplated and articulated objectives of the project according to the PEOPLE model presented in chapter 2. The objectives had to be not only specific, motivating, actionable, relevant and timely but also researchable within the context of participant Aboriginal communities and their environment. Research is essentially about creating knowledge and using it for the betterment of society. Several questions come to mind: what is knowledge? Who is creating knowledge and whose knowledge? What are the methods of knowing? Who is the 'knower' and what is the 'known'? Can the knower and known be the same? Raising these epistemological questions helps us to realise that there are different methods of knowing.

Objectivist research

Often research is dominated by the objectivist epistemological perspective, which follows the positivist paradigm. When we say 'objectivist epistemological perspective' we are referring to some of its assumptions such as stable reality, value neutrality, objectivity, observability, measurability, generalisability, universality and reductionism. It is also referred to as a positivist paradigm. It often uses experiments and tests, and lends itself well to quantitative research methods and techniques. Such dominant objectivist and positivist research paradigms have been critiqued because they ignore sociocultural, economic, political and similar contexts. They do not offer scope to include people's meanings and experiences. Although they appear to be preoccupied with testing hypotheses and theories, they seem to be far from real settings. They are known for breadth but lack depth, and negate other forms of knowledge (Guba & Lincoln 1995).

Constructivist research

The constructive epistemological perspective in some ways is opposite to objectivist research. Unlike objectivist research, it does not claim to be objective as its very nature is subjective. The constructivist epistemological perspective creates and recognises other forms of knowledge. It is influenced by theories such as symbolic interactionism, phenomenology, hermeneutics, feminism and critical inquiry. It recognises meanings, experiences and interactions and the interpretation of people. It assumes that the reality is unstable and focuses on social processes. It is value-driven. It recognises historical, political and cultural contexts, and analyses power, privilege, position from a social justice perspective. Hence action and change is part of research. Under the constructivist perspective, the researcher is just an instrument, who provides voice for participants and their perspectives. It follows flexible research design and inductive approaches. This perspective lends itself to qualitative research methods such as observation, case study or ethnographic studies. It challenges the assumptions of the objectivist/positivist paradigm in terms of the nature of reality, who can know, what knowledge is and who can produce it.

An indigenous alternative approach to research

In addition to the objectivist and constructivist epistemological perspectives, it is important to recognise and acknowledge an indigenous alternative approach to research. Foley (2003: 48) has observed that Western epistemological approaches are culturally unacceptable to the indigenous epistemological approach to knowledge. About indigenous epistemological approach, Rigney (1997: 3) notes:

> Indigenous people are at a stage where they want research and research designs to contribute to their self-determination and liberation struggles, as it is defined and controlled by the communities. In privileging the first perspective models of indigenous qualitative research methods, we not only provide processes to keep their indigenous identities and knowledges safe, but also provide space for hope and the potential of moving forward to the realisation of a non-colonial research future.

Rigney further explains that Indigenous people see, think and interpret the world and the world's realities in differing ways from non-indigenous people because of their experiences, history, cultures and values (1997: 8). Weber-Pillwax (2001: 49–50) identifies six research principles for Indigenous research:

1 All forms of living things are to be respected as being related and interconnected.
2 The source of a research project is the heart/mind of the researcher, where the unselfish motives in the researcher ensure benefits for everyone.
3 The foundation of indigenous research lies within the reality of the lived Indigenous experience and are grounded in real people as social beings rather than the world of ideas.
4 Any theories developed or proposed are based upon and supported by indigenous forms of epistemology.
5 Indigenous research is grounded in the integrity of indigenous people and communities and therefore cannot undermine the people or communities.
6 The languages and cultures of indigenous peoples are living processes.

REFLECTIVE EXERCISE 6.3
By reading relevant research methods books, compare and contrast the objectivist epistemological perspective, the constructivist epistemological perspective and the indigenous epistemological approach. Identify their theoretical/ideological bases, assumptions, strengths and weaknesses.

A mixed methods approach

Instead of being ideologically bound by only one type of research or only one source of knowledge creation, you may believe in employing a mixed methods approach to research that uses the strength of each research approach and overcomes their weaknesses. According to Creswell and Plano Clark (2007: 5),

> Mixed methods is a research design with philosophical assumptions and methods of enquiry. As a methodology, it involves philosophical assumptions that guide the direction of the collection and analysis and the mixture of qualitative and quantitative approaches in many phases of the research process. As a method, it focuses on collecting, analyzing, and mixing both quantitative and qualitative data in a single study or series of studies. Its central premise is that the use of both approaches in combination, provides a better understanding of research problems than either approach alone.

For the purpose of this research, mixed methods research design is the one that combines the objectivist epistemological perspective, the constructivist epistemological perspective and the indigenous epistemological approach. It is important that research helps indigenous people to empower, self-determine and liberate themselves from oppressive experiences, including all forms of colonisation.

As a social worker, I reflected upon the role that research plays in empowerment and disempowerment and was committed to the use of multiple and participatory research methods. I have been guided by the work of Guba and Lincoln (1989) on the use of case studies and by the growing literature on indigenous research. Accessing data through a variety of methods and building collective knowledge has been a very significant influence. Rejecting the subject–object dualism that underpins much research has enabled research to be a collaborative effort between myself and other participants and has led to dismissing a singular dominant focus of the research.

Research ethics

Research often raises ethical questions, and it is important to conduct research according to research ethics. In this regard, the AASW (2010) Code of Ethics is an excellent aid as it relates to research that sets parameters for observing the conventions of ethical scholarship but unequivocally expresses that the research will 'Place the interests of research participants above the social worker's personal interests or the interests of the research project' (5.5.2.2). In addition, the code states that 'Social workers will honour Aboriginal and Torres Strait Islander knowledge and ensure that research conducted with Aboriginal and Torres Strait Islander peoples and communities is based on established Indigenous research protocols' (5.5.2.1).

On the political environment

As the research design allowed, it was important to look at the prevailing sociopolitical context. The project was undertaken at a time of considerable political uncertainty in relation to Aboriginal Australians at the national level. Some of the events relating to Aboriginal issues included: a greater focus on accountability in ATSIC; a Commission of Audit appeared to be signalling a shift of many responsibilities to the states; a review of ATSIC itself; questions as to the commitment of the Howard Coalition Government to Native Title legislation; criticisms of the Minister (Senator John Herron) by the Social Justice Commissioner (Mick Dodson); legislative changes to ATSIC, which were initially blocked by the Senate; pejorative comments ('Aboriginal industry') by the Minister; a reserved decision by the High Court in relation to the Wik peoples' Native Title claim; the resignation of some members of the Aboriginal Reconciliation Council; a cut of $414 million in the ATSIC budget; the thirtieth anniversary of the Wave Hill walk-off; an impassioned speech by the Governor-General calling for reconciliation; the first Aboriginal Olympic gold medallist; a speech by the Independent Member for Oxley calling for the abolition of ATSIC; the report of the 'Stolen Generations' inquiry; a call by the Minister for Education (Western Australia) for 'forced hostel' education of Aboriginal children; and uncertainty over continuation of funding of Community Development Employment Programs.

Indigenous people had limited political voice. Aboriginal inequality and lack of access and equity in the political systems was also noted. At the Federal Government level, for example, there had never been an Aboriginal in the House of Representatives. At the local government level in New South Wales, there were 177 councils (and the Lord Howe Island Board) with 1808 local government councillors. Of these councillors, eleven were Aboriginal persons who identify with the Aboriginal community. Aboriginal people therefore comprised approximately 0.6 per cent of the elected representatives throughout New South Wales even although they represented 1.24 per cent of the New South Wales population. Aboriginal people were significantly underrepresented in home ownership, in political structures and in a range of other areas.

On race and ethnicity

Much is written and theorised around the concepts of race and ethnicity (see for example Halstead 1988; Hollinsworth 1998; Miles 1989). Castles (1996: 19–20) writes:

> There is a confusing plethora of literature on race and racism. For instance the useful collection of Rex and Mason (1986) of theories of race and ethnic relations includes Weberian, Marxist, anthropological, pluralist, rational choice, sociobiological, symbolic interactionist and identity theory approaches. These are mainly sociological theories but one can find the works of philosophers, historians, economists, jurists, psychologists, discourse analysts and cultural theorists. Any study of racism is necessarily inter-disciplinary for a full understanding can be achieved only through examination of all factors – historical, economic, political, social and cultural – which make up any given situation of racism.

PERSONAL REFLECTION

My thinking was that race was predominantly a social construct rather than a biological construct but draws helpful perspectives from a wide range of disciplines, including psychological, sociological, economic and political perspectives. Race and ethnicity involves physical/organic, social/relational, mental/emotional and spiritual/existential components used in a way that creates a 'racial' identity. I have been influenced by Halstead's (1988) six-type classification of racism, McConnochie, Hollinsworth & Pettman's (1988) approach to institutional racism, Kovel's (1970) concept of aversive racism, reading about the eugenics movement and my experience with Indigenous communities.

Research design

In this case, it was important to develop a mixed methods research design consisting of objectivist, constructivist and Indigenous epistemological perspectives. The sample of ten Indigenous communities was determined by the Binaal Billa Regional Council Steering Committee on the basis local government issues. The selection of the local government areas was a consequence of the location of the Aboriginal communities selected. The social work researcher looked at the ten selected Indigenous communities and respective local government areas.

There were in excess of fifty possible Indigenous communities in the Binaal Billa ATSIC Region. The Steering Committee wanted to select Indigenous communities that they considered represented a cross-section of relationships between local government and Indigenous people. They predicted that some of the areas selected had close and beneficial relationships between local government and the Indigenous community while others had adversarial relationships. The Indigenous communities were urbo-rural, small rural and former Aboriginal reserves. Some were resettlement communities while others were former missions on traditional land areas controlled by particular nation-groups, and others were areas of mixed background.

The thinking of the Steering Committee was to obtain a diverse sample. In research terms, the sample selection was somewhat random, somewhat stratified and somewhat purposive. The selection of the sample was based on their own lived knowledge of the communities, their understanding of local government, personal anecdotes, stories and narratives. A complex process of negotiating with their constituency (Indigenous people) included a reading of the 'climate' of the particular Indigenous communities and their receptiveness to a project planned by the ATSIC Regional Council, then undertaken by a non-Indigenous researcher.

The plan was to use participatory research methods and select respondents from the ten communities and their respective local governments by using purposive and snow-ball sampling methods. Transect walks, participatory diagramming, ethnobiographies, interviews with key informants and community meetings and consultations with a number of participants were planned. These are different methods of collecting (qual-itative) data from and about communities by engaging local people. Data collection from secondary sources such as relevant legal documents, statistical information from the Australian Bureau of Statistics and local media was planned. To collect data from these sources, appropriate instruments such as observation, interview and consultation guidelines were planned and appropriate qualitative and quantitative data analysis was contemplated. Due to paucity of space, these cannot be elaborated here. How the researcher translated all this thinking into action is discussed in the next section.

Doing of a social work researcher

PERSONAL REFLECTION

As a social work researcher, my research activities were driven by my interest and commitment to working with Aboriginal communities, the terms of research specified by the steering committee and my thinking about the research project and design as discussed above. It is important to recall the PEOPLE model discussed in chapter 2. Following the informed consent, it was essentially research participants and the research team putting together their labour in the research participants' environment according to the objectives of the project and the flexible research design. The following discussion shows how we implemented the research design in an empowering and emancipatory manner.

Secondary data collection and analysis

The project was initiated with a legal and library search in relation to local government agreements, regional agreements and the law as it affects local government. International bodies of literature were reviewed with respect to regional agreements in Australia, Canada and New Zealand. A thorough knowledge and reading of local government legislation, grants commission requirements and federal–state fiscal relations was undertaken. The analysis showed that that rates from ratepayers formed a small portion of the budgets of some shires and that Indigenous land councils and housing corporations were disadvantaged by comparison to other organisations (e.g. churches, charitable and benevolent groups and home-owning pensioners). Such anomalies were noted, and these and similar results led to other lines of thinking and doing.

Further secondary data collection and analysis was undertaken in the areas of rates, services, employment and Aboriginal people's contribution to, and expenditure from, local government in light of the Grants Commission's 1995–96 *Annual Report*

(Local Government Grants Commission 1996; adjustment grants were not included). Conservative parameters were adopted. The analysis did not claim to be precise but rather to give an indication of directions and trends from the available data. Where appropriate, these approximations were extrapolated to give an indicator of total benefits possible over the Binaal Billa Regional Council area. How these findings were used for advocacy and brokerage is discussed below. It needed to be noted that councils are answerable to their constituents and that funds from the Grants Commission were untied.

Data collection through consultations

Indigenous researchers and the social work researcher designed and conducted two types of consultation. One was with the community groups, and the other was with the local government. The designs had much in common in terms of the information being sought. Group facilitation and public speaking were part of the consultation phase. By using a snowball sampling technique, community members were accessed through the Indigenous community organisations. The design for Aboriginal communities specifically adopted a participatory research approach. The Indigenous community consultations varied in numbers. Of 250 possible people at Nanima (Wellington), in excess of seventy people attended the public meeting organised by the Nanima Aboriginal Council. At Cummeragunja the attendance at the public meeting was six. The public meetings were supplemented by individual interviews conducted at appropriate places in order to ensure representation across a range of ages, interests, genders and commitment to the community.

To consult the local government, key persons at various councils were identified and interviewed. It was *negotiated* and *brokered* with the general manager of the shire or municipality and in some situations also included the mayor and senior staff. The attendance at these consultations varied according to size of the local government, the availability and accessibility of elected representatives and local individual, political and social considerations. These consultations were more formal than the Indigenous community consultations and tended to follow the semi-structured assessment tool more precisely.

In both types of consultation, the objective was to *enable* the community and local government representatives by creating the opportunity to comment on the current existing relationships and to express areas that they felt could be developed for the mutual benefit of the Aboriginal community and local government. At the conclusion of the consultations (which were undertaken separately), no attempt was made to *negotiate* or *mediate* the sometimes differing views of the Aboriginal community and local government over local issues. The areas for mediation and negotiation were delineated and a process for the future recommended.

Following the consultations, the research team *advocated* a 'blueprint' for the development of the relationship between the local government and its Aboriginal community(s).

The consultation data analysis and the major findings

The analysis indicated that the relationships with individual local Aboriginal communities and local government varied along a continuum and that each community had its unique features. At one end of the continuum was communities and local government where a consultative, cooperative and constructive relationship existed to the benefit of all local government constituents, including Indigenous people. At the opposite end of the continuum, there was hostility, antagonism, lack of consultation and lack of constructive interaction between local government and Aboriginal communities. Some local government bodies ignored the presence of Aboriginal communities within their boundaries, citing as their rationale that no rates were charged and therefore no services were provided. These councils overlooked their responsibilities towards Aboriginal members of the public within their boundaries. The funding apportioned to the shire on a population and disadvantage basis by the New South Wales Local Government Grants Commission was not considered by these shires. As they considered the analysis, some shires recognised the error of thinking and the responsibility to all constituencies within the shire boundaries.

On reflection, the research team was of the view that the research project contributed to achieving the objectives set by the steering committee.

The research process involving and leading to action and change

Education and awareness-raising

Through the research process, educating both Indigenous people and local government was an important role. It appeared that some Indigenous communities in the research had little understanding of local government and its operations, while some local governments were well informed of the statistical features of their Indigenous communities but less well informed of the realities of everyday life in the Indigenous communities or of the aspirations of those communities. I saw these phenomena in terms of different ways of knowing and considered that part of the research outcome was an educative and awareness-raising role.

Pointing out funding displacement and its opportunity costs – structural barriers

The research pointed out funding displacement as an opportunity cost. In communities that were former Aboriginal reserves, much of the infrastructure (water, sewerage and roads) that would normally be provided by local government had been provided by ATSIC. Funds that could have been usefully employed in the training and development of Aboriginal people or placed in business enterprises controlled by Aboriginal people had been used to provide basic services that could reasonably have been expected to be provided by local government. This was a result of legislation relating to land. This funding displacement meant that Aboriginal people continued to be disadvantaged in health, housing, economic independence and service provisions. Possible ways to address some of the structural disadvantages were suggested.

Empowerment and a checklist for negotiation

Empowering Indigenous people was a critical 'doing' through the research process. The research identified the factors from the Australian and international literature (see Dolman 1997) for the purpose of achieving satisfactory agreements with varying levels of government as: willingness; bargaining power; unity; information and research; timing; communication; and geopolitical realities (claimants are less likely to receive a favourable settlement when there are competing non-Indigenous developmental interests at stake). A subset of other relevant factors included: experience in settlement development (the degree of existing poverty and despair among claimants and the urgency of development pressures will shape outcomes); knowledge of existing models (the demonstration effect of other local agreements can influence negotiating positions); and public attitudes (public support for claims either locally or nationally can lead to significant alliances).

This set of knowledge was developed into a checklist for negotiating with local governments with respect to a variety of local issues. Some local governments had a consultation process and model in place to ensure that Aboriginal people were included in local government and had a say in important issues that affected either them specifically or the community more generally. Other local governments were marked by a lack of involvement with the Aboriginal community and in some instances by a disregard for their involvement in, or contribution to, local government. In one community, Aboriginal consultation was said to occur on Indigenous matters, but the person who was consulted on all occasions was not accepted by the Indigenous community as being Aboriginal and certainly not as representing the community's views. The community saw the person as enabling the local government to say they had

consulted with the Indigenous community. Aboriginal communities and local government could, and were willing to, improve their relationship. Towards this the checklist
for negotiation was developed.

Advocacy and brokerage relating to employment

The research process led to advocacy. With notable exceptions, Aboriginal people were
marginalised from many local government services. Local government bodies failed
to *negotiate* (or negotiated in inappropriate ways). They had failed to develop means by
which to include Aboriginal people as full participants in local government and, in
some instances, failed to adequately discharge responsibilities in relation to employment obligations to Aboriginal people. Rates, land acquisition, heritage protection,
services, housing and employment were the dominant concerns of the Aboriginal
communities. There was willingness by Aboriginal people and of many within local
government to acknowledge the need for improvements and to look constructively for
ways and means to forge and further better relationships.

Within the ten communities researched, there was potential to develop relationships that would advance both Aboriginal people and whole local government, including closer consultation, an increase in the number of Aboriginal employees in local
government, enhancing the representation of Aboriginal people elected to local government councils and commercial development in such areas as tourism, housing, environmental protection, small business development, heritage and cultural protection.
For each of the ten local governments and communities, the research advocated a
tentative plan and mechanisms for furthering appropriate mediations or negotiations.

Employment, income and related benefits

Aboriginal people were underrepresented as employees in local government in the
areas reviewed by this research. The report *Mainly Urban* (House of Representatives
Standing Committee on Aboriginal and Torres Strait Islander Affairs 1992; recommen-
dation 30) recommended that local government employ Aboriginal and Torres Strait
Islanders in at least the same proportion as they occur in the workforce at the local
government area. Mostly that was not the case, as shown in table 6.1.

The research findings were calculated using very conservative cost–benefit
parameters ($30 000 per job per year). On this analysis, an additional twenty-five
to thirty-one positions would be available to Aboriginal people in the ten councils
reviewed – representing an income shift to Aboriginal people from $750 000 to
$930 000 per annum. Quite apart from the monetary implications, the advantages
are the training, experience, education, pro-social modelling and development that
can be accessed by Aboriginal people through local government. These are typically

Table 6.1 Representation of Aboriginal people as employees in local governments

Local government area	Total population (Grants Commission figure)	Aboriginal population (% Grants Commission)	Shire workforce as in consultation	Aboriginal employees as stated in consultation	Aboriginal people in shire workforce (%)
A	2 950	3.98	45	2	4.4
B	7 270	6.14	80	6	7.5
C	5 240	7.14	120	20	16.6
D	36 430	5.6[a]	258	5	1.9 10 additional jobs
E	21 860	2.61[b]	180	3 or 4	1.6 2 additional jobs
F	7 720	8.26	180 (include retirement village 85)	2 (include 1 at retirement village)	1.1 Up to 12 additional jobs
G	5 290	2.98	60	Nil	Nil Additional 2 jobs
H	2 450	5.50	35	2 (I)[c] 5 (council)	5.7%[d]
I	57 310	1.82	495	12	2.42
J	9 520	8.17	120	5 (all labouring)	4.16 Additional 5 jobs

a Council estimate: 10 per cent.
b Council estimate: 7 per cent.
c As identified by community consultation.
d Council estimate: 5.7 per cent; the council's figure would be 14 per cent. The local Indigenous community did not recognise three employees identified by the council as Indigenous.

not valued in standard cost–benefit analysis. These are the 'hidden benefits' that neither a surrogate market technique nor a productivity technique or contingent valuation technique can reliably calculate.

There was a clear need for Aboriginal people to occupy management, technical and professional positions in local government. The research noted that where Aboriginal people were employed by local government, they tended to be in labouring and/or lower-paid and lower-skilled employment. The consultations also revealed that in some locations the Aboriginal community did not apply for local government positions as they perceived (whether correctly or incorrectly) that their opportunity to obtain employment in local government was negligible. The view was expressed by some Aboriginal people that local government was prepared to employ Aboriginal people on short-term programs funded by other sources but would not employ Aboriginal people as part of their full-time workforce. Some comments by local government authorities tended to confirm the views held by the Aboriginal community.

Equal Employment Opportunity Monitor

Acting on this research, the Binaal Billa Regional Council for several years engaged local government in a voluntary Equal Employment Opportunity Monitor (developed as part of this project), so that the employment of Aboriginal people in local government was monitored on an annual basis. The intent was to develop an awareness in local government (in Freirian terms 'conscientisation') and assist in obtaining and retaining Aboriginal employment in local government. Significant improvement in levels of Indigenous employment in local government had occurred, and the process was controlled within the ATSIC Regional Council. A specific outcome of this research, in relation to employment, was the employment of an Indigenous consultant to develop Indigenous employment in the REROC (Riverina East Regional Organisation of Councils – an amalgam of thirteen councils) area.

Advocacy and brokerage relating to land, rates and housing

Rates charged

Some anomalies that disempowered Aboriginal organisations were noted. Where an Aboriginal Lands Council made a claim on unclaimed Crown land, some local government authorities began charging rates (both land and service rates) from the day on which the property passed to the possession of the local Aboriginal Lands Council. No rates are paid on the unclaimed Crown land while it remains the property of the Crown, but as soon as ownership is established by the local Aboriginal Lands Council, rates were charged despite there being no development and few (if any) services to that land. Local Aboriginal Lands Councils had a financial disincentive to claim former Crown land as the land immediately became rated. This led to one lands council being in receivership with the primary creditor being the local government, which had not collected rates on twenty-four unserviced, undeveloped, former Crown lands blocks that had been claimed for their heritage value.

Subsidy denied

The majority of Indigenous housing was owned, maintained and/or managed either by Aboriginal Housing Corporations or by the Local Aboriginal Land Council. The majority of the Aboriginal people in the housing were in some way or other dependent upon

Commonwealth Income Support benefits and were on low incomes. However, in the general community, where housing is owned by an eligible pensioner, the rates were generally charged at half the land rates (by the local government), the state government paid one quarter of the land rates and the other quarter was effectively subsidised by local government. However, where a house was owned by an Aboriginal Housing Corporation or a local Aboriginal Lands Council and was rented by an eligible pensioner, in general, full rates were charged to the Aboriginal Housing Corporation or the Local Aboriginal Lands Council by the local government. The tenant may have been an eligible pensioner, but this anomaly meant that to a significant extent the Aboriginal Housing Corporation or the local Aboriginal Lands Council was subsidising the pensioner in their housing rather than the subsidy being from the state government and local government. Where a local Aboriginal Lands Council could not (or would not) pay the rates to local government, at the expiry of twelve months, the local government could claim the arrears from the State Aboriginal Lands Council who reduced the allocation to the Local Aboriginal Land Council by the amount of the arrears (and the local government claimed amount).

Costs saved

Supreme Court cases involving the Nungara Cooperative Society Ltd and the Maclean Shire Council (1991) and the Toomelah Cooperative Ltd and the Moree Plains Shire Council (1996) suggested that cooperative societies may be considered as public benevolent institutions and could be exempt from rate payments. These legal precedents were largely unknown to Aboriginal communities and provided a powerful bargaining point for Aboriginal communities with local government. In one consultation, the general manager acknowledged that he knew of these two legal cases but that the council had not applied the effects of those decisions 'as we have not been asked to by the Aboriginal community'. Advocacy led to that situation being rectified at a cost saving to the Indigenous community of $80 000.

A new legal project

A further specific outcome of this pilot project was that the Binaal Billa Regional Council sponsored a legal project (undertaken by the lawyer on this research) that drafted a set of model rules that would enable Aboriginal housing organisations and other Indigenous organisations to have objectives that complied with the terms and conditions required to satisfy the requirements for the charitable and benevolent bodies section of the New South Wales *Duties Act 1997* (section 275). The situation on former Aboriginal reserves varied. In some instances, local government indicated that as Aboriginal reserves paid no land rates or were rated as one property, no services were provided, or charges were made to that community as if that community was a private individual landholder. The significance of this was that (in some instances) local government perceived its responsibility to cease at the gates of the former Aboriginal reserve and that the provision of infrastructure and/or services was the responsibility of other organisations (principally ATSIC).

The concepts involved in council rating were difficult to explain to Indigenous communities. Consistent with the concept of moving from the verbal to the visual, a picture representation was undertaken.

Recognition of legitimate revenue

Rate revenue was a significant, but not exclusive, part of most local governments' budgets. Local government budgets in rural inland New South Wales involved a local government equalisation component whereby funds were distributed on the basis of 'horizontal equalisation' (based largely on population numbers and road lengths) to ensure that the differential capabilities of local governments in raising revenue and the cost differentials in the delivery of services, including to the needy and socially dis-advantaged, were recognised. Hence it could be argued that councils were receiving a revenue stream via the Grants Commission for Aboriginal people who lived within their boundaries and that the 'no rates, no services' approach negated recognition of this income stream. In one former Aboriginal reserve, using the most conservative of parameters, the existence of that reserve in the local government added approximately $110 000 in funding via the Commonwealth Grants Commission. It is certainly the case that roads, noxious weeds services, library services and other services were available to the Aboriginal communities and that they shared in the general benefits of the shire, but it was nevertheless an important recognition of Aboriginal people's financial con-tribution to shire budgets simply by virtue of living within the boundaries of the shire.

Recognition of Indigenous communities

This research noted that one council showed its commitment to Indigenous Australians and 'acknowledges and grieves for the loss by Indigenous people of their land, their children, their health and their lives' and the Council 'supports Indigenous and non-Indigenous people working together for a treaty or other instrument of recon-ciliation' and 'recognises the valuable contribution ... made by Indigenous people and look forward to a future of mutual respect and harmony'. In the ten communities visited, no such commitment existed. Empowered by this knowledge from the research, eight years later this symbolic but important recognition has been implemented in at least six local governments of the Binaal Billa Region and variations of the commitment in two other local governments.

PERSONAL REFLECTION

The 'doing' as a social work researcher (as distinct from other disciplines involved in research) shows that social work research is not concerned only with data collection, analysis and findings but also has an emancipatory agenda that involves advocacy and empowerment. In this research, I was concerned with finding out the nature of the relationship and the dynamics of that relationship, but I was additionally concerned to ensure that the relationship developed. The road would be made by the local government and Indigenous communities walking together towards a shared future in which the diverse contributions were valued. It shows the recognition of the importance of dialogue, agreement and achievement. It may be noted that this research was not just the social worker's thinking and doing but also equally emanated from and influenced his being, which is discussed in the next section.

REFLECTIVE EXERCISE 6.5

Critically discuss how the research process led to action and change in Aboriginal communities. What factors led to such action and change?

■ 'Being' of a researcher

PERSONAL REFLECTION

Interest and commitment

As stated earlier, I have a long-standing interest in Aboriginal issues. I was highly motivated and committed to conduct this research from emancipatory and empowering perspectives. A project such as this cannot be conducted without significant interest, strong motivation and commitment to the cause. Subsequent to the project, a Steering Committee member confided that his selection from the tenders was based less on research skills and research methodology and more on 'someone that could know our heart'. I do not claim that I know the 'heart' of Aboriginal people or communities, but the Steering Committee member's comment supports my interest in and commitment to improving the conditions of Aboriginal people.

Belief in diversity, its strengths and utilisation

I strongly believe in diversity. Although diversity is a complex concept and has several dimensions, in this research context, my belief in diversity has helped to bring together diverse epistemological perspectives (objectivist, constructivist and indigenous), inter-disciplinary and intercultural knowledge and interdisciplinary professionals, including people from Aboriginal communities.

Practical common sense (prudence) and temperance

In the social work profession, it is important to develop the virtues and qualities of prudence and temperance. These qualities are always evolving, and it is nearly impossible to claim that one has mastered them. Over a period of life and professional experience, I have learned to be prudent and temperate. When to act and not to act or when to commit or omit are difficult decisions in most of the complex situations, and there is no foolproof tool that allows one to make correct decisions. Perhaps reflective experience is one guide towards it.

Hope

I believe in hope. Hope provides energy for action, and hopelessness pacifies the action. The objectives of this research – self-determination, collaborative relationship, service development and utilisation and reconciliation – were hopes for me. I believe that these can be achieved and conditions in Aboriginal communities can be improved.

Commitment to social justice issues and anti-racist and anti-oppressive values

My theological orientations and professional socialisation have helped me to be conscious of social justice and anti-racist and anti-oppressive values. Poverty, inequality and discrimination deeply concern me. My being as a white man in regard to the issues of white and black racism, coloniser and the colonised, and oppressive structures is critical to me in the conduct of this research.

Fortitude

It is important to cultivate courage. Transacting from my own comforts of living conditions to Indigenous communities' living conditions, although temporarily, requires courage. Witnessing extremely deprived conditions in the midst of prosperity and the ability to withstand years of exploitation and oppression, hoping to change that condition at whatever level and through whatever means (in this case research), requires fortitude. Without it I would not have entered Aboriginal communities.

The description of my being in terms of these virtues, although they are not presented in any particular order, is presented as an example in the research context. It is neither comprehensive nor inclusive of all aspects of my being that is relevant to this research. The next section shows the dynamics of my being, thinking and doing.

Dynamics of thinking and doing and being

PERSONAL REFLECTIONS

I undertake research that I want to do and have practical outcomes for which I have and/or can acquire the skills to ensure the best outcome for and with the participants. In approaching a research project, I used the PEOPLE (see chapter 2) model that considers thinking and doing and being, the participants (including myself), the environmental scan, the project objective, the process and labour and the evaluation, which must include (for me) practical outcomes. While my being drew on thinking and doing, the following discussion shows that my doings and field observations challenged my being and that there was a critical dynamic occurring among my being, thinking and doing, and doing and thinking.

Meeting deficiencies

In considering this research project, I had deficiencies in the area of knowing the legal structures related to ratings and local government. I needed to put together a team that had that specific knowledge. I also recognised that I would need well-respected Indigenous co-researchers to provide the entry into communities and to ensure that the research (and myself) was not 'colonising'. I recognised that the Indigenous researchers would also be helpful with some of the local government consultations as they would pro-socially model intelligent, capable and committed Indigenous people to councils who might not have shared that perspective. However, for an Indigenous co-researcher, the issue of his being was firmly within the Indigenous community, and he struggled with the changing nature of that identity; in particular the concept of being listened to and being a co-contributor to the research rather than an 'assistant'. He began to understand that his life experiences had conditioned him to accepting himself as lesser and with lesser aims and goals. His challenge to being in this context was to consider his Indigenous knowledge as being at least as important to the research process as the ability to do library searches, design data-collection instruments, read statistical data and so on, which are part of Western research design skills.

Challenges to my being and its influence on my thinking and doing

In this research project, several aspects of my being was challenged and that influenced by thinking and doing. Some examples of such challenges are discussed below.

Challenge to epistemological diversity

A challenge to my being was to constantly attempt to ensure that the foundation of the research lay in the lived Indigenous experience that is grounded in real people and real situations as social beings rather than in the world of ideas. This was not the same priority for the local government councils, who were familiar with the world of ideas and to applying Western research methods and approaches. This was most challengingly brought out when the research project attempted to develop a 'negotiating/mediating package' for local government and Indigenous communities. It was quite simple to develop a package that would show the principles and methods used by councils negotiating with local interest groups (i.e. the principles of how local governments negotiate with Indigenous people). However, the project researchers did not have the skills and ability to develop a similar program that showed how Indigenous people negotiated with local councils. Issues of power and authority, timing and decision-making within the Indigenous community and how these were represented to those outside the community were different. Assumptions such as that all forms of living things are to be respected as being related and interconnected are supported by Indigenous forms of epistemology (see Weber-Pillwax 2001: 49–50) were not necessarily assumptions shared by councils. A strictly positivist design would be simple and may have greater reliability and validity but would reduce the type and quality of information and the range of people who could benefit from the research. The challenge to being involved valuing all the different sets of skills and different contributions arising from the different sources of knowledge. Despite such challenges to my thinking, doing and being, I persisted on epistemological diversity, which helped to observe and include a full range of mental/emotional and spiritual/existential factors at the Indigenous community consultations, and develop the negotiation guidelines suitable to Aboriginal communities.

Challenge to sociocultural diversity

My being was challenged when I considered the extent to which the language and culture of Indigenous people are living processes. In some communities, the local language has been eradicated entirely since the invasion and settlement of the area. Many Indigenous people expressed their concern that their culture was being lost either through active suppression or through the influence of the dominant culture 'swamping' the Indigenous culture. Although I recognise that cultures and language change and that change is inevitable and much change is positive, nevertheless it is profoundly challenging to witness the diversity of language and culture being lost. It seemed to me that a reduction of the human language, culture and biodiversity was occurring and being replaced by a blended monoculture rather than a rich diversity of cultures and languages.

Challenge to prudence and temperance

I experienced several critical incidents in the research project that challenged my prudence and temperance. In one community consultation, at a large meeting, a serious, loud, disruptive verbal altercation occurred between a younger man and a respected male elder. In the public setting, my immediate thoughts were that I ought to have intervened and adopted a peace-making or mediating role (doing). However, this would have reinforced the idea of the 'white man' solving the altercation by intervention. I seemed to be the person most concerned by the altercation, and others appeared to be interested observers and, at times, noisy supporters. The public meeting seemed to be in danger of degenerating into an ugly and unproductive verbal fight. I was torn between intervening and imposing control and allowing the matter to resolve itself. I decided not to intervene as my experience with Indigenous communities had suggested that there is often posturing and loud altercations that end in their own resolution. I was enormously helped by an Indigenous sessional co-researcher, who urged me to let it run.

At the conclusion of what I perceived to be the worst of the ten consultations with Indigenous communities, two senior Indigenous women who had not contributed at all to the consultations approached me to indicate that the directions suggested were the correct ones and that they would see that they were completed. My Indigenous staff member indicated that these women were the real power and authority in the community and that it had been a most successful consultation.

In another situation, the ethics application required by my university imposed a set of research restrictions that make pursuing important, community-initiated and tangential avenues of enquiry more difficult. In one consultation, the issues that the community wanted to develop were well beyond the authorisation of the ethics application but were the dominant concern of the community. It highlighted the clash between research 'owned' by institutions and researched 'owned' by communities. It was important and uncomfortable, and I kept evaluating whether I was making prudent and temperate decisions. I do not know whether I acted correctly. 'Pure' research of a positivist nature seems to have a greater certainty as to process and to predictability. Research for social workers is far more inductive and less certain as to either the pathway or the outcome. I was acutely aware that this research had a political component to it and that I might not have understood the particularities of the politics.

Challenge to hope

My being was also challenged around the virtue of hope. In some communities, the level of poverty and dysfunction was acute and an atmosphere of hopelessness prevailed. In some places it manifested itself in depression and suicidal ideation. To questions such as 'Tell me what it is like living in . . .?' and 'What could make things different?' there were very different answers that indicated mental/emotional and spiritual/existential elements. The sense of identity was bound to 'country'. One person said, 'We are the river people – but we see the river dry up through irrigation – and we die with it.' Another commented on how their land was being starved of water and the trees were dying, which had specific meaning for Indigenous people. Others remarked on the forced removal from former reserves, which had no services provided to them. They recalled how these reserves had been their home and the sadness they felt at seeing them in such states of disrepair. One group expressed dismay that the 'mission' hospital and the 'mission' school bell had been removed by local government without any consultation. These were symbols of stability, and the Indigenous community wanted them back. It was challenging to provide realistic, hopeful future options that were not simply the dreams of a 'white man' who did not live in the community. I used an approach that helped to return the bell to the community. The community saw this as a real outcome and a symbol of hope and change for the future.

Challenge to multiple roles – researcher and change agent

Often I found it challenging to combine the role of a researcher and a social worker facilitating advocacy and change. It indicated the conflict for the social work researcher who was involved in advocacy and negotiation while undertaking research. There is a limited sense of remaining apart from the subject matter, as may be considered essential in a strictly positivist approach. The social worker researcher was involved in action and in that regard undertakes research that is different from many other forms of research in other disciplines. The social worker researcher, at the core of his/her being, desires to know and understand and critically reflect, then wants to change unjust situations. However, the challenge for me was that the symbol (in this case the bell) might create hope for the future but is really insufficient when compared to the overall needs of the community. In the face of gross neglect and poverty, if the symbol is all that occurs, the symbol itself becomes part of the process of maintaining injustices and the prevailing hegemony.

Challenge to social justice, anti-racist and anti-oppressive values

My sense of social justice was challenged when the financial analysis revealed structural barriers and disadvantages for Aboriginal communities. Such practices as 'no rates, no services', building arrears, diverting money from allocated purposes, non-consultation and non-implementation of legal provisions that are meant to protect Aboriginal people militated against social justice, anti-racist and anti-oppressive values. Raising awareness of these issues led to the recognition of issues and some action plans to address them.

I was challenged around my construction of race and ethnicity. Before this research, I had accepted views of race without critically considering the origin of racial and ethnic paradigms and indeed their capacity for replicating and maintaining existing hegemonies and inequalities. I was profoundly challenged at the level of guilt. As I considered the reality of the removal of land and of children and the levels of institutionalised racism (e.g. the rating system and disincentives to own the land), I began to appreciate that I had been (through ignorance) complicit in this injustice and a beneficiary of it. I began to understand the issues of land and compensation as issues of human rights and justice rather than just political or social problems. I began to question the notion of race and its underpinnings in the biological sciences and its outworking in the social sciences. The eighteenth- and nineteenth-century scientific notions of race built on biological or organic characteristics (e.g. skin colour, facial features, origins) had led to unjust social, economic and political structures. I began to re-evaluate how the way knowledge from one area (e.g. the biological sciences) was used in another area (e.g. the social sciences), and I began to requestion concepts such as 'social evolution'. I wanted to abandon any notion of race and consider all people as part of the human race. However, the corollary of that view would be to weaken the place of Indigenous people in Australia as they would lose their communal and national identity. As I began to re-evaluate the premises on which race and ethnicity are based, I recognised that to abandon the concept of race and ethnicity entirely would have significant effects at personal (sense of significance and identity) and political (sense of solidarity) levels. To endorse its current premises has other consequences, including perpetuating and entrenching stereotyping and discrimination.

Overall, I came away from some of the Indigenous consultations profoundly moved and uplifted by the fortitude and prudence and especially the charity, faith and hope that I saw – and which occasionally left me in tears. From some of the local government consultations, I saw the virtues identified by Lewis in the representatives who were seeking just and positive ways to redress what they saw as poverty and dispossession within the constraints that they had. Others, it seemed to me, lacked any hope and some lacked charity. Constant self-reflection and self-monitoring, as well as monitoring of the team members, was required. The issue of being (self) was inseparable from the research focus. In this research, thinking and doing and being were inseparable at all times. It was not possible to do without thinking, or to think without being moved to action. Fundamental to both was the sense of being that looked forward with a degree of hopefulness. Although the primary role of the pilot research might have had a system linkage focus, advocacy for and the emancipation of disadvantaged communities was an outcome.

REFLECTIVE EXERCISE 6.7

What were the critical challenges to the social worker's being? Did this reading influence your thinking doing and being? If yes, how? If not, why?

Conclusion

As stated in the introduction, this chapter aims to discuss role social work research and the role that a social work researcher plays or should play in initiating action and change, and how conscious use of being, together with thinking and doing, facilitates that process. Towards achieving that aim it provided the brief description of the project in terms of its objectives, the ATSIC Binaal Billa Regional Council's Steering Committee requirements, how the research agenda fitted the researcher's values and professional commitments, and a summary of research methods followed. Developing regional agreements with a focus on self-determination and reconciliation was a challenging objective that created hope in Aboriginal communities and in me.

The thinking of the researcher showed the relative strengths of objectivist, constructivist and indigenous epistemological perspectives, and the need to bring these perspectives and their research methods together to achieve the objectives of the study. The thinking also included being cognisant of the socioeconomic, political, cultural and racial contexts within which the study was conducted. While the mixed methods approach was the most appropriate, part of the research design in terms of the ten indigenous communities to be studied was determined by the Steering Committee.

According to the research design, the data were collected from secondary sources, community consultations, interview and participatory research methods. An important part of this research process – doing – was initiating action and change. The data-collection process was emancipatory and empowering, at least to some extent, and the analysis further strengthened that change process. The awareness-raising of funding displacement and opportunity costs, legitimate revenue, a checklist for negotiations, lost employment opportunities, legal anomalies, the employment opportunity monitor, rates charged, subsidies denied, costs saved and the need for recognition were important steps towards action and change. This analysis to some extent facilitated advocacy and empowerment.

Some aspects of the being of the researcher discussed were his interest and commitment, belief in diversity, prudence and temperance, hope and fortitude. The analysis of the dynamics of his thinking, doing and being showed how the field realities challenged the researcher's being and changed his thinking and doing in relation to epistemological choice, research design, the role performance as a social work researcher and the change agent, community consultation and unjust, racist and oppressive practices. On the whole it highlighted the significance of the conscious use of being, along with thinking and doing, in social work research leading to action and change.

In concluding, we hope that this chapter helps readers to critically reflect on epistemological issues, the use of empowering and emancipatory research methods and how consciously they can use their being in social work research and action.

▦ Questions and exercises

1 What did you learn from this chapter?
2 If you were to develop a research design for your research project, what aspects of this chapter would be useful to you?

3   Can social workers perform the roles of researcher and change agent at the same time? Critically discuss what the challenges are and how this aim can be achieved.

4   What knowledge, skills and attitude do you need to reflect on and consciously use your thinking, doing and being in social work research?

7

Being in the context of reflective practice as a social work leader, manager, administrator

THIS CHAPTER IS about how social workers can assume leadership positions in human service organisations and make a difference. Traditionally, (social) welfare administration was considered as one of the methods of social work practice, which intersects with all social work practice methods. Organisational and administrative systems are needed to deliver services at individual, family, group and community levels. The nomenclature 'welfare administration' has changed to 'human service organisation practice' in recent times (see Jones & May 1992; Gardner 2005; Hughes & Wearing 2007; McDonald et al. 2011; Ozanne & Rose 2013). However, irrespective of the nomenclature, it is important to note that large organisations, both government and non-government, are needed and exist to systematically organise, administer and manage welfare or human services programs, including:

- government human services departments
- community child protection/welfare services
- ageing and disability
- mental health and hospitals
- non-government organisations such as Red Cross, Mission Australia, Anglicare, Centacare and so on.

Large numbers of social workers practise within these organisational contexts. Although the majority of social workers practise at the front line, which is important, it appears that training for social workers and their contribution to administration and management in organisations is inadequate and minimal. Few social workers take higher-level leadership positions in organisations. This trend needs to change. A small number of social workers who assume such leadership positions seem to turn their back on social work and identify with the ethos of top-down administration and management, forgetting core social work values and principles. Since many social workers begin and remain at the frontline level, leadership and management positions are often occupied by people other than social work professionals, who seem to have entirely different orientations (e.g. managerialism) that are sometimes contrary to social work values and principles. This creates a difficult situation for social workers as they have to negotiate between organisational and professional frameworks, which may be contradictory or different. We believe that such organisational contexts can be changed if social workers themselves aim for, and are trained to, lead the human services organisations at various levels. With right commitment, passion and vision, they can be capable of changing bureaucratic institutions to humanising organisations.

This chapter shows, as an example, how a social worker as an administrator, manager and/or leader defined and worked with participants; scanned the environment of an organisation; worked with and modified set objectives; initiated and enacted work processes through people and systems; and evaluated outcomes. In doing so, it will reflect on core value dilemmas and practical decisions under bureaucratic and sociolegal pressures.

First, it will consider key aspects of a social work leader, manager and/or administrator in terms of conceptual clarity and differences. Second, it presents the organisational context and the social worker's thinking. Third, it shows what the social worker did by using selected tasks or challenges. Finally, it reflectively shares the social worker's being, which enabled him to think and act, and act and think, the way he did to set goals and achieve them by leading change in the organisation. We hope that it inspires social workers to become leaders in their chosen area.

■ Chapter objectives

After completing this chapter students should:

- appreciate the fundamentals of social work leadership, management and administration
- consider the constraints and attributes of working in such a role, and
- consider and apply aspects of being that are relevant to working as a leader, manager and/or administrator in social work.

REFLECTIVE EXERCISE 7.1

Identify social workers who are in leadership positions in human service organisations.

Would you like to assume a leadership position in your social work career? If yes, what kind of social work leader would you like to become, and what is driving you? If not, why not?

▓ Main themes and concepts used

The main theme of this chapter is how a social worker tried to combine the roles of an administrator, manager and leader, and initiated necessary changes in a large organisation. It also shows the reflections on the social worker's thinking, doing and being.

Understanding the terms: administrator, manager, leader

There are a number of ways of understanding 'administrator, manager and leader' in the context of social work practice. For the purposes of this chapter and as reflected in actual practice, the terms 'administrator', 'manager' and 'leader' have been used to denote a complex practice function. Theoretical distinctions have been made between these roles, as discussed in table 7.1 on p. 175 (see Wood et al. 2006: 384; Keeling 1972; Zastrow 2003: 21; Drucker 1981).

For example, Keeling (1972) argues that 'administration' and 'management' contrast in key areas and lie at opposite ends of a spectrum. Wood et al. (2006: 384) do not mention administration in their conception of a manager or leader, and make the simple distinction that management is 'doing things right' while leadership is 'doing the right things, and inspiring, guiding and motivating people'.

In practice, social work administrators, managers and leaders perform a range of functions that require the skills of an administrator (in Keeling's terms) and a manager and leader (as discussed by Wood et al. 2006). Cloushed et al. (2006: 8), in writing specifically about management in social work, use the three terms interchangeably while recognising that others will make distinctions and use language differently. Drucker (1981) described management as 'getting things done through people'. It can be argued that this definition encapsulates the three major influences and schools of thought on management:

- the human resource focus of management (emphasis on people)
- the objectives-based school of management (things), and
- the process-oriented philosophy of management (getting things done).

Hepworth, Rooney and Larsen (2002) say that the social worker who is a manager of services has a wide and disparate role that requires multiple focuses and multiple roles, including the roles of system developer, researcher and systems maintenance role.

The social work administrator, manager or leader's work

The social work administrator, manager or leader's work may include:

- setting agency objectives
- analysing social conditions in the community

- making decisions about services to be provided
- establishing organisational structures
- administering finances
- securing funds
- monitoring processes
- recruiting and supervising staff
- transforming social policy.

In the context of a government organisation there are pressures to be an administrator and a manager (in Keeling's 1972 terms) requiring literacy and numeracy skills; avoiding embarrassing mistakes while seeking success; being both arbitrator and protagonist in different circumstances; both conforming and experimenting simultaneously; using legal and quasi-legal skills while considering economic and socioeconomic factors; working with hierarchical delegations while wanting to develop maximum commitment and delegation; and having roles that are defined by both responsibility and tasks.

▥ Case study

The analysis for this chapter will focus on the social worker leadership experiences of the author (Bill Anscombe) in a large, complex and multi-programmed organisation that operated within statutory and fiscal requirements, as well as in a highly turbulent and politicised environment. The organisation had the following statutory responsibilities:

- the prevention of child abuse and early intervention for families
- child protection and out-of-home care (OOHC) of children who have been removed from their parents or caregivers
- welfare and disaster relief, and
- building community and social capacity as both a funder of services and a provider of direct services.

The role of the social worker in this case involved the leadership, management and administration of child protection and welfare services across an area of 588 000 square kilometres with a dispersed population of about 400 000 people. Of this population, more than a thousand children were in out-of-home care, and there were 14 000 reports of child abuse and neglect per year. There were 168 staff in the area, of whom 113 were direct caseworkers. Services were provided from twenty-five locations, including a number of one- or two-person locations in very small rural areas. The operating budget was approximately $14 million, and the social worker had significant influence over the $39 million grants budget.

PERSONAL REFLECTION

While social workers significantly contribute to the welfare and well-being of people, their contribution to administration and management of organisations is limited in terms of training and practice (see Bilson & Ross 1999, McKay 2002 and Clarke & Newman 1997 regarding the reaction to the domination of managerialism).

I had been fortunate to pursue a course of study in public management (not social work management) that had exposed me to the classical theories of management, including Fayol and the critique by Drucker (1977), the scientific management of Taylor (1911), concepts espoused by Weber (1947), human relation theories, including Follett (see Zander & Zander 2000), McGregor (1960) and Likert (1967).

I was attracted to concepts of transformational leadership (involving individualised consideration – mentoring and coaching; intellectual stimulation; the encouragement of innovation and creation; inspirational motivation; articulating an appealing and inspiring vision; and idealised influence – role-modelling through a sense of meaning and challenge). I realised that, with a vast area and multiple service delivery centres not linked well by accessible transport, my previous transactional leadership (whereby the leader sets goals, standardises practices and establishes routines and procedures, and has close and regular contact) was unlikely to be sustainable.

Social work managers and leaders often work in bureaucracies (Watson 1980; Garston 1993). They operate in differing contexts, with differing frameworks and differing styles, including autocratic, democratic, laissez-faire and others (Hersey & Blanchard 1988; Blake & Mouton 1964). Financial and legal requirements and procedural matters have turned some managers and leaders from being helpers of front-line workers to inhibitors and inspectors of front-line workers. The differences between administration and management have been articulated and have profound practical implications. Drawing on Keeling's (1972) analysis, table 7.1 summarises the distinction between administration and management and extends it to leadership in social work.

Current social work administrator/manager/leaders operate in an environment of managerialism and neo-liberalism. By managerialism, we mean the application of the managerial techniques of business to the running of other organisations, including government departments, not-for-profit organisations and others (faith-based or religious). By neo-liberalism, we mean the philosophy that advocates open markets, privatisation and deregulation with an enhanced role for the private sector. Managerialism has been critiqued on the grounds that it distorts basic values, has a belief in the market mechanisms, inappropriately mixes public and private management and values and inappropriately uses a consumer metaphor and structural issues (e.g. Ife 1995, 1997; Cloushed et al. 2006).

Table 7.1 Comparing administration and management to the social work leader

Criteria	Administration	Management	Social work leader
Objectives	Infrequently reviewed and changed; parliamentary legislative goals	Detailed short-term goals and targets – reviewed frequently	In consultation with participants and mindful of the environment, frequently reviewed and changed to meet participant expectations
Success criteria	Mistake avoidance	Success seeking	Creatively, enabling and empowerment of participants to learn by successes and mistakes (doing) while ensuring systemic expectations are met
Resource use	Secondary task: to be used within parliamentary and Treasury guidelines	Primary task	Focus on the use of, and linkage to, existing resources and the generation and creation of new resources for empowering the participant
Structure	Role defined by responsibility; limited delegation as defined by Treasury regulation and legislation; hierarchic structure	Roles defined by task; maximum delegation	Egalitarian, anti-hierarchical and participatory structures
Roles	Arbitrator	Protagonist	Catalyst and social change agent
Attitudes	Passive; time insensitive; risk avoiding; procedural; conformity to standards	Active; seeks opportunities; exploits opportunities; results oriented; experimental	Human rights and social justice focus; empowering; proper process oriented and anti-oppressive
Skills	Legal or quasi-legal; literacy	Economic or socioeconomic; numeracy	Enabling and empowering skills; literacy and numeracy skills; and the doing skills of Zastrow (2003)

Source: adapted from Keeling 1972: 152

PERSONAL REFLECTION

Partly through my social work commitment and its emphasis on human beings, my preference has been to use situational leadership (Hersey & Blanchard 1988) as it encompasses a focus on both the leader and the follower. It recognises that the leader may have power and authority related to position or finance, but it can also be related to charisma, expert knowledge, academic achievement or acceptance. I take the view that power and authority (like structure) is a neutral concept – it is neither good nor bad – but can be used in order to create humanising organisations and maximise individual opportunity. Mullaley (2006) provides approaches to fighting structures by being part of them. For me, the social work leader has values that are consistent with the goals and purposes of social work. There are conflicts and tensions in practice between administration, management, leadership and social work (e.g. the value of social justice may be in conflict with a Treasury goal of efficiency, or the needs and program needs at the individual level may be at odds with the corporate goal of uniformity and consistency of service) but they are conflicts and tensions that provide opportunity for humanising organisations and maximising individual opportunity. Social work that is empowering allows for the consideration of multiple goals arising from many sources rather than the narrow consideration of one goal arising from one source.

According to the position description, the co-participants (managerially referred to as stakeholders) included children at risk of harm, children in OOHC, families (both birth families and foster care families), communities (ranging from urbo-rural to rural to remote), staff, interagency relationships (both government and non-government), the agency (the organisation) and the government. Some of the participants were clearly defined and known (such as individual children in care, current service providers) while others were more abstract (such as potential employees, service providers and carers). In order to better understand each participant's expectations of the social work leader and of the organisation, it was important to construct an ecomap. Using this information, meetings were held with the various participants or representatives of participants to confirm or challenge their initial expectations.

The social work leader had formal responsibilities as indicated in the job description, including Treasury regulations, legislation and agreements. In commencing the position, it was also recognised that the social worker would need to bring together three geographic and organisational areas with three different cultures into one area with state-wide objectives. This posed a number of challenges, particularly as the workforce had been depleted, leaderless and in transition for some time. In parts of the region there had been a culture of autocratic leadership and some evidence of vicarious trauma of staff and clients occasioned by administrative decisions.

PERSONAL REFLECTION

I was determined to pro-socially model inclusive and human-centred leadership. As I considered the size of the region, I intended to follow a transformational rather than transactional style of leadership (Bass 1990; Bass & Steidlmeier 1998; see also literature on geographically dispersed teams, such as Duarte & Snyder 2006). I had serious self-doubts about my capacity to undertake the position. I considered that I had the virtues required for the position but recognised that I would need to self-monitor, particularly with respect to fortitude and hope. I had deficiencies in not having had 'hands-on' experience in child protection and child welfare; no recent experience of industrial or administrative law; no established reputation in the organisation; and few established networks of power and influence within the organisation. I recognised that I aimed to build a cohesive team that saw clients and service providers of the organisation as co-participants and partners rather than adversaries and opponents – and that this was contrary to (then) existing practice.

REFLECTIVE EXERCISE 7.2
Write what distinctions, if any, you draw between a leader, a manager and an administrator.
   What do you think of as the characteristics of a good leader, a good manager, a good administrator? How does s/he use power? How does s/he influence? How does s/he communicate both decisions and care?
   Is there a difference in the approach to goals as a leader compared with a manager and administrator?
   Is there anything specific about a social work leader/manager/administrator?

The environmental scan

On the first day, it was prudent to undertake an environmental scan informed by a range of written material and access to some key informants. While the environmental scan covered a very wide range of issues including finances, inter-governmental relationships, restructuring and systemic developments, the reflective analysis in this chapter is limited to two issues: staffing and OOHC. Of the hundred caseworker positions (providing front-line child protection services), fifteen positions were unfilled, fifteen positions were filled by untrained temporary staff without the required minimum qualifications, four were on return-to-work programs following serious injury or distress and five were stood down or suspended on pay pending resolution of allegations.

On analysis, 1045 children in the region were in OOHC having been removed from their caregiver or birth parents. Of these, 49.7 per cent were Indigenous, which far exceeded the expected rate on the basis of population statistics. There were significant variations. The environmental scan lead to thinking about the differential rates of children in OOHC, which showed that two adjacent communities with almost equal population size, similar age and ethnicity components, similar employment profiles and similar other characteristics (based on Australian Bureau of Statistics analysis and a standard community profile), had very different outcomes with respect to children in OOHC. The larger community had twenty-one children in OOHC while the smaller community had fifty-eight children in OOHC.

Two other areas also had very different proportions of children in OOHC. One area had a population base of 85 000 and had a young age profile with high numbers of Indigenous people and a total of eighty children in OOHC. Another area, with a population base of 40 000 people, an older age profile (meaning that there were fewer children) and a lower percentage of Indigenous people, had 108 children in care. The ABS Socio-Economic Index for Advantage (SEIFA) for the two areas suggested that the situation 'should' have been reversed. The explanation from key informants (the presence of a major hospital in the smaller location) was not supported by analysis of the OOHC register. These differential rates, for no obvious reason, were of concern. It confirmed the belief that child protection practice involves both individual and social factors. Parton, Thorpe and Wattam (1997: 67) have written:

> What is considered child abuse for the purpose of child protection policy and practice, is much better characterised as a product of social negotiation between different values and beliefs, different social norms and professional knowledge and perspectives about children, child development, parenting. Far from being a medico scientific reality, it is a phenomena where moral reasoning and moral judgements are central.

Studies revealed that different professionals faced with child maltreatment and neglect scenarios applied significantly different standards regarding what constituted either child abuse or child neglect. In practice, child protection often focuses upon individuals rather than social, cultural and ideological issues.

PERSONAL REFLECTION

My thinking was that there are children, families and neighbourhoods that lack resources and have significant economic, community and social pressures affecting the issues of safety and well-being of children. Although these include drug and alcohol use, domestic violence, mental illness and changes in family structures, researchers identify poverty as the most detrimental sociodemographic risk indicator in determining children's life chances (Golombok 2000; Shonkoff & Phillips 2000) with it affecting health, education, housing, access to goods and services, and employment.

I reflected on risk. Risk has displaced need as the core principle of social policy formulation and welfare delivery (Kemshall 2002). Western society is increasingly risk averse, being predicated on the culture of safety (Furedi 1997) and framed by the precautionary principle ('better safe than sorry'). Human beings do not always act in acceptable, logical and rational ways. Alcohol and drug use, mental health concerns, family violence, unemployment, poverty, disability and other factors intersect to make the family a complex place in which children and young people develop.

Risk and childhood

No child grows up in a risk-free environment, and whether a risk-free environment – even if possible – would be desirable is arguable. Although all children experience some degree of risk, most children are at the lower end of the risk continuum. The management of risk using actuarial and deductive methods has increased. These approaches have an underlying logic and thinking in which there are two ways to be right and two ways to be wrong when comparing actual reabuse to the prediction of reabuse. Figure 7.1 is adapted from Dale, Thompson & Woods (2001: 87).

In child protection, if a prediction does not accurately predict reabuse (Box 3), then the consequence for individuals could be very serious and might include death or serious injury. Predictions of reabuses that do not occur (Box 2 – false positives) are very costly in dollar and human terms as children and young people and their families are subjected to unnecessary state intervention. The relative occurrence of behaviour is the base rate that dramatically influences the outcomes of the right or wrong/predicted or actual decision table. Behaviour with a high or nil base rate is easier to accurately predict than correctly predicting infrequent but possible events.

Despite limitations in human decision-making (such as the influence of recency/primacy issues, the confirmatory bias and overconfidence), clinical intuition and a clinical understanding of the unique circumstances of each case is a valuable complement to the actuarial grounding that can occur using risk predictions and base rates.

	Actual	
	Yes – reabuse	No – No reabuse
Prediction Yes – reabuse	Right (1)	Wrong (2)
No – no reabuse	Wrong (3)	Right (4)

Figure 7.1 Predicting risk of reabuse in child protection matters

My thinking about the relationship between clinical judgements and risk measures was informed by the debate in social work on evidence-based practice or evidence-aware practice (Otto & Ziegler 2008: 274; Gibbs & Webb cited in Plath 2006: 66; Trevithick 2005, 2008). There are important questions as to the elements that constitute evidence-based practice, the nature of evidence itself, the standard against which evidence is assessed and whether evidence-based practice is possible and desirable in complex, multidimensional and multi-agency situations. However, the social work leader has to implement practices and approaches in this contested terrain and in the current state of knowledge and evidence. The social work leader with strong social justice virtues uses this knowledge to engage with the difficult task of developing resources and processes for the empowerment of people.

The above reflection about the child protection system also highlights the dilemmas of the social work leader. It could legitimately be argued that the majority of the organisation's child protection work was short-term and crisis-driven. Short-term targeted intervention is the favoured model of managerialism and, rather than solve entrenched family, community and social issues, it *manages* short-term crises. More clients can be seen within time-limited goals and objectives. Managers become translators of policy into instrumental objectives that are evaluated and monitored to ensure compliance. Resource-intensive therapeutic work over the long term is often overtaken by short-term emergency responses. In short, the urgent replaces the important and the mechanical application of processes replaces the focus on human beings. Although a singular modality of intervention is unlikely to fit the needs of all clients of the organisation, short-term approaches might not be as suitable for long-term and chronic problems in families. Developing sustained, long-term work with families who have high levels of dysfunction that might affect intergenerational dysfunction rather than managing short-term incidents was a priority.

It was important to consider the implications in OOHC of the risk and short-term approach in the light of the differential rates of children in OOHC. If many of the children in OOHC who had been predicted as being at risk would not be reabused, *then* enormous harm at enormous human, social and financial cost was being caused to children and their families. Although agencies and the community might 'feel' safe, the estranged children and their birth families are paying the real cost. Short-term safety and long-term welfare and well-being must be considered.

Risk assessing came originally from actuarial studies in insurance for shipping. Risk profiles use the idea of the frequency or likelihood of an event and the seriousness or severity to the individual or organisation of that event. How applicable do you think these concepts are to areas of human need?

Try the following exercise

A and B are part of a criminal gang and are arrested. A and B cannot communicate with each other in any way. The police do not have enough evidence to convict them on the most serious charge. They expect to sentence A and B both to a year in prison on a lesser charge. However, at exactly the same time, the police offer A and B the opportunity to betray the other by saying that the other committed the crime. If A and B both betray each other, each serves two years in prison. If A betrays B but B remains silent, A will be set free and B will serve three years in prison. If B betrays A but A remains silent, B will be set free and A will serve three years in prison. If A and B both remain silent, both will only serve one year in prison (on the lesser charge).

In an actuarial sense, the best outcome is for both to stay silent (two years gaol in total) whereas the other options lead to three years or four years gaol in total. But of course the actuarial calculations do not take account of trust, betrayal, self-interest and other human qualities. What will you do?

Doing as a leader/manager/administrator

One of the first tasks of the social work leader was to approve the funding for seven children taken into care. M (named changed) was a single mother living in poor quality rental accommodation in a small rural community with her seven children (aged 2–12 years) receiving a total of $1281 per fortnight in income security. Depressed, with no family support, basic literacy, no work skills and tired, she attended the organisation threatening self-harm. The children were placed in foster care, and her income was reduced to $480.20 per fortnight). A foster carer took all seven children and received a tax-free allowance of $2450 per fortnight as the foster care allowance of (then) $350 per fortnight per child. The carer received $2450 per fortnight more than the birth mother of the children for caring for them. Using this case example shed light on some significant practice issues. It was noticed that the foster parent did not cooperate with the organisation in encouraging restoration of children to their birth mother after the mother had shown changes and the capacity to care for her children. Examining the situation and applying an economic analysis indicated that there is a financial incentive (for the carer) for the children to be retained in OOHC and a perverse incentive for the carer *not* to cooperate with family restoration.

The social work administrator/manager/leader in child protection work is confronted with challenges that require careful thought and are often postulated in a binary (either/or) way. Thinking systemically/logically and laterally/creatively allows them to be reframed and alternative approaches and explanations considered. This thinking can reframe the debate about risk and evidence-based practice away from immediate risk of harm to include long-term well-being and to an approach that incorporates both actuarial risk analysis and clinical judgement. Such thinking will look to approaches other than short-term intervention. Rather than celebrating the rising numbers of children in care being evidence of children's safety, it may well be an indicator of wider social policy failure. The administrator (in Keeling's (1972) terms) would be risk averse and follow procedures whereas the manager may be much more risk tolerant and allow for local solutions, and the social work leader will look for outcomes that are just and endorsed by the participants.

Having undertaken the environmental scan, which included the organisational goals, the resources available, the values, the nature of the communities served and the current realities, it was important to prioritise objectives. The highest priorities were staffing and arresting the rapid increase in OOHC growth, especially at the identified high-growth offices of the region. These priorities were made because it was believed that inadequate staff (in numbers or training or support) results in poor services. Some children were being unnecessarily brought into care in some locations with the consequent disruption to birth families and children and unnecessary cost to the State.

PERSONAL REFLECTION

Within my first week, I wrote to all staff with an outline of my 'being' (who I was) and my one-year objectives. My detailed and written personal objectives included:
- bringing the staff vacancy rate back to less than 10 per cent
- developing strategies that would recruit staff for long-standing positions that were unfilled
- reducing the number of children in OOHC by 10 per cent and having every child in care with a 'Life-Storying Book'
- having a management structure with reasonable spans of control in place, and
- having all accounts (except the operating budget) in credit.

In the organisation, there were few established routines, and constant demands from individuals, contracted service providers, staff, small group and large group public representation, staff management and supervision. There was no structure of management, and one of the roles of the social work leader was to enable and develop first-time managers who were newly appointed and were making the transition from caseworker to leader/manager/administrator. The doing in the position involved all the social work roles identified by Zastrow (2010): enabling, brokering, advocating, empowering, activism, mediating, negotiating, educating, coordinating, researching, group facilitating, public speaking. Some of the core tasks involved: brokering services; mediating and negotiating; educating and researching; coordinating emergency responses; group facilitation; advocacy; budget matters; staffing and 'difficult-to-fill' locations, as described below.

Brokering services

Brokering services, which involves linking individuals and groups with the services or personnel that they need, is one core task.

Mediating and negotiating

Mediating involves intervening in disputes between parties in order to help them find compromise, reconcile differences and reach contractual or covenantal agreements by remaining neutral and making sure that both parties in a dispute understand their

Table 7.2 Micro-, mezzo- and macro-level skills

Level	Example
Micro	Individual complaints by clients and staff
Mezzo	Negotiating new memoranda of understanding with the health organisation, juvenile justice, aged, disability and home care
Macro	Interstate agreements regarding cross-border issues

positions by clarifying, recognising miscommunications and helping the parties present their case clearly.

Negotiating involves bringing together those who are in conflict over one or more issues in order to arrive at a compromise and mutually agreed solution, but the negotiator may be aligned with one side or the other.

Mediating and negotiating skills were required at the micro, mezzo and macro levels (see table 7.2).

Educating and researching

Educating involves information-giving and teaching new and adaptive skills. This was done at the individual level through coaching and at group and community level. The role of educating was done both formally and informally. Research was conducted in relation to OOHC, kinship care and Indigenous foster care.

Coordinating emergency responses

This involves ensuring that there is no duplication of services or conflict in objectives or, where there is conflict between objectives, that the conflict is managed effectively. Staffing for coordinating emergency responses was an important responsibility. Potential emergencies included flooding, bushfires and the defusing of World War II explosives found in a deceased estate.

Group facilitation

Group facilitation included small, project-driven groups and larger, ongoing ones. Public speaking involved representation including interorganisational forums, community meetings, action and lobby groups, service-provider groups and at State functions. These often involved public speaking either in person or on radio.

Advocacy

As an advocate, the social work leader represented the region at a state-wide level and the organisation at interorganisational and community forums.

I was concerned that the doing would become so consuming that the opportunity for reflection would be lost. Fortunately, the long-distance driving required by the position provided the opportunity to reflect and think about the issues of the region and plan interventions.

Budget matters

It was recognised that the operating budget may be a problem from the perspective of the organisation. Over the first few months, the social work leader developed a defence for not addressing the issues of the operating budget. An administrator operating to Treasury regulations and organisational standards may simply have implemented cost savings and cost cutting.

As a social worker leader, I took the view that a basic inequity and unfairness existed between rural and urban communities. The Resource Allocation Model (RAM) was urbo-centric and unrealistic and based upon the simple formula of the operating budget being 15 per cent of the area salary budget. Having decided that those responsible for the budget allocation were finance-oriented, had little knowledge of non-metropolitan practice and would be unlikely to be amenable to arguments based on service delivery and human well-being, I argued a very simple cost analysis using the reality of practice to mount a defence and advocate for change. I saw this issue as an opportunity also to educate about rural social work practice and to negotiate a just outcome for rural areas. Of the many examples developed, two will illustrate the effects of doing skills of researching, advocating, activism and negotiating in developing a defence that led to a changed RAM.

Operating budget – example 1
The salary of a manager was (say) $80 000/year – 15 per cent of that figure was $12 000 per year. A manager in an urban area with all her/his staff located in the same building had $12 000 as an operating budget, which was based on his/her salary. The manager in one office in my area had office locations at a great distance from the base. The person travelled the equivalent of 48 000 kilometres per year and thereby consumed the total budget provided under the RAM (using the Public Service casual user rate of 24 cents per kilometre). Only two of the six locations were accessible

within the same day, and each of the other four required staying overnight, which also needed to be part of the notional $12 000.

Operating budget – example 2
New staff required training, which was undertaken centrally and paid for regionally. Training of a new staff member required six full weeks of attendance in Sydney at the state award capital city allowance and a minimum of six return airfares. These costs were to be met from the area's operating budget. But offices located in metropolitan areas did not incur such operating costs as they were able to access training within a train journey on a daily basis.

These examples are indicative of how an urbo-centric approach adversely affects service delivery. These and other examples were defensible in the finance reviews that occurred quarterly and caused a revision of the RAM.

REFLECTIVE EXERCISE 7.4
Consider the different skills that are used in the above examples. You might like to reflect upon the need to challenge deeply entrenched but unfair assumptions. You might like to reflect upon the need to meet the demands of those outside of the social work arena by using the terms and means that will be understood by them. You might like to reflect upon the analytic skills needed to understand the issues.

Staffing and 'difficult-to-fill' locations

Staffing the area and particularly the 'difficult to fill' locations was a priority. Staffing rural and remote locations involves issues at the personal, societal, professional and community levels. The social work leader developed and promoted the following statement: 'To have an effective service requires the right people, with the right skills, in the right place, at the right time, with the right remuneration, with the right leadership, with the right objectives, with the right processes, doing the right things and with the right supervision and support.'

Operating as a social work leader/manager/administrator, evidence indicated that obtaining and retaining skilled, qualified and experienced staff was a major issue in rural and remote areas. Rural communities are underserviced (Chapman & Greenville 2002). Governments have adopted a range of strategies to address the inability to obtain staff in many locations. The approach taken in this particular case was to trial creative and innovative ways of filling (particularly Indigenous) vacancies.

Some locations are difficult to staff. After consultation with a wide range of others and some research, the following profiling matrix was developed to determine 'difficult to staff' locations:

- failure of merit selection: a position has been advertised without success or the candidature does not meet the minimum criteria for the position
- staff mobility: high staff mobility or where staff do not complete the period necessary to ensure satisfactory service delivery to the community
- experience of staff: staff appointed are typically in their early years or first year of service
- the experience of managers: managers appointed to difficult-to-staff locations are typically in their first managerial position
- staff morale: staff morale in the difficult-to-fill locations may be perceived as being low
- availability of casual staff: availability can be affected by two major factors – non-availability due to the remote location, and the reluctance of casual workers to work in locations owing to prior experience or the location's reputation.

When this matrix of factors exists, the community is disadvantaged by not having the positions filled, by receiving an inadequate service from a distant location or by having positions filled by staff who were inexperienced or ill-qualified. It is a peculiarity of the way society is organised that the most challenging service positions in the areas of greatest social exclusion are often filled by the persons of least experience or capacity.

Potential strategies included:

- incentives
- tenure – with a right of transfer at the end of the tenure period
- sabbatical leave
- spouse/partner transfer (to accommodate dual-income families)
- alternative work schemes (which involve the trading of junior positions to allow for the appointment of a more senior position)
- directed transfers
- partnership arrangements: working with local communities and local organisations to develop partnership arrangements that build the social cohesion and social capital of particular locations.

Consider the following three examples related to staffing.

Example 1: Indigenous child protection worker

Filling the only position as an Indigenous caseworker in a small town of 1600 people of whom 58 per cent were Indigenous was extremely difficult. It met each of the criteria of the matrix. Additionally, the housing rental cost was high for a small, fibro home in an unattractive neighbourhood and not in the secured and fenced area of the government services compound. The position had been filled for six weeks in a period of fourteen months. Services were being offered from a town some 150 kilometres away on an 'as needed' basis with a purely casework model of intervention that responded to crisis situations. The underlying issues of poverty, neglect, dispossession, substance abuse and oppression were not being addressed.

The social work leader managed the process but was constrained by urbo-centric legislation and procedures (such as being required to ask all candidates exactly the same questions; adherence to centralised advertising; and standardised costs of and approaches to recruitment). Within these parameters, a number of additional Indigenous recruiting strategies were undertaken.

The previous appointee had exited following a very short time (six weeks), citing community pressures. She said she could not see anything 'ever' changing, and she felt 'unsafe'. A former worker had left the position following threats and violence to the worker's family. There was a lack of safety for one worker and a lack of hope for another. The community wanted a live-in service. However, the physical safety of the staff member and their family had to be assured, given the comments of the previous two occupants. An agreement was reached whereby the community covenanted to value any new worker and recognised the community's responsibility to keep that person and their family safe. This covenant was put to the representative group.

Equally significant was a change to the job description. In child protection, the most difficult decisions involve the removal of children following abuse. These are decisions that can influence aspects of the wider community and raise a range of emotional and behavioural responses. In small, isolated communities, child removal decisions are often volatile and staff are especially vulnerable. The job description for this location was altered so that the highly volatile decisions on removal were taken outside the community with the consequent protection of the worker in the community.

With these features in place, advertisements were placed in the required newspapers and in Indigenous newspapers. A brochure was developed for community agencies and placed throughout the community. Aboriginal radio was used with Aboriginal staff from other locations. These were beyond the normal highly centralised recruitment processes and incurred additional expense.

Current Aboriginal staff assisted in identifying people in the community with the relevant skills and abilities to be able to undertake training and work in the organisation. A culturally appropriate information package was developed. An Aboriginal person was the contact person for the position and convened the selection panel, which had more Aboriginal people than non-Aboriginal people. The interviews were conducted in friendly places, and interview questions were rigorously assessed for cultural appropriateness. Information packages were widely available and an information session was run that assisted the applicant in making a written application. Feedback was given to all who enquired. An orientation day occurred with a barbeque lunch at a community location where prospective applicants could meet the panel members before the interviews. These approaches lessened the difficulty of the subsequent interview, where the very nature of asking direct questions of Aboriginal people may be culturally inappropriate.

The position was filled, and the subsequent training occurred.

Example 2: Aboriginal mentoring and education

Indigenous staff members were employed without the tertiary qualifications expected of all other caseworkers. This approach recognises that there are many forms of knowledge. While they have cultural knowledge and life experience, they frequently do not have the casework skills and wider social work skills needed for performing all aspects of the position. These formal academic deficiencies are evident when communities do not receive funding or other supports because the worker is not able to undertake analysis and make submissions as a consequence of inappropriate literacy or education levels.

Mentoring was directly provided for Indigenous employees of the organisation. The mentoring revolved around:

- the employees understanding their place in the child welfare system
- an overview of the various movements and history of child welfare including theoretical perspectives
- an understanding of the characteristics of children
- a brief child development overview and the significant influences on children
- holistic multidimensional assessment skills
- communication and interviewing skills
- organisational and time management skills
- creative thinking skills
- case management skills
- skills in genograming and ecomapping
- negotiating skills and risk assessment skills.

The program developed thinking and doing and being of Indigenous staff in a dominant 'white' bureaucracy. This mentoring program recognised the difficulty in separating work from the community, particularly where there was a large number of one's own family living in the community. While the mentees assessed the program very highly (using a positivist assessment) and while all outputs nominated were achieved, the real test was the effect of the program on work performance, the mentee's satisfaction with the role, the community's acceptance and respect for the mentees and the organisation, and the contribution made to the community and the lives of children and young people. In this regard, an unsolicited email from the immediate supervisor of the mentees stated: 'We are already seeing the benefits of the mentoring program. N— [mentee's name] and C— [mentee's name] are pleased with the program and we are seeing the changes in both of them already. I appreciate your efforts very, very much.'

Example 3: Out-of-home care and staffing through a social work mobile unit

Recruiting and training paid staff and assessing and developing foster carers in rural and remote areas are difficult. Some of the failure to attract staff is due to the uniqueness of rural and remote practice and the myths, fears and assumptions of potential employees. The objectives of the social work Mobile Student Unit were:

- to expose social work students to rural and remote practice
- to recruit, train and assess potential foster carers and develop current carers
- to develop a mobile cohesive student unit
- to undertake limited life-storying work with OOHC children, and
- to undertake a community assessment of four communities.

The anticipated outcomes of the project were the assessment of potential foster carers; training new foster carers; developing the skills and values of current foster carers; life-storying work completed; four community analyses completed; the organisation to be seen as a preferred employer among university students; and heightened awareness by students of the innovative practices.

The evaluation of the first rural Mobile Student Unit were thirty-eight new carers trained as against a target of twenty-four; fourteen new carers trained and fully assessed against the organisational step-by-step assessment modules as against a target of eight; six staff members of the Department of Community Services (DoCS) trained in step-by-step assessment and life-storying work; three children's programs run; six current carers refreshed through training; four community analyses completed; fourteen children with life-storying work undertaken as against a target of twelve; four carers trained in life-storying work; community speaking opportunities (press, service groups); approximately forty hours of travel (by car).

The following comments were made by students engaged in the program:

> The main lesson learned was that a difference can be made, and that with inspiration things can change; the mobile unit was excellent; the people we met and the concrete results we achieved were well worth the stress of the project; in the beginning the

confidence that we had in ourselves as leaders, trainers and as effective social workers was limited compared to the confidence that we have discovered; there are already children who have been placed in the care of newly registered carers; current foster children will benefit from the training of their foster carers and the life story work that will continue; overall, the Mobile Student Unit was a most valuable and unique experience; we found ourselves trying to find our potential in an atmosphere where expectations were high and not negotiable.

REFLECTIVE EXERCISE 7.5

Hepworth, Rooney and Larsen (2002) refer to the role of linking. Can you think of ways in which you could link different needs with resources similar to the example above? Think of your local area and the infrastructure and people in it. Now imagine that you have a child in need of care and support. Think whether there is any possible link between the child and (say) the local newspaper, school, church, sporting club, service groups and so on. How might needs and resources be brought together creatively?

■ Reflecting on being as a social worker leader/manager/administrator

Organisational being

Staff, communities, individuals and agencies have their own sense of being (identity, hopes, frustrations, characteristics). The social work leader is part of an organisation that has a sense of being. Most organisations have a set of formal values, and all have informal values. Most have a formal code of behaviour, and all have informal codes of behaviour. All organisations have interrelationships and intrarelationships and are subject to various formal and informal accountabilities.

In reality, the being of the organisation is frequently synonomous with the local staff and local issues. The organisation's sense of being, despite policies and procedures emanating centrally, is embodied by local staff. The 'mantra' (the right staff in the right place and so on) became accepted (in varying degrees) throughout the region and furthered the importance of all staff pro-socially modelling the values and beliefs and approaches that we wished to develop.

The sense of being varied. In the Indigenous caseworker recruitment, the being of the new caseworker was not known other than that s/he would be Indigenous. The being of the community in which the new worker was placed was known both statistically and experientially.

With the Indigenous mentees, their being was known. Through assessment, engagement and collaboration, new self-concepts were able to be developed that particularly affected the mental/emotional, social/relational and existential/spiritual development.

The social work group involved many different senses of being. The students were coming to terms with being a social worker, with remote living and with the blurred boundaries of the personal and the professional (illustrated by a night of drinking that had some professional implications).

Challenges to social work: leader's being

PERSONAL REFLECTION

As a social work leader, I found it a constant challenge to respond optimistically to entrenched and intergenerational poverty and the neglect of individuals and communities. It was a challenge to be the organisational representative in the face of legitimate complaints about policy and service delivery. I recognised the importance of maintaining the cardinal and theological virtues – especially hope and charity. But it is one matter to seek forgiveness for a wrong as an individual and quite another as the representative of an organisation in the highly charged world of politics. Not having the freedom to act unilaterally in the best interests of the child or family but having to appropriate some degree of a corporate identity was a challenge to my sense of being. It was a challenge to balance the situation of individuals in need with the legitimate need of the organisation to protect itself. There were times when I needed greater fortitude (when dealing with the hostility of individual aggrieved parents, staff members or whole communities) and when I needed prudence, temperance and justice. As I reflected upon the contractual nature of much employment, I recognised the real ownership by organisations and fear by the staff and the very real potential of that person to serve the interest of the organisation rather than the interests of the public. The writings of Freire and liberation theologians and biblical writings were important in resisting becoming part of oppression rather than part of liberation.

In this position the social work leader had to read, think and act in a transformational leadership/management role (see Bass 1990 and Avolio et al. 1991). It was simply not possible to transact daily or even weekly with such a wide and diverse constituency. The response was to set the transformational goals and put in place the mechanisms for their achievement. This was a real challenge to the social worker's being as it meant that, despite regularly setting the objectives and providing the mechanisms, it was difficult to have a well-developed sense of the person or persons or agency that would deliver on the objectives. It was not possible to know the virtues (in the cardinal and theological sense) of all the carers who would deliver daily foster care services to children in need. I developed an informal checklist around the virtues that proved very useful in dealing with difficult situations – but it would have been difficult to implement systematically in the organisation. It quickly become clear that there were no 'one-stop', universal solutions but rather a series of well-considered, well-implemented, principled, creative approaches that recognised diversity and uniqueness.

My greatest challenge to being was being asked to continue in the job for a further year. I had set myself a one-year agenda, which I had communicated to all staff on my first day, including that I would leave the area well set up for the next person by staffing the area, getting the OOHC issues resolved, balancing the budgets (except the operational budget) and having the structural changes completed. The demands of work had been physically exhausting, and this was confirmed by my medical practitioner. When I applied the social/relational element, I considered that I had committed to a course of action (one year) and that to extend the time would leave me open to criticism that I had not kept my word. I was also concerned about increasing centralisation and the consequent diminution of diversity and responding appropriately to unique circumstances. The organisation was adopting evidence-based practice where evidence meant research/ empirical evidence largely to the detriment of appreciating the many other forms of knowledge and participant-led needs. At the mental/emotional aspect of my being, I could see increasing control over staff, communities and the individuals where one form of knowledge and one approach of contractual social obligation would occur.

I also considered the spiritual/existential aspects. Within my own Christian framework, worth is not measured by income, position or activity. As I was able to set things in place, another administrator/manager/leader would be able to dismantle them. While I could contribute to and make changes within the lives of individuals and communities and make a significant ontological difference, few of the changes would amount to much in an eternal and teleological perspective. I missed my family life, my work in refugee resettlement, at the residential college and through my local church, and these, for me, were of greater eternal and temporal significance.

The challenge for the leader/manager/administrator social worker involves implementing 'top down' directives and approaches. The real potential exists for the social work leader to be oppressive and to impose solutions and processes. The professional social work leader/manager/administrator uses thinking, doing and being across the micro, mezzo and macro levels utilising knowledge appropriated from many sources and ensuring that no single source of knowledge or single orientation dominates. It is possible, for example, to give a primary allegiance to (say) an economic view of the role and balance the budgets to the detriment of (say) service delivery. It would be possible to focus on the staff rather than on the outcomes and consequences for clients. It would have been possible to consider the rising rate of children in OOHC as a cause for celebration of children being safe rather than a measure of wider systemic or policy failure. It would have been possible to take a political perspective and have a primary allegiance to the organisation rather than to the more ill-defined notion of the public. It would have been possible to have a primary allegiance to foster carers rather than birth families.

Bringing together disparate knowledge drawn from many sources and appreciating its diversity rather than seeking to impose either a false unity or a synthesis of such knowledge remains a challenge for the social work leader. One of the deficiencies of this approach is that others might not perceive the administrator/manager/leader as being predictable and consistent. Individual situations that have similarities might not lead to identical outcomes. In a sociopolitical climate where predictability and consistency of outcomes are valued and desired, the social work leader's approach means that the individual circumstances and dynamics rather than the imposed procedures and policies are significant in determining action and outcomes. This can be perceived by others as lack of consistency rather than appreciation of diversity. At the macro level, there is a sociopolitical need for consistency. At the individual level there is a need for individualised, creative approaches. Centralism and proceduralism might create consistency but might also negate diversity and creativity and justice.

Indigenous being and context

The social work leader/manager/administrator accepts that inequality has both structural and individual causes. Structurally, the rising rate of children in OOHC may be unacceptably high and may be substantially caused by State intervention in predominantly low-income families. Where once the racial composition of children (their sense of being as black, white, half-caste and so on) was a reason for State intervention, the current criteria may include calculations of risk, drug and alcohol use by parents, and poverty. This approach might not find immediate and positive resonance with other areas of service delivery, which are implicitly being criticised for (say) poor income support or inappropriate housing, mental health or law enforcement policies. Thinking and doing and being in child protection means considering a range of factors (income support, health policy, housing, approaches to domestic violence, gambling policy and so on) that are within the province of others and for whom child protection is not their primary objective. Bringing together knowledge from many sources and recognising that reducing (say) gambling or poverty may have a very positive influence on reducing the incidence of children coming into care and an equally negative effect upon the revenue of the Treasury and highlights the often competing priorities of organisational and governmental intervention.

The social work leader (and others) recognises differences to be acknowledged and valued without seeking to resolve differences or impose a synthesis or false unity. It also allows for gaps in current knowledge. The mentoring program, for example, was aimed at 'accelerating learning' and was driven by the needs (as perceived by the organisation) of the mentees. The thinking for the program was founded upon two theoretical positions and a gap in knowledge. It was important that Indigenous epistemology and Indigenous knowledge be valued and incorporated in order to counter the 'colonising' effect of Western-style mentoring. A limited literature failed to assist with the question of whether there were distinctive differences between mentoring and Indigenous mentoring.

PERSONAL REFLECTION

Hill et al. (2001) identified Indigenous workers as subject to a range of conflicting and contradictory expectations, and workers develop strategies that are oppositional, separational, integrational or compromised – in order to be able to work within bureaucracies. I used this limited knowledge of Indigenous workers with Freire's (1975) concept of consciencisation. I accepted that the mentee/mentor relationship implied a power differential based on work experience but wanted to avoid a power differential based on race or the debilitating effects of 'colonising' education. The approach acknowledged mutuality and respected differences and exceptionality. The mentees' lived experience and cultural knowledge was a resource against which new knowledge presented to them could be evaluated. I was attempting to have an approach whereby different types of knowledge were valued for what they were all able to bring to any particular situation without trying to set up the knowledge as oppositional, separational, integrated or compromised – but rather having an appreciation of how the diverse knowledge bases could lead to new, exciting and creative outcomes.

This approach offers a way forward in obtaining, training, developing and retaining the people. It was recognised that the shift in the macro-sociopolitical environment to contractual relationships and a more flexible workforce has also meant a change in the sense of vocation (being) – whereby many positions are now jobs done for money rather than vocations that have an element of service and commitment. Social work, with its commitment to social justice and (for me) a bias to the poor, is an alternative orientation. Practical social policy in the area of staffing rural and remote locations involved addressing this sociopolitical shift and the urbo-centric decision-making. It involved recognising other sources of knowledge and motivation and action that led to localising real solutions. The three examples in the staffing of rural and remote locations have highlighted both the successes and difficulties in balancing good service delivery in areas of, arguably, the greatest need and the greatest oppression, and reflect the interconnectedness of thinking, doing and being.

REFLECTIVE EXERCISE 7.6
When you are in a position of not having all the information that you would want
(e.g. not knowing how Indigenous mentoring operates), how do you make decisions,
and how do you protect against merely repeating the practices of the past?

The influence of history on organisational being

The social work leader/manager/administrator values quantitative and qualitative approaches and applies critical reflection. This was particularly the situation in considering the differential rates of children in OOHC. A quantitative approach based on statistics showed anomalies. The explanations from key informants were not supported by other evidence. What was noticeable was that defensive practices had developed and that local management was excessively risk averse and took the precautionary principle to the extreme. Understanding history provided the additional information that made sense of the rates of OOHC. This particular local office had been subjected to a centralised, intrusive and blaming approach to the death of a child some six years earlier. The incident and its legacy had instilled fear. Although the management and many staff had changed, the historic legacy led current management and staff to react to any matter with extreme caution and to take actions that would immediately protect a child but would create many more children in care (i.e. false positives).

The question that no leader likes to face is: what are an acceptable failure rate and acceptable consequences where human decision-making and unpredictable human behaviour are involved?

Being as a social work leader, manager and/or administrator involves living with uncertainty and facing the consequences while being clear about one's goals. Statistically, the increase in the rate of OOHC was arrested and numbers of children receiving OOHC declined by more than 10 per cent. The staff vacancy rate among the 113 positions – an increase of 13 per cent in front-line staff numbers – was 8 per cent (down from arguably 37 per cent) with no temporary unqualified staff, no return-to-work staff and no outstanding disciplinary matters. The changed staffing resulted in significant change and an empowered and confident service delivery.

▦ Conclusion

The social work leader/manager/administrator faces value dilemmas (whether to be active or passive; risk-taking or risk averse; corporate goal-driven or human rights/social justice oriented) and is challenged by knowledge and demands from multiple sources. Key information in making a decision may be missing or is unclear and/or contested. Organisational values (formal and informal) may be the antithesis of the values of others or the social work leader. The social work leader/manager/administrator has the opportunity to consider differing knowledge, differing focuses and orientations without seeking to balance them or to unify them. Adopting multidimensional approaches allows the truly diverse positions and knowledge to be valued and contribute to the outcomes. The social work leader will have to make decisions – but will be making them on the broadest possible knowledge and value base. As illustrated by the examples, there are tensions between fiscal outcomes and service delivery outcomes for individuals and communities and tensions between the demands of centralised employment processes and the needs of localised employment and recruitment.

PERSONAL REFLECTION

Sometimes I met these tensions through following both centralised processes and supplementing them with localised additional processes. At other times I have prioritised one set of demands above another. On further occasions, the response has been to advocate for change. I was challenged by the different perspectives (the legitimate top-down demands of the political and administrative system and the legitimate bottom-up demands of clients and communities). I was challenged by the different ideologies and approaches related to child protection and OOHC and the 'evidence' advanced in support. I was profoundly challenged by Parton, Thorpe and Wattam (1997: 67), who argue that child abuse 'is a product of social negotiation between different values and beliefs, different social norms and professional knowledge . . . is a phenomena where moral reasoning and moral judgements are central'.

The social work administrator/manager/leader is a part of that social negotiation and is informed by the values of social work and my own qualities of being related to the virtues.

Social worker administrators/managers/leaders will need to continue to bring thinking–doing–being to the multidimensional and multilayered nature of their work within a perspective that focuses on the critical importance of human beings rather than simply on processes designed to create consistency and uniformity. A singular approach, whether it is driven by urbo-centric demands or by economics, or by a singular model of welfare service delivery (such as short-term intervention) or by discipline-specific ideology, needs to be rejected. The complexity and uniqueness of social work management, administration and leadership requires the bringing together of approaches that value and dignify individuals, families, communities, staff and agencies.

■ Questions and activities

Activity 1

Imagine that you are starting in a real organisation of your choice for the first time. What is the essential information you need to have? You might like to select an agency and research it.

You may like to consider: history (when it was founded and why it exists); mandate (under what auspices and legislation does it operate); what its stated values are; what its purpose and clients/stakeholders are; what its sources of funding are and how it operates financially; what its purposes and objectives are; what its stated values are; how it is structured and who really holds power and influence; what is its size; how is it staffed (considering volunteers, qualifications, duty statements and so on); how consumers/service users are able to participate; and how it is seen by the wider community.

Using your skills in unobtrusive observation, consider the following related to your chosen organisation: what is the knowledge on which it relies; whether there is a discernible moral system is operating; how truth is conceived and practised (e.g. anything is acceptable as long as it is not found out); what the organisational beliefs are; do collective assumptions exist that cannot be challenged; how new ideas are generated and adopted; acceptable ways of expressing dissent exist; do 'folk theories and logic' exist that must be accepted; how change is generated.

Activity 2

Consider the following:

> 'A leader is the (wo)man who has the ability to get other people to do what they don't want to do and enjoy it.'
>
> Harry S Truman, quoted in *The People's Almanac* (1975)

> 'Leadership is the lifting of a (wo)man's vision to higher sights, the raising of a (wo)man's performance to a higher standard, the building of a (wo)man's personality beyond its normal limitations. Wishing won't make it so; doing will.'
>
> Peter F. Drucker, *The Practice of Management* (1955)

> 'I have to follow them, I am their leader.'
>
> French politician Alexandre Auguste Ledru-Rollin (1807–74)

> 'The art of leadership ... consists in consolidating the attention of the people against a single adversary and taking that nothing will split up that attention.'
>
> Adolf Hitler, *Mein Kampf* (1925–26)

How do you react to these quotes? What are the essential characteristics that you would like a social work leader/manager/administrator to possess, and what characteristics will you display in your areas of leadership?

8

Reflections on thinking, doing and being: future of social work practice

IN THIS CHAPTER we reflect on what we have tried to accomplish in this book and foreflect on social work practice. For the act of reflecting about the future, we coin the word 'foreflect' (see chapter 2). It is organised into three parts. The first part discusses the significance of focusing on being along with thinking and doing in social work practice. The second part focuses on the reflective social work practice model and how we have applied it to five social work practice methods. Finally, in the third part, we share some possibilities of building being in social work education and practice.

▥ Chapter objectives

The chapter highlights the significance of being in terms of developing it, using it and reflecting on it. After studying this chapter, readers should be able to reflect on:

- the importance of focusing on being
- the overview of the reflective social work practice model and the way it was applied at five social work practice methods
- future social work education and practice focused on being.

▥ Main themes and concepts used

The core theme that flows through this concluding chapter is the zest of the book; that is, reflections on thinking, doing and being, and future directions in terms of research, education and training. No new terms are introduced here. Most of the concepts, such as reflection, reflective practice, thinking, doing and being, have been defined and discussed earlier (see chapters 1 and 2). We believe the theme of the book itself is inviting the social work fraternity in making it.

▪ Significance of 'being' in social work

Our reflections on the preceding seven chapters suggest that being plays a pivotal role in social work practice and that it also facilitates reflection on practice. If being is so critical, why has it not come to the fore in social work so far? It would be incorrect to assume or argue that social work does not include being or that social workers do not use their being in practice.

In fact, being is not new to social work. The use of the phrase 'thinking, doing and being' in social work literature and practice suggests that the presence of being is very much acknowledged. It is used to some extent to discuss the self of a social worker, the use of social worker's self in professional practice, professional development of a social worker and self-care of a social worker. However, social work education, practice and research over the years has mostly been preoccupied by thinking and doing; that is, theory and practice, and doing and thinking, which is practice and theory linkages to knowledge use and creation. It might not be an exaggeration to observe that sometimes in practice it is only thinking or only doing, bereft of each other. The being aspect of social work has remained behind or hidden and underdeveloped. Why is this the state in the contemporary professional social work?

This question calls for a brief recapitulation of and reflection on the way the social work profession has evolved, developed and spread over a period of one century within the contexts of science and technological advancements and consequent growing industrialisation, colonisation and neocolonisation and social, cultural, economic and political changes. As discussed in chapter 1, responding to the ills of industrialisation and urbanisation, (professional) social work originated through voluntary efforts of a small numbers of individuals. In the midst of wealth creation and prosperity, poverty, homelessness, deprivation and difficult living conditions existed. Out of their love, compassion, genuine concern and commitment, these individuals tried to do something to help the needy in their immediate surroundings. Such committed efforts led to the formation of voluntary organisations such as Charity Organisation Societies and Settlement Houses and eventually the birth of the social work profession through formal training, practice and knowledge creation, and the dissemination of professional social work from the UK and USA to many other countries. Although these efforts are laudable, the force of expanding professional social work has not kept pace with growing social problems and needs in many communities.

Professionally trained social workers have been relentlessly working in a range of complex and challenging sectors and settings. For example, these are large government welfare departments, health departments, particularly hospitals, mental health and disability and ageing, family and community services, particularly, child welfare and protection, juvenile justice and corrections, voluntary organisations and communities. Significant knowledge creation and use has occurred in terms of social work theory and practice. Between Mary Richmond's book, *Social Diagnosis* (1917), and Bob Mullaly's book, *Radical Social Work* (2006), a paradigm shift occurred in how social workers think and work (see also Fook 1993; Ferguson & Woodward 2009). Similarly, social work knowledge around critical social work, empowerment and strengths-based practice, human rights and social justice, social development, anti-oppressive and anti-discriminatory practice, feminist and postmodern social work, ecological or green social work, international social work, reflective practice, a range of counselling and therapies (e.g. solution focused, narrative and so on) and evidence-based practice is emerging. Social workers use this knowledge base in training as well as in practice by different degrees, depending upon their own understandings and field contexts. In their practice they perform several roles by using a range of skills (see table 1.2 in chapter 1). It is also important to acknowledge the argument about and knowledge emerging from practice to theory and the contribution of reflective practice towards it. While reflectively summarising in this way, it may be noted that there is a great diversity in the application of knowledge across different practice sectors and settings.

Social work theory and practice, and practice and theory linkages, are not uniform across all sectors and field settings. However, social workers have significantly engaged in practice (a lot of doing). Despite such engagement, social problems such as poverty, relative deprivation and inequality, mental health issues, domestic violence and child abuse and neglect have not reduced due to a combination of structural factors. In many instances their practice is informed and constrained by organisational contexts and knowledge frameworks. Consequently the professional life and practice of some social workers appear to have been routinised. For example, consider the practice settings such as mental health, disability, child protection, ageing and so on, where often standard diagnostic tools determine decisions. Social workers' own sense of judgement and what they think themselves about the overall situation and their clients' feelings, emotions and judgements seem to play a very small role in deciding. These and similar cultures of practices need to be critically examined. Do many social workers practice in this way? If they do, why do they do so?

First, social work theory and practice and practice and theory discussion and linkages in a binary form need to be questioned in terms of their adequacy, suitability and effectiveness. They are relevant, but they alone may not be enough. Second, knowledge frameworks in terms of diagnostic tools that draw on positivism alone, and that convert social workers into instruments, need to be reconsidered. Third, ideological foundations of the ethical frameworks of the social work profession and their limitations need to be reexamined. Fourth, the way social work has been professionalised and professional social workers are prepared need to be analysed. Fifth, the hidden and neglected concepts of being need to be developed and used in practice.

As discussed in chapters 1 and 2, by and large, contemporary social work practice is dominated by all the five factors. Its linear preoccupation with theory–practice and practice–theory linkage, decisions guided and bound by managerialism and scienti- cism, procedure-oriented, rule-bound practice and way of preparing social workers, and least regard for or consideration of a being of a practitioner altogether appear to be affecting both quality and quantity of social work. For example, although discussion about theory and practice and practice and theory linkage is good, some social work practitioners' experiences have suggested the gap between theory and practice, and practice and theory, and such a gap has led to questioning the whole approach. Under the influence of managerialism and scienticism, changing organisational culture has negatively affected or compromised the functions of social workers.

Similarly, Kantian categorical imperative and Bentham's utilitarian ideas have profound influence on the social work profession and its code of ethics. Under Kant's categorical imperative principle, irrespective of varied situations, a set of injunctions are non-negotiable, unconditional and non-contingent, and they must be applied universally. For example some of these imperatives are: 'do unto others as you would expect them to do to you'; 'treat people as ends in their own right' and 'never as a means to an end only'; and, as a way of respect, allow people to self-determine themselves. Although these imperatives or principles appear good, Kant's (1964) approach does not help to resolve if moral rules are inconsistent or in conflict with each other, but social workers face such conflicts in the field. It does not address cultural relativism issues and does not recognise the ambiguous, messy, indeterminate and uncertain nature of social life (Rossiter 2006). It disconnects the decision-maker from the real world (Crigger & Godfrey 2011). In the same vein, consequentialism/utilitarianism focuses on consequences and acts, and undermines motives and the actor. It does not define the nature of what is good in social life. By following majority views, it can disregard well-respected virtues and ways of behaving (Harstell 2006; Houston 2012). For benefi- cial outcomes any methods can be justified. If the consequences are not known or uncertain, it is not fair to judge an action as right or wrong. The principle of utilita- rianism is antithetical to the core social work value of human dignity and worth. How have this theory–practice debate, between managerialism, scienticism, Kantian and utilitarian principles, influenced and shaped the being/self of a social worker?

When we ask some of our social work students about their career plans or what they would like to do after the degree, some say they want to work in a hospital or a school and some others say they want to start a private practice. Further, when we ask why they want to pursue that career path, often their response includes a long pause. It may be difficult to articulate what drives them to do so. Some also believe that the market is fine and the user must pay; there is nothing wrong in it. Despite professional training and practice, there appear to be social work identity crises and deprofessionalisation forces. On the whole, in spite of so much significant engagement in the field, the social work profession's outcome is not generally as discernible as it should be.

On the basis of our observation and analysis, a partial explanation of these phenomena may be offered. We think that the social work profession, education and practice have lost their way by not focusing on the being of a social worker. Being of a social worker can be strengthened by developing certain virtues. The virtue theory is broadly influenced by the Platonic and Aristotelian notions of what is excellent (areté), what is practical and wise (phronesis) and what typifies human flourishing (eudaimonia), although Aristotle first emphasised good of the larger community, then good of the individual (Aristotle 1976). Aristotle's doctrine of mean provides the basis for virtues. Prudence or temperance of a worker helps to choose between two extremes in a balanced way that suits the situation. Virtuous practitioners should be able to steer their thinking and practice and practice and thinking in a balanced way. Virtue-led practice will also empower them to deal with the limitations of the organisational, managerial and other ideologically driven contexts that are conducive neither for their practice nor for their clients. To the extent possible, it is also important to focus on the being of clients or people social workers work with.

These reflections are not theoretical arguments. They are also not our assumptions. To demonstrate their applicability in practice, as discussed in chapter 2, we have developed a reflective practice PEOPLE model and illustrated its use in practice across the social work practice methods. The following section recapitulates that exercise.

REFLECTIVE EXERCISE 8.1

Do you think the social work profession and its education and practice has lost its way? Whatever is your response, why do you think so?

Why do you think focus on the 'being' of a social worker is needed?

▓ The reflective social work practice model and its application

As discussed in chapter 2, reflective practice is overused and often misunderstood or differently understood by social workers. The discussion of the concept of reflective practice clarified that reflection involves deep and critical thinking about the past practice event in order to improve and/or replicate good practice. Further reflective practice requires the use of those critical reflections for better practice and generating practice-based knowledge. A reflexive practitioner is the one who has become proficient in using reflective practice. Reflective practice benefits in many ways, provided it is practised the way it should be. It helps to improve oneself and others.

While discussing several theoretical underpinnings of reflective practice (John Dewey's, Donald Schon's, David Kolb's, David Boud's and others' – see chapter 2 and table 2.1), we have proposed a reflective social work practice model that tries to blend being, thinking and doing of a social worker with five important, closely connected segments of their work, which has been abbreviated as PEOPLE (participants, environment scan, objectives, process and labour and evaluation). It also includes an analytical framework to track the role of being in directing thinking and doing and doing and thinking around the PEOPLE model. Participants include both a social worker and people with whom s/he works. The model suggests building relationship, working together to scan their environment, set objectives, follow appropriate processes to achieve set objectives and evaluating with a focus on being along with thinking and doing. It can be applied at any level, irrespective of whether social workers work at the individual, community or group levels. When social workers employ such a model, does it make any difference to their understanding and practice? Does it improve their practice? Does it make conscious their being and strengthen it? Practitioners need to consider and address these and similar questions. Being is an untapped potential in every social worker. The future of social work lies in building and consciously using it.

What has been tried in this book is rudimentary, and it has been done by following the post-fact analysis method. However, we believe that these not so ideal examples may encourage others to bring their being to the social work practice agenda. In chapter 3, in the context of working with individuals and families, the social worker worked with a complex case. Looking at the facts and issues in the case, one wonders why such a civilised, well-developed society produce and harbour sexual deviants, people with alcohol, drug and mental health issues, and enact rules, procedures and remedies that seem more often to penalise victims than perpetrators. The social worker's mandated role was to supervise Ixx to ensure that he followed post-release parole conditions and, in the event of violation of any conditions, to invoke the legal process. To meet the conditions, it was an easy option to separate the children from the family and not bother about their mother at all. Often legal systems are rule-bound procedural square boxes, which in the name of doing good lay a vicious track that make it difficult for people to escape. It requires courage, conviction and commitment to laterally think and act out of and beyond the square box and critically examine the process of achieving the final goal of facilitating safe and happy family for both parents and children. Reflections on the social worker's thinking, doing and being show how he used his judgement, temperance and fortitude to expand the scope of his work and include the whole family to work with under the resource-constrained environment. Social workers on a daily basis work with hundreds of such difficult cases. It is a real challenge for them to consciously use their being to confront complex issues or enormous needs and find creative ways to address them to uphold human rights of and social justice for people they work with.

REFLECTIVE EXERCISE 8.2

Revisit chapter 3. If the social worker had worked only according to the mandated roles, imagine what would have been the outcomes. How did the use of the social worker's being make a difference to the case?

Chapter 4 shows how the reflective practice model can be applied while working with groups. Group work is a fascinating, engaging and deeply rewarding both for the worker and members of the group. Group work can be educational, developmental, remedial/therapeutic, recreational and mutually supportive. It can be practised in open settings such as communities and neighbourhoods, and closed settings such as hospitals and prisons. The formation and development of and setting tasks/objectives for the group, and participatory achievements of the group objectives, are important, and they differ from one group context to another. The role of the group worker and members are critical. In this group work example, the social worker shows the unique challenges he faced in organising the group work sessions with to-be-released inmates in the private prison setting. It was an unconventional setting for practising participatory, liberating and emancipatory group work. The prison atmosphere, both physical and social, its rules, regulations and restrictions, appeared most unconducive for group work practice. Some workers might accept the situation as is, and some others might simply not initiate any group work process as the prison setting itself might appear repulsive to a social work ethos.

Undeterred by the challenges of the prison culture, the changes such as removal of the surveillance camera, bringing the food that was cooked outside and breaking the silence of the group members so that they could say something and participate in the group process introduced by the group worker appeared radical in the given context and circumstances. Working with the prison authorities on the one hand and working with the group members on the other hand, and the overall outcome of the group work process provide insightful and encouraging experiences.

The experience suggests that merely thinking and doing is not adequate to help inmates think about the transition from dependent life to independent life and to mentally prepare for anticipated pitfalls and take steps to avoid falling back. The analysis shows that, when being is consciously practised along with thinking and doing, what a difference it does make. Although group work is a very powerful method and it is highly satisfying work, it appeared to have lagged behind in terms of research, literature and practice. We hope this example encourages many social workers to engage in practising group work by focusing on being.

REFLECTIVE EXERCISE 8.3

Revisit chapter 4. If the group worker had worked only according to the prison rules and regulations, imagine what would have been the outcomes.

Reflect on how the use of social worker's being made a difference to the practise of group work.

Group work and community work are closely connected in some respects. Group work naturally feeds into community work, depending upon the nature of community practice. How the social worker reflectively practised with communities is discussed in chapter 5. Among social workers, like group work, community work or practice (also referred to as community organisation and development) is not as popular as practice with individuals. Many social workers appear to find comfort in practising with individuals rather than the other methods. It appears that (Australian) social workers have neglected their practice with communities. Why does such a state exist in the profession and practice? It is important to reflect on this critical question. What kind of social worker's being is needed or needs to be developed for community practice?

Although one example of community practice is discussed in chapter 5, a few important observations may be made. Thinking of community practice is different from doing community practice with passion, vision and commitment. Practising with communities at the grassroots level in rural remote areas in utterly deprived conditions is particularly noteworthy. It requires courage, commitment and something more than social work theory and practice. Many local-level communities have been neglected for years, and social workers, given their value premise, naturally need to be there. But mostly they are not. Whatever little community development practice occurs, it often occurs from the top-down perspective; more often than not, needs and plans are defined and designed somewhere else, but not in communities. What kind of a social worker's being is needed to initiate participatory community practice whereby people themselves determine their priorities and issues? Towards achieving that, people's capacities have to be built and an enabling environment needs to be created by engaging community people. Due to globalisation and similar forces, there appears to be a trend of declining communities, particularly in terms of culture and diversity. Thus community practice also involves retaining and developing community identity as articulated by communities themselves. Part of the identity also includes community harmony and diversity. In the discussed case, although the government project agenda was to address illicit drug use in communities, the social worker creatively altered that agenda to meet felt issues and needs of the communities and at the same time tried to achieve the objectives. As an outsider, a social worker who is practising community development under the resource-constrained environment, particularly the local personnel, faces a difficult task. Here the social worker has shared what he has tried and how his being was in play while accomplishing what he has accomplished as a community practitioner.

REFLECTIVE EXERCISE 8.4

Recapitulate the thinking, doing and being of the social worker in chapter 5. Why do you think many social workers do not opt for community practice? How did the use of the being of the social worker make difference in the community practice?

The next case discussed in the book is about social work research. Chapter 6 argues that social work is a research-oriented profession with a difference. Unlike other social research, social work research aims to achieve action and change. It is empowering and emancipatory. Every social worker should be able to or needs to demonstrate this type of research in their practice. However, by and large, social work research is mostly relegated to social work academics. Practitioners need to significantly engage in research, and the very nature their practice is conducive to such engagement. Acceptance of diverse research methods and reflective social work practice provide ample scope for social workers to undertake action and change-oriented research. Do social workers undertake such research? If not, why not?

In chapter 6, the social worker demonstrates how his research project was participatory, action- and change-oriented. It followed diverse research methods and raised significant anomalies related to rates and services and structural issues. How existing structures oppress Aboriginal communities and that what they are doing appears to be normal and fair are well exposed through this research. Most importantly, the analysis shows that merely research knowledge and skills are inadequate to undertake such research. The social worker's interest and commitment to the cause and value orientation as to what type of research he does or does not undertake are important part of his being. His reflections also show how the field realities challenged his being and altered his thinking and doing in regard to the choice of research methods, research design, role performance as a change agent, community consultation and unjust and oppressive practices. Many lessons can be learned from this research. We hope it inspires other social workers to undertake research to act and change.

REFLECTIVE EXERCISE 8.5
Review chapter 6. Plan a research project to bring change in your practice setting.

The last social work method discussed in chapter 7 was traditionally known as social welfare administration, and now it seems to have changed to human service organisation. Whatever the nomenclature, (welfare) states have developed large administrative systems and organisations to deliver a range of social services to people. Large number of social workers were trained and employed in such organisations to the extent that social work was labelled as an agent of state control at front lines. Although that might be disputable, it has been observed that social workers are often unable to or unwilling to assume administrative leadership positions in such organisations. It is important to reflect on why such a situation exists in the profession and in professional social work preparation. As pointed out in chapter 7, the minority of social work professionals who attain administrative leadership positions then seem to forget social work ethos and values, and identify more with the management and top-down control, and as a consequence some turn out to be agents of oppression. Contrary to this seeming trend, we argue that social workers need to assume transformative leadership in human service organisations and welfare administration. It is possible to develop such leadership by focusing on the being of a social worker.

As an example, chapter 7 demonstrates the social worker's transformative leadership in challenging and changing some of the bureaucratic and administrative practices in difficult circumstances and trialling some innovative approaches relating to the number of children under State care, staff recruitment and retention, and funding allocation. With such power and position, perhaps, a lot more could be done to humanise organisations and their administrative systems.

As insiders, social workers have a great opportunity to demonstrate their leadership and challenge and change certain practices that enhance people's well-being. Challenging bureaucratic structures is easier said than done. That is where the role of the being of a social worker comes in. In this chapter the social worker narrates some of the challenges to his being and the fine lines between the oppressor and the liberator. On the whole, the social worker's experience may encourage some social workers to aspire for transformative leadership and initiate change in the organisational and administrative practices.

REFLECTIVE EXERCISE 8.6
Review chapter 7. What kind of leader you want to become in human service organisations? Why do you think there are only a small number of leaders with a social work background in human services organisations?

In each of the social work methods chapters (chapters 3 to 7) the social worker has demonstrated the application of the reflective social work practice model in terms of PEOPLE and has also shown how his thinking, doing and being was applied at each aspects of the PEOPLE. Some might question the categorisation of social work methods in terms working with individuals, groups and communities, social work research and welfare administration/management/human service organisations as some social workers tend to use these methods in a generic and integrated form. Not only may additional practice methods be added but also such methods as social work research and welfare administration may be regarded differently as they act as service methods for practising the first three methods. Social work research and welfare administration/management are needed in all the first three methods. Some aspects of policy practice are captured in the community development and welfare administration/management chapters.

There are limitations to this book and to the model and social work methods discussed here. We do not pretend to claim that we have captured what being is or that we are successful in building the concept of being. We only have made an attempt towards that end. A lot more research and work need to be done to develop the concept of being and use it in practice. The reflective social work practice model and our analysis are not perfect. Although emerging from practice and reflections on it, it has yet to be trialled by practitioners in the field. The concept of being needs to be refined, and alternative views about it in the social work context need to be addressed. Many other social workers may demonstrate the use of their being in some other different and better ways. It is important to constructively critique, improve and do better. This book is an initial step towards that direction. However, we firmly believe that the development and use of being in social work will enhance the quality of practice and produce discernible outcomes. We hope our initial attempts encourage other social work educators and practitioners to see the potential of the conscious use of being in social work and further contribute to the development of being.

Future of social work practice

What inspires social workers to do inspiring work? What inspires social workers to follow the pursuit of excellence in their practice? The contemporary unequal world needs contagious social work practice that quickly spreads to address social justice and human rights issues. Despite claiming to be a global profession, social work has generally remained a 'containious' profession, mostly and meagrely in urban pockets. Earlier we have remarked that professional social work seems to have lost its way from many perspectives. These may be deprofessionalisation, globalisation, managerialism, lack of indigenisation, growing inequality, poverty, relative deprivation, development of other competing professions, diffused identity and so on. Equally, efforts are being made to further professionalise, to seek registration and regulation, to initiate collaborative activities, to bring social development on the agenda and to develop standards and ethical codes, at least in some parts of the world. Some challenges for the social work profession are:

- how to professionalise without depersonalising its practice (Under the positivism, evidence-based and market-dominated practice, depersonalised practice is a real danger.)
- how to extend and expand from remedial/clinically oriented practice to developmentally oriented practice (Many have warned that if the profession does not expand to include social and community practice, it may split into two different professions.)
- how to progress beyond theory–practice and practice–theory limited binary focus (Further progress for the profession seems to have stuck in this binary node.)

Among many other efforts, as argued earlier, we believe that the social work profession and practice can address these challenges by focusing on the being of a social worker. Just professionalising, clinical/remedial work and a theory and practice and practice and theory focus, although important, are not sufficient.

About thinking, doing and being, Anscombe (2009) has argued that 'if you think and don't do – you are useless; if you do and don't think – you are dangerous; fundamental to thinking and doing is being'. Here we do not assume or argue that social workers do not have being or virtues. Our quest is to look for ways to strengthen and bring being or basic qualities – what we call virtues – to the fore to consciously use them. How to find equal and explicit place for being along with thinking and doing? This book has demonstrated that it can be accomplished, yet it is a challenge and a crucial task for the social work profession to embrace it in its own interest and that of society.

Strategies

For the social work profession and social workers, we envisage two main strategies to embrace being-focused and virtue-led practice. First, systematic research is needed to explore and understand the development of the social worker's being and virtue-led practice. Second, necessary changes are needed in social work education and training so as to help social workers develop their being with a focus on virtues.

Research

In regard to the first strategy, a reasonably acceptable concept of being and virtues needs to be developed. As stated earlier, being is an underdeveloped and underutilised concept in social work, although often referred to along with thinking and doing. Being has existential and metaphysical connotations in the discipline of philosophy. In social work being is not understood in that way. So, social work must develop its own disciplinary or interdisciplinary concept of being. In chapter 1, we have clarified our concept of being, which includes the dimensions of physical/organic, social/relational, mental/emotional and spiritual/existential (see figure 1.1). It needs to be further discussed, debated, critiqued and refined by the professional social work community.

As we have tried to show, if the concept of being is delimited in terms of virtues, it is important to identify and define the specific virtues that we are looking for in social workers. What are the core virtues? Why only certain specific virtues? Where do you find them? How can you develop and build them in social workers? These are fundamental research questions, and we must find convincing answers to them within and beyond the professional social work community. It is important to look at social workers who have inspired others and achieved excellence and to study what virtues they have with a view to building similar virtues in others. It is also important to confirm through inductive and deductive processes that virtue-led social work practice leads to better processes and outcomes.

Education and training

Informed by such research, through the second strategy, necessary changes need to be introduced in the professional accreditation standards, code of ethics and social work education and training. If some aspects of being and virtues are already there in an implicit or indirect way they need to be expanded and made more explicit. It may necessitate curricular changes in certain subjects or courses. From that perspective it is also important to examine the social work code of ethics and the curriculum. Although building being and developing virtues is a long-term process, during professional socialisation ways and means of building being and developing virtues needs to be considered. Appropriate learning and teaching strategies, exposure to and analysis of good cases and examples during and after the course through professional development activities are in order.

Although both strategies appear challenging and demanding tasks for social work professional bodies, practitioners, educators and researchers, they are practical tasks. We believe implementation of these strategies will help prepare virtue-led practitioners and practice that can make a difference in the lives of people, communities and organisations in whatever they do and achieve inspiring excellence.

REFLECTIVE EXERCISE 8.7

Do you think social work should focus on virtue-led practice? What do you think of the strategies suggested, and what other strategies could be employed to initiate virtue-led practice?

▥ Conclusion

This final chapter has summarised the significance of being in social work practice. It has provided an overview of the reflective social work practice model and some reflections on the way it was applied while working with individuals and families, groups, communities, in human service organisations, administration and management and when undertaking research. Neither the model nor the efforts to apply it in practice are perfect. But the possibility and potential are evident. Towards bringing being into the main frame of social work practice along with thinking and doing, research could be undertaken to develop the concept of being and virtues relevant for the discipline and profession of social work. It also calls for necessary changes in professional standards and social work education and training. For the social work profession, education and practice and for social workers, we believe, it is a promising direction.

▦ Questions and exercises

1 Critically review the book.

2 What have you learned by reading this book? Make a list of learning and insights gained from this book.

3 What is the main message of the book? Do you agree or disagree with that message? Critically discuss.

4 Develop some strategies to build your being in terms of virtues, and try to practise them in your field placements or in practice and discuss with your supervisor.

5 In your view, what should be the future direction for social work practice and the social work profession?

References

AASW (1999). *AASW Code of Ethics: 2nd Draft for Consultation*. Canberra: AASW.

—— (2010). *Code of Ethics*. Canberra: AASW.

—— (2012). *Australian Social Work Education and Accreditation Standards*. Canberra: AASW.

—— (2013). *Practice Standards*. Canberra: AASW.

Agnew, R. & White, H. (1992). 'An empirical test of general strain theory.' *Criminology*, vol. 30, pp. 475–99.

Akers, R. (1994). *Criminological Theories: Introduction and Evaluation*. Los Angeles: Roxbury Press.

—— (1998). *Social Learning and Social Structure: A General Theory of Crime and Deviance*. Boston: Northeastern University Press.

Allan, J., Briskman, L. & Pease, B. (2009). *Critical Social Work: Theories and Practices for a Socially Just World*. Sydney: Allen & Unwin.

Allport, G. W. (1964). *Pattern and Growth in Personality*. New York: Holt, Rinehart & Winston.

Alston, M. (2009). *Innovative Human Services Practice*. Melbourne: Palgrave Macmillan.

Anscombe, A. W. (2009). 'Consilience in social work: Reflections on thinking, doing and being' (doctoral thesis). Wagga Wagga, NSW: Charles Sturt University.

Aristotle (1976). *Nicomachean Ethics*. Harmondsworth: Penguin.

Arnd-Caddinton, M. & Pozzuto, R. (2006). 'Understanding the use of self in social work practice.' *Socialinis Darbas*, vol. 5, pp. 108–15.

Atkinson, T., & Claxton, G. (eds). (2000). *The Intuitive Practitioner on the Value of Not Always Knowing What One is Doing*. Buckingham, UK: Open University Press.

Australian Bureau of Statistics (2001). *ABS 2039.0 – Information Paper: Census of Population and Housing – Socio-Economic Indexes for Areas, Australia, 2001*.

Australian Social Work (2013). *Australian Social Work* (Journal of AASW), Special section on social work enabling sustainable and ecological living, vol. 66, no. 2, June 2013.

Avolio, B. J., & Bass, B. M. (1991). *The Full Range Leadership Development Programs: Basic and Advanced Manuals*. Binghamton, NY: Bass, Avolio & Associates.

Baines, D. & Benjamin, A. (2007). *Doing Anti-Oppressive Practice: Building Transformative, Politicized Social Work*. Manitoba: Fernwood Publishing Co.

Baldwin, M. (2004). 'Critical reflection: Opportunities and threats to professional learning and service development in social work organizations.' In N. Gould & M. Baldwin (eds), *Social Work, Critical Reflection and the Learning Organization*. Aldershot: Arena.

Bandura, A. (1977). *Social Learning Theory*, Englewood Cliffs: Prentice Hall.

Banks, S. (2006). *Ethics and Values in Social Work*, 3rd edn. Basingstoke: Palgrave Macmillan.

Basava International Foundation (2009). *Vachanas of Basavanna*. London: Basava International Foundation.

Bass, B. M. (1990). 'From transactional to transformational leadership: Learning to share the vision.' *Organizational Dynamics*, Winter, pp. 19–31.

Bass, B. M. & Steidlmeier, P. (1998). 'Ethics, character and authentic transformational leadership.' <http://cls.binghampton.edu/BassSteid.html> (retrieved 1 April 2008).

Bauman, Z. (1991). *Modernity and Ambivalence*. New York: Ithaca.

Becker, H. (1973). *Outsider: Studies in the Sociology of Deviance*. New York: Free Press.

Belbin, M. (1981). *Management Teams*. New York: John Wiley & Sons.

Bilson, A. & Ross, S. (1999). *Social Work Management and Practice*. London: Jessica Kingsley Publishers.

Blake, R. & Mouton, J. (1964). *The Managerial Grid*. Houston: Gulf Publishing.

Bolton, G. (2010). *Reflective Practice Writing and Professional Development*, 3rd edn. London: Sage Publications.

Borton, T. (1970). *Reach, Touch and Teach*. London: McGraw-Hill.

Boud, D., Keogh, R. & Walker, D. (1985) *Reflection: Turning Experience into Learning*. London: Kogan Page.

Boud, D. & Walker, D. (1998). 'Promoting reflection in professional courses: The challenge of context.' *Studies in Higher Education*, vol. 23, no. 2, pp. 191–206.

Bowles, W., Collingridge, M., Curry, S. & Valentine, B. (eds) (2006). *Ethical Practice in Social Work: An Applied Approach*. Sydney: Allen & Unwin.

Bradshaw J. (1972). 'A taxonomy of social need.' In G. McLachlan (ed.), *Problems and Progress in Medical Care*. Seventh series. NPHT/Open University Press.

Braithwaite, J. (1989). *Crime, Shame and Reintegration*, Cambridge: Cambridge University Press.

Briskman, L., Latham, S. & Goddard, C. (2009). *Human Rights Overboard*. Melbourne: Scribe Publications.

Brookfield, S. D. (1987). *Developing Critical Thinkers: Challenging Adults to Explore Alternative Ways of Thinking and Acting*. San Francisco: Jossey-Bass.

Brown, J. (1992). *Counselling and Social Work*. Buckingham: Open University Press.

Bruce, L. (2013). *Reflective Practice for Social Workers: A Handbook for Developing Professional Confidence*. Maidenhead: Open University Press.

Camilleri, P. (1996). *(Re)Constructing Social Work: Exploring Social Work Through Text and Talk*. Aldershot: Avebury.

Cashmore, J. & Paxman, M. (1996). *Wards Leaving Care: A Longitudinal Study*. Sydney: NSW Department of Community Services.

Castles, S. (1996). 'The racisms of globalisation.' In E. Vasta & S. Castles (eds), *The Teeth are Smiling: The Persistence of Racism in Multicultural Australia*, Sydney: Allen & Unwin, pp. 12–45.

Chapman, L. & Greenville, A. (2002). 'Profiling rural Australia: Impact of changes in the agricultural sector in rural towns.' *Australian Commodities*, vol. 9, no. 1, pp. 234–49.

Cheers, B., Darracott, R. & Lonne, B. (2005). 'Domains of rural social work practice.' *Rural Society*, vol. 15, no. 2, pp. 234–51.

Chenoweth, L. & McAuliffe, D. (2012). *The Road to Social Work and Human Services Practice*. Melbourne: Cengage Learning.

Chizmar, J. & Ostrosky, A. (1998). 'The one-minute paper: Some empirical findings.' *Journal of Economic Education*, vol. 29, no. 1, pp. 3–10.

Clark, D., Beck, A. & Alford, B. (1999). *Scientific Foundations of Cognitive Theory and Therapy*, New York: Wiley.

Clarke, J. & Newman, J. (1997). *The Managerial State: Power, Politics and Ideology in the Remaking of Social Welfare*. London: Sage Publications.

Cleckley, H. (1941). *The Mask of Sanity: An Attempt to Reinterpret the So-called Psychopathic Personality*, St Louis: Mosby.

Cloushed, V., Mullender, A., Jones, D. & Thompson, N. (2006). *Management in Social Work*. Basingstoke: Palgrave Macmillan.

Cloward, R. & Ohlin, L. (1960). *Delinquency and Opportunity*. New York: Free Press.

Cohen, J. (1983). 'Incapacitation as a strategy for crime control: Possibilities and pitfalls.' In M. Tonry & N. Morris (eds), *Crime and Justice: An Annual Review of Research*. Chicago: University of Chicago Press.

Cohen, S. (1972). *Folk Devils and Moral Panics*. London: McGribbon & Kee.

Connolly, M. & Harms, L. (2009). *Social Work: Contexts and Practice*, 2nd edn. Melbourne: Oxford University Press.

Cournoyer, B. (2000). *The Social Work Skills Workbook*, Belmont, CA: Brooks/Cole.

Cowie, A. P. (1993). *Oxford Advanced Learner's Dictionary*. Oxford: Oxford University Press.

Cowlishaw, G. (2004). *Blackfellas, Whitefellas and Hidden Injuries of Race*. Malden: Blackwell Publishing.

Cox, D. (1995). 'Social development and social work education.' *Social Development Issues*, vol. 17, nos 2/3, pp. 1–18.

Cox, D. & Pawar, M. (2013). *International Social Work: Issues, Strategies and Programs*, 2nd edn. Thousand Oaks, CA: Sage.

Cox, J. R. & Willard, C. A. (1982), *Advances in Argumentation Theory and Research*, Carbondale: Southern Illinois University Press.

Creswell, J. W. & Plano Clark, V. L. (2007). *Designing and Conducting Mixed Methods Research*. Thousand Oaks, CA: Sage.

Crigger, N. & Godfrey, N. S. (2011). *The Making of Nurse Professionals: A Transformational, Ethical Approach*. Sudbury, MA : Jones & Bartlett Learning.

Crisp, B., Anderson, M., Orne, J. & Green, L. P. (2004). 'Learning and teaching assessment: Reviewing the evidence.' *Social Work Education*, vol. 23, no. 2, pp. 199–215.

Crittenden, P. & Ainsworth, M. (1989). 'Child maltreatment and attachment theory.' In D. Cicchetti & V. Carlson (eds), *Handbook of Child Maltreatment*. New York: Cambridge University Press, pp. 432–63.

Dale, C., Thompson, T. & Woods, P. (2001). *Forensic Mental Health: Issues in Practice*. Great Britain: W. B. Saunders.

Dalrymple, J. & Burke, B. (2006). *Anti-Oppressive Practice: Social Care and the Law*. Berkshire: Open University Press.

Davies, M. (1994). *The Essential Social Worker: A Guide to Positive Practice*. Vermont: Arena.

De Bono, E. (1985). *Six Thinking Hats*. Boston: Little, Brown & Co.

Dempsey, K. (1990). *Smalltown*. Oxford: Oxford University Press.

Dewane, C. J. (2006). 'The use of self: A primer revisited.' *Clinical Social Work Journal*, vol. 34, no. 4, pp. 543–57.

Dolman, K. (1997). *Indigenous Regional Agreements – International and Comparative Indigenous Regional Agreements*, Sydney: UNSW Press.

Dominelli, L. (2002). *Feminist Social Work Theory and Practice*. Basingstoke: Palgrave Macmillan.

—— (2003). *Anti-Oppressive Social Work Theory and Practice*. Basingstoke: Palgrave Macmillan.

—— (2012). *Green Social Work: From Environmental Crisis to Environmental Justice*. Cambridge: Polity Press.

Drucker, P. (1977). *Management*. London: Pan.

—— (1981). *The Principles of Management*. São Paulo: Pioneira Thomson.

Duarte, D. L. & Snyder, N. T. (2006). *Mastering Virtual Teams*. San Francisco: Jossey-Bass.

Durkheim, E. (1950). *The Rules of Sociological Method*. Trans. Sarah A. Solovay & John H. Mueller. New York: Free Press.

Edwards, J. A. & Bess, J. M. (1998). 'Developing effectiveness in the therapeutic use of self.' *Clinical Social Work Journal*, vol. 26, no. 1, pp. 89–105.

Eysenck, H. (1977). *Psychology is About People*, New York: Penguin.

Farrugia, D. (2013). 'The reflexive subject: Towards a theory of reflexivity as practical intelligibility.' *Current Sociology*, vol. 61, no. 3, pp. 283–300.

Fattah, E. A. (1997). *Criminology: Past, Present and Future*. Basingstoke: Macmillan Press.

Ferguson, I. & Woodward, R. (2009). *Radical Social Work in Practice: Making a Difference*. Bristol: Policy Press.

Fitzgerald, M. (1994). 'Theories of reflection for learning.' In A. Palmer, S. Burns & C. Bulman (eds), *Reflective Practice in Nursing*. Oxford: Blackwell Science.

Flandreau West, P. (1989). *The Basic Essentials – Protective Behaviours, Anti-Victimisation and Empowerment Process*. Adelaide: Essence Publications.

Flaskas, C. (2004). 'Thinking about the therapeutic relationship: Emerging themes in family therapy.' *Australian and New Zealand Journal of Family Therapy*, vol. 25, no. 1, pp. 13–20.

Foley, D. (2003). 'Indigenous epistemology and Indigenous standpoint theory.' *Social Alternatives*, vol. 22, no.1, pp. 44–52.

Fook, J. (1993). *Radical Casework: A Theory of Practice*. Sydney: Allen & Unwin.

—— (1999). 'Reflexivity as method.' In J. Daley, A. Kellahear & E. Willis (eds), *Annual Review of Health Social Sciences*, vol. 9.

—— (2002). *Social Work: Critical Theory and Practice*. Thousand Oaks: Sage.

— (2004). 'Critical reflection and transformative possibilities.' In L. Davies & P. Leonard (eds), *Social Work in a Corporate Era: Practices of Power and Resistance.* Aldershot: Ashgate, pp. 16–30.

— (2007). 'Reflective practice and critical reflection.' In J. Lishman (ed.), *Handbook for Practice Learning in Social Work and Social Care,* 2nd edn. London: Jessica Kingsley Publishers.

— (2012). *Social Work: A Critical Approach to Practice.* London: Sage Publications.

Fook, J. & Askeland, G. A. (2006). 'The "critical" in critical reflection.' In S. White, J. Fook & F. Gardner (eds), *Critical Reflection in Health and Welfare.* Maidenhead: Open University Press.

Fook, J. & Gardner, F. (2007). *Practising Critical Reflection: A Handbook.* Maidenhead: Open University Press.

Frank, J. D. (1982). 'Therapeutic components shared by all psychotherapies.' In J. M. Harvey & M. M. Parks (eds), *Psychotherapy Research and Behaviour Change.* Washington DC: American Psychology Association.

Freire, P. (1975). *Pedagogy of the Oppressed.* Harmondsworth: Penguin.

French, J. R. P., Jr, & Raven, B. (1968). 'The bases for social power.' In D. Cartwright (ed.), *Studies in Social Power.* Ann Arbor, MI: University of Michigan Press.

Furedi, F. (1997). *Culture of Fear: Risk-taking and the Morality of Low Expectations.* London: Continuum.

Gardner, F. (2005). *Working with Human Service Organisations: Creating Connections for Practice.* Melbourne: Oxford University Press.

Garston, N. (ed.) (1993). *Bureaucracy: The Three Paradigms.* Boston: Kluwer.

Garvin, C. (1997). *Interpersonal Practice in Social Work: Promoting Competence and Social Justice,* Boston: Allyn & Bacon.

Gergan, K. (1999). *An Invitation to Social Construction.* Thousand Oaks, CA: Sage Publications.

Gibelman, M. (1999). 'The search for identity: Defining social work – past, present, future.' *Social Work,* vol. 44, no. 4, pp. 298–310.

Gibbs, G. (1988). *Learning by Doing: A Guide to Teaching and Learning Methods.* Oxford: Further Education Unit, Oxford Polytechnic.

Gill, O. (1977). *Luke Street: Housing Policy, Conflict and the Creation of the Delinquent Area.* London: Macmillan.

Golombok, S. (2000). *Parenting: What Really Counts?* East Sussex: Routledge (UK) & Taylor & Francis Group.

Goffman, E. (1961). *Asylums: Essays on the Social Situation of Mental Patients and Other Inmates*. New York: Anchor Books.

Gottfredson, M. & Hirschi, T. (1990). A *General Theory of Crime*. Redwood City, CA: Stanford University Press.

Gray, M., Coates, J. & Hetherington, T. (eds) (2013). *Environmental Social Work*. Abingdon: Routledge.

Gray, M. & Webb, S. (2013). *Social Work Theories and Methods*, 2nd edn. London: Sage Publications.

Gray, M. & Webb, S. (eds) (2010). *Ethics and Value Perspectives in Social Work*. Basingstoke: Palgrave Macmillan.

Groth, A., Hobson, W. & Gary, T. (1982). 'The child molester: Clinical observations.' *Journal of Social Work and Child Sexual Abuse*, vol. 1, no. 1–2, pp. 129–44.

Grove, W. (1985). 'The effect of age and gender on deviant behaviour: A biopsychosocial perspective.' In A. Rossi (ed.), *Gender and the Life Course*. New York: Aldine.

Guba, E. G. & Lincoln, Y. S. (1989). *Fourth Generation Evaluation*. Newbury Park: Sage Publications.

—— (1995). 'Competing paradigms in qualitative research.' In N. K. Denzin & Y. S. Lincoln (eds), *Handbook of Qualitative Research*. London: Sage Publications.

Habermas, J. (1974). *Theory and Practice*. London: Heinemann.

—— (1987). *Knowledge and Human Interest*. Cambridge: Polity Press.

Hagan, J. (1989). *Structural Criminology*, New Brunswick: Rutgers University Press.

Halstead, M. (1988). *Education, Justice and Cultural Diversity*. London: Falmer Press.

Hanson, R. K. & Thornton, D. (1999). *Static 99: Improving the Predictive Accuracy of Actuarial Risk Assessments for Sex Offenders*. Ottawa: Public Works and Government Services Canada.

Harms, L. (2007). *Working with People: Communication Skills for Professional Practice*. Melbourne: Oxford University Press.

Hartsell, B. (2006). 'A model for ethical decision-making: The context for ethics.' *Journal of Social Work Values and Ethics*, vol. 3, no. 1.

Harvey, D. (1990). *The Condition of Post-Modernity: An Enquiry into the Origins of Cultural Change*. Oxford: Blackwell.

Healy, K. (2005). *Social Work Theories in Context: Creating Frameworks for Practice*. Basingstoke: Palgrave Macmillan.

—— (2012). *Social Work Methods and Skills: The Essential Foundations of Practice*. Basingstoke: Palgrave Macmillan.

Healy, L. (2008). *International Social Work: Professional Action in an Interdependent World* (2nd edn), New York: Oxford University Press.

Healy, L. M. & Link, R. J. (eds). (2012). *Handbook of International Social Work: Human Rights, Development, and the Global Profession.* New York: Oxford University Press.

Henderson, P. & Thomas, D. (2002). *Skills in Neighbourhood Work*, New York: Routledge.

Hepworth, D. H., Rooney, R. H. & Larsen, J. A. (1997). *Direct Social Work Practice: Theories and Skills.* 5th edn. Pacific Grove, CA: Brooks/Cole–Thomson Learning.

—— (2002). *Direct Social Work Practice: Theory and Skills.* 6th edn. Pacific Grove, CA: Brooks/Cole.

Hersey, P. & Blanchard, K. H. (1988), *Management of Organizational Behavior: Utilizing Human Resources,* 5th edn. Englewood Cliffs, NJ: Prentice-Hall.

Heydt, M. & Sherman, N. (2005). 'Conscious use of self: Tuning the instrument of social work practice with cultural competence.' *Journal of Baccalaureate Social Work,* vol. 10, no. 2, pp. 25–40.

Hick, S. F., Fook, J. & Pozzuto, R. (2005). *Social Work: A Critical Turn.* Toronto: Thompson Publishing.

Hill, P., Wakeman, J., Mathews, S. & Gibeon, O. (2001). 'Tactics at the interface: Australian Aboriginal and Torres Strait Islander health managers.' *Social Science and Medicine,* vol. 52, no. 3, pp. 467–80.

Hirschi, T. (1969). *Causes of Delinquency.* Berkeley: University of California Press.

Hollinsworth, D. (1998). *Race and Racism in Australia.* Katoomba: Social Science Press.

House of Representatives Standing Committee on Aboriginal and Torres Strait Islander Affairs (1992). *Mainly Urban: Report of the Inquiry into the Needs of Urban Dwelling Aboriginal and Torres Strait Islander People.* Australian Government Publishing Service, November 1992.

Houston, S. (2012). 'Engaging with the crooked timber of humanity: Value pluralism and social work.' *British Journal of Social Work,* vol. 42, no. 4, pp. 652–68.

Howells, K. & Day, A. (1999). *The Rehabilitation of Offenders: International Perspectives Applied to Australian Correctional Systems.* Trends and Issues in Crime and Criminal Justice, no. 112. Canberra: Australian Institute of Criminology.

Hubble, M. A., Miller, S. D. & Duncan, B. L. (1999). *The Heart and Soul of Change: What Works in Therapy.* Washington, DC: American Psychological Association.

Hughes, M. & Wearing, M. (2007). *Organisations and Management in Social Work.* London: Sage Publications.

Hugman, R. (2010). *Understanding International Social Work: A Critical Analysis.* Basingstoke: Palgrave Macmillan.

—— (2013). *Culture, Values and Ethics in Social Work: Embracing Diversity*. Abingdon: Routledge.

Hugman, R. & Smith, D. (1995). 'Ethical issues in social work: An overview.' In R. Hugman & D. Smith (eds), *Ethical Issues in Social Work*. London: Routledge, pp. 1–15.

Ife, J. (1995). *Community Development: Creating Community Alternatives – Vision, Analysis and Practice*. Melbourne: Longman.

—— (1997). *Rethinking Social Work: Towards Critical Practice*. South Melbourne: Addison Wesley Longman.

—— (2002). *Community Development*. Sydney: Pearson Education.

—— (2012). *Human Rights and Social Work: Towards Rights-based Practice*. Melbourne: Cambridge University Press.

—— (2013). *Community Development in an Uncertain World: Vision, Analysis and Practice*. Melbourne: Cambridge University Press.

International Association of Schools of Social Work (2014). 'New international definition of social work.' <http://www.iassw-aiets.org/nidosw-20140221> (retrieved 6 March 2014).

International Federation of Social Workers & International Association of Schools of Social Work (2004). *Ethics in Social Work, Statement of Principles*. Bern, Switzerland: IFSW.

Jacobs, P., Brunton, M. & Melville, M. (1965). 'Aggressive behaviour, mental subnormality and the XXY male.' *Nature*, no. 208, pp. 1351–2.

Jeffery, C. (1971). *Crime Prevention Through Environmental Design*. Beverley Hills, CA: Sage.

Jenkins, A. (1990). *Invitation to Responsibility*, Adelaide: Dulwich Centre.

John Howard Society of Alberta (2002), 'Sex Offender Treatment Programs.' <http://www.johnhoward.ab.ca/pub/respaper/treatm02.pdf> (retrieved 30 April 2014).

Johnson, D. & Johnson, F. (2000). *Joining Together: Group Theory and Group Skills*. Boston: Pearson.

Jones, A. & May, J. (1992). *Working in Human Service Organisations: A Critical Introduction*. Melbourne: Longman Cheshire.

Jones, D. N. & Truell, R. (2012). 'The global agenda for social work and social development: A place to link together and be effective in a globalized world.' *International Social Work*, vol. 55, no. 4, pp. 454–72.

Kant, I. (1964). *The Groundwork of the Metaphysics of Morals*, New York: Harper & Row.

Keeling, D. (1972). *Management in Government*. London: Allen & Unwin.

Kemshall, H. (2002), *Risk Social Policy and Welfare*. Buckingham: Open University Press.

Kendall, K. (1993). 'Program evaluation of therapeutic service at the prison for women.' <http://www.csu.scc.gc.ca> (retrieved 1 April 1999).

Kenny, S. (1994). *Developing Communities for the Future: Community Development in Australia*, South Melbourne: Nelson.

Knott, C. & Scragg, T. (2013). *Reflective Practice in Social Work*, 3rd edn. London: Sage/LM.

Koch, T. & Harrington, A. (1998). 'Reconceptualising rigour: The case for reflexivity.' *Journal of Advanced Nursing*, vol. 28, no. 4, pp. 882–90.

Kohlberg, L. (1969). *Stage and Sequence: The Cognitive-Developmental Approach to Socialization*, New York: Rand McNally.

—— (1973). 'The claim to moral adequacy of a highest stage of moral judgment.' *Journal of Philosophy*, vol. 70, issue 18, pp. 630–46.

—— (1981). *The Philosophy of Moral Development*. New York: Harper & Row.

Kolb, D. A. (1984). *Experiential Learning: Experience as the Source of Learning and Development*. Englewood Cliffs: Prentice Hall.

Kondrat, M. (1999). 'Who is the "self" in "self-aware": Professional self-awareness from a critical theory perspective.' *Social Services Review*, vol. 73, pp. 451–76.

Kovel, J. (1970). *White Racism: A Psychohistory*. New York: Pantheon.

Krech, D., Ballachey, E. & Crutchfield, R. (1962). *Individual in Society: A Textbook of Social Psychology*. New York: McGraw-Hill.

Lawrence, J. (1976). 'Introduction. Australian social work: In historical, international and social welfare context.' In P. J. Boas & J. Crawley (eds), *Social Work in Australia: Responses to Changing Context*. Melbourne: Australia International Press & AASW.

Lax, W. D. (1996). 'Narrative, social constructionism and Buddhism.' In H. Rosen & K. T. Kuehlwein (eds), *Constructing Realities: Meaning Making Perspectives for Psychotherapists*. San Francisco: Jossey-Bass.

Lean, M. (1995). *Bread, Bricks, and Belief: Communities in Charge of Their Future*, West Hartford: Kumarian Press.

Lee, J. A.B. (2001). *The Empowerment Approach to Social Work Practice*. New York: Columbia University Press.

Leighninger, L. & Midgley, J. (1997). 'United States of America.' In N. S. Mayadas, T. D. Watts & D. Elliot (eds), *International Handbook on Social Work Theory and Practice*. Westport: Greenwood Press.

Lemert, E. (1967). *Human Deviance, Social Problems and Social Control*. Englewood Cliffs: Prentice Hall.

Levine, M. & Perkins, D. (1987). *Principles of Community Psychology: Perspectives and Applications*. New York: Oxford University Press.

Lewis, C. S. (1960). *The Four Loves*. London: Harvest Books.

—— (2001). *Mere Christianity*. London: HarperOne.

Likert, R. (1967). *New Patterns of Management*. New York: McGraw-Hill Book Company.

Lister, L. (1987). 'Contemporary direct practice roles.' *Social Work*, vol. 32, pp. 384–7.

Litvack, A., Bogo, M. & Mishna, F. (2010) 'Emotional reactions of students in clinical field education: An exploratory study.' *Journal of Social Work Education*, vol. 46, no. 2, pp. 227–43.

Loeber, R. & LeBlanc, M. (1990). 'Towards a developmental criminology.' In N. Morris & M. Tonry (eds), *Crime and Justice*, vol. 23, Chicago: University of Chicago Press.

Lyons, K., Hokenstadt, T., Pawar, M., Huegler, N., & Hall, N. (eds) (2012). *The Sage Handbook of International Social Work*. London: Sage Publications.

McArdle, J. (1993). *Resource Manual for Facilitators in Community Development*. Melbourne: Employ Publishing Company.

McBeath, G. & Webb, S. A. (2002). 'Virtue ethics and social work: Being lucky, realistic, and not doing one's duty.' *British Journal of Social Work*, vol. 32, no. 8, pp. 1015–36.

McConnaughy, E. A. (1987). 'The person of the therapist in psychotherapy practice.' *Psychotherapy*, vol. 24, pp. 303–14.

McConnochie, K., Hollinsworth, D. & Pettman, J. (1988). *Race and Racism in Australia*. Katoomba: Social Science Press.

McDonald, C., Craik, C., Hawkins, H. & Williams, J. (2011). *Professional Practice in Human Service Organisations: A Practical Guide for Human Service Workers*. Sydney: Allen & Unwin.

McGregor, D. (1960). *The Human Side of Enterprise*. Sydney: McGraw-Hill.

McGuire, J. (2013). 'What works to reduce reoffending: 18 years on.' In L. A. Craig, L. Dixon & T. A. Gannon (eds), *What Works in Offender Rehabilitation: An Evidence-based Approach to Assessment and Treatment*. Chichester: Wiley-Blackwell.

McGuire, J. & B. Rowson (eds) (1996). *Does Punishment Work?* London: Institute for the Study and Treatment of Delinquency.

McKay, R. (2002). 'New managers feel unprepared for the role.' *Community Care*, September, p. 14.

McKinnon, J. (2013). 'The environment: A private concern or a professional practice issue for Australian social workers.' *Australian Social Work*, vol. 66, no. 2, pp. 156–70.

Maidment, J. & Egan, R. (eds) (2004). *Practice Skills in Social Work and Welfare*. Sydney: Allen & Unwin.

Maier, N., Solem, A. & Maier, A. (1975). *The Role Play Technique: A Handbook for Management and Leadership Practice*. La Jolla, CA: University Associates.

Mapp, S. C. (2007). *Human Rights and Social Justice in a Global Perspective: An Introduction to International Social Work*. New York: Oxford University Press.

Markowitz, F., Bellair, P., Liska, A. & Liu, J. (2001). 'Extending social disorganization theory: Modelling relationships between cohesion, disorder and fear.' *Criminology*, vol. 39, pp. 293–320.

Marlatt, G. A. & Gordon, J. R. (eds) (1985). *Relapse Prevention: Maintenance Strategies in Addictive Behaviour Change*, New York: Guilford Press.

Marshall, W. L. (2005). 'Therapist style in sexual offender treatment: Influence on indices of change.' *Sexual Abuse: A Journal of Research and Treatment*, vol. 205, no. 17, pp. 109–16.

Martinson, R. (1974). 'What works? Questions and answers about prison reform.' *Public Interest*, vol. 10, pp. 22–54.

Martyn, H. (ed.) (2000). *Developing Reflective Practice: Making Sense of Social Work in a World of Change*. Bristol: Policy Press.

Marziali, E. & Alexander, L. (1991). 'The power of the therapeutic relationship.' *American Journal of Orthopsychiatry*, vol. 61, pp. 383–91.

Matza, D. (1960). *Becoming Deviant*, Englewood Cliffs: Prentice-Hall.

Maynard-Moody, S. & Musheno, M. (2000). 'State agent or citizen agent: Two narratives of discretion.' *Journal of Public Administration Research and Theory*, no. 10, pp. 329–58.

Mead, G. H. (1934). *Mind, Self and Society*. Chicago: University of Chicago Press.

Mendes, P. (2005). 'The history of social work in Australia: A critical review.' *Australian Social Work*, vol. 58, no. 2, pp. 121–31.

Merton, R. (1968). *Social Theory and Social Structure*. New York: Free Press.

Midgley, J. (1995). *Social Development*. London: Sage Publications.

—— (2014). *Social Development: Theory and Practice*. London: Sage Publications.

Midgley, J. & Conley, A. (2010). *Social Work and Social Development: Theories and Skills for Developmental Social Work*. New York: Oxford University Press.

Miles, R. (1989). *Racism*. London: Routledge & Kegan.

Moon, J. (1999). *Reflection in Learning and Professional Development: Theory and Practice*. London: Kogan Page.

—— (2004). *A Handbook of Reflective and Experiential Learning: Theory and Practice*. London: Routledge Falmer.

Mowbray, M. (1996). 'Community work practice and a case for the renovation of community work education.' *Australian Social Work*, vol. 49, no. 2, p. 3.

Mullaly, B. (2006). *The New Structural Social Work: Ideology, Theory, Practice*. New York: Oxford University Press.

Muran, J. C., Samstag, L. W., Ventur, E. D., Segal, Z. V. & Winston, A. (2001). 'A cognitive-interpersonal case study of a self.' *Journal of Clinical Psychology*, vol. 57, no. 3, pp. 307–30.

Mussen, P. (ed.) (1983). *Handbook of Child Psychology*, vol. 1, New York: Wiley.

Narayan, D., Rietbergen-McCracken, J. (1998). *Participation and Social Assessment: Tools and Techniques*, Washington, DC: World Bank.

National Gang Centre (2004), 'Highlights of the 2004 National Youth Gang Survey.' <https://www.ncjrs.gov/pdffiles1/ojjdp/fs200601.pdf> (retrieved 24 June 2014).

Nash, M. (2009). 'Histories of the social work profession.' In M. Connolly & L. Harms (eds), *Social Work: Context and Practice*. Melbourne: Oxford University Press.

Newman, O. (1973). *Architectural Design for Crime Prevention*. Washington DC: US Department of Justice National Institute for Law Enforcement and Justice.

NSW Local Government Grants Commission (1996), *1995–96 Annual Report*, Department of Local Government, Sydney.

Norton, M. (1976). 'Trends in social work education: The experience of a decade, 1965–1975.' In P. J. Boas & J. Crawley (eds), *Social Work in Australia: Responses to Changing Context*. Melbourne: Australia International Press & AASW.

Nungera Cooperative Society Ltd vs Maclean Shire Council (1991). *Aboriginal Law Bulletin*, issue 78, Aboriginal Law Research Unit, UNSW, Sydney, 1997.

O'Connor, J. & McDermott, I. (1997). *The Art of Systems Thinking: Essential Skills for Creativity and Problem-solving*. San Francisco: Thorsons Publishing.

O'Hara, A. & Pockett, R. (2011). *Skills for Human Service Practice:Working with Individuals, Groups and Communities*, 2nd edn, Melbourne: Oxford University Press.

O'Hara, A. & Webster, Z. (2006). *Working with Individuals, Communities and Organizations*. Melbourne: Oxford University Press.

O'Malley, P. (1996). 'Post-social criminologies: Some implications of current political trends for criminology theory and practice.' *Current Issues in Criminal Justice*, vol. 26, no. 1, pp. 26–38.

Osburn, L. (1999). 'Power to the profession: A study of a professional association's exercise of power over tertiary education' (PhD thesis). Armidale, NSW: University of New England.

Otto, H. & Ziegler, H. (2008). 'The notion of causal impact in evidence-based social work: An introduction to the special issue on what works?' *Research on Social Work Practice*, vol. 18, issue 4, pp. 273–7.

Owen, J. (1993; 2003). *Program Evaluation: Forms and Approaches*. St Leonards: Allen & Unwin.

Ozanne, E. & Rose, D. (2013). *The Organizational Context of Human Service Practice*. Melbourne: Oxford University Press.

Parton, N., Thorpe, D. & Wattam, C. (1997). *Child Protection: Risk and the Moral Order*. London: Macmillan.

Pavlov, I. P. (1906). 'Scientific study of the so-called psychical processes in the higher animals.' In W. Dennis (ed.) (1948), *Readings in the History of Psychology*. Century Psychology Series. East Norwalk, CT: Appleton-Century-Crofts, pp. 425–38.

Pawar, M. (2000). 'Social development content in the courses of Australian social work schools.' *International Social Work*, vol. 43, no. 3, pp. 277–88.

—— (2010). *Community Development in Asia and the Pacific*. New York: Routledge.

—— (2013). 'Water insecurity: A case for social policy action by social workers.' *Australian Social Work*, vol. 66, no. 2, pp. 248–60.

—— (2014a). *Social and Community Development Practice*, New Delhi: Sage.

—— (2014b). *Water and Social Policy*, Basingstoke: Palgrave Macmillan.

Pawar, M. & Cox, D. (2010a). 'Social development.' In Pawar, M. & Cox, D. (eds), *Social Development: Critical Themes and Perspectives*. New York: Routledge.

—— (2010b). *Social Development: Critical Themes and Perspectives*. New York: Routledge.

Pawar, M., Sheridan, R. & Hanna, G. (2004). 'International social work practicum in India.' *Australian Social Work*, vol. 57, no. 3, pp. 223–36.

Payne, M. (1997a). *Modern Social Work Theory*. London: Macmillan.

—— (1997). 'United Kingdom.' In N. S. Mayadas, T. D. Watts & D. Elliot (eds), *International Handbook on Social Work Theory and Practice*. Westport: Greenwood Press.

—— (2005). *Modern Social Work Theory*. Basingstoke: Palgrave Macmillan.

Peck, S. (1982). *People of the Lie: The Hope for Healing Human Evil*. London: Rider.

Piaget, J. (1983). 'Piaget's theory.' In P. Mussen (ed.), *Handbook of Child Psychology, Vol. 1*, New York: Wiley.

Pierson, J. & Thomas, M. (2010). *Dictionary of Social Work*. Maidenhead: Open University Press.

Plath, D. (2006). 'Evidence-based practice: Current issues and future directions.' *Australian Social Work*, vol. 59, no. 1, pp. 56–72.

Poulter, J. (2005). 'Integrating theory and practice: A new heuristic paradigm for social work practice.' *Australian Social Work*, pp. 199–212.

Preston-Shoot, M. (2007). *Effective Groupwork*, 2nd edn. Basingstoke: Palgrave Macmillan.

Pulla, V. (2012). 'What are strengths based practices all about? In V. Pulla, L. Chenoweth, A. Francis & S. Bakaj (eds), *Papers in Strengths Based Practice*, New Delhi: Allied Publishers.

Reichert, E. (2011). *Social Work and Human Rights. A Foundation for Policy and Practice*, 2nd edn. New York: Columbia University Press.

Richmond, M. (1917). *Social Diagnosis*. New York: Russell Sage Foundation.

Rigney, L. (1997). 'Internalisation of an Indigenous anti-colonial cultural critique of research methodologies. A guide to Indigenous research methodologies and its principles.' *Journal of American Studies*, vol. 14, no. 2, pp. 109–22.

Roberts, A. R. & Ottens, A. J. (2005). *The Seven Stage Crisis Intervention Model: A Road Map to Goal Attainment, Problem Solving and Crisis Resolution*. Oxford: Oxford University Press.

Rogowski, S. (2010). *The Rise and Fall of a Profession*. Bristol: Policy Press.

Rolfe, G., Freshwater, D. & Jasper, M. (2001). *Critical Reflection for Nursing and the Helping Professions: A User's Guide*. Basingstoke: Palgrave Macmillan.

Rolfe, G., Jasper, M. & Freshwater, D. (2011). *Critical Reflection in Practice: Generating Knowledge for Care*. Basingstoke: Palgrave Macmillan.

Rossiter, A. (2005). 'Discourse analysis in critical social work: From apology to question.' *Critical Social Work*, vol. 6, no. 1, pp. 1–11.

—— (2006). 'The "beyond" of ethics in social work.' *Canadian Social Work Review*, no. 23, pp. 139–44.

Rothman, J. & Tropman, J. E. (1987). 'Models of community organization and macro practice perspectives: Their mixing and phasing.' In F. M. Cox, J. L. Erlich, J. Rothman & J. E. Tropman (eds), *Strategies of Community Organization: Macro Practice*, 4th edn. Itasca, IL: F. E. Peacock Publishers.

Rowlings, C. (1997). 'Europe.' In N. S. Mayadas, T. D. Watts & D. Elliot (eds), *International Handbook on Social Work Theory and Practice*. Westport: Greenwood Press.

Ruch, G. (2000) 'Self and social work: Towards an integrated model of learning.' *Journal of Social Work Practice*, vol. 14, no. 2, pp. 99–111.

Sack, J. (2002). *The Dignity of Difference*, London: Continuum.

Schmalleger, F. (2008), *Criminology Today*, Upper Saddle River, NJ: Prentice Hall.

Schon, D. (1983). *The Reflective Practitioner*. London: Temple Smith.

Seidel, S. & Blythe, T. (1996) 'Reflective practice in the classroom.' Unpublished article, Project Zero/Massachusetts Schools Network.

Seligman, M. E.P. (2002). *Authentic Happiness*, New York: Free Press.

Shaw, C. R. & McKay, H. D. (1969). *Juvenile Delinquency and Urban Areas*. Chicago: University of Chicago Press.

Sheppard, M. (2007). 'Assessment: From reflexivity to process knowledge.' In J. Lishman (ed.), *Handbook for Practice Learning in Social Work and Social Care: Knowledge and Theory*, 2nd edn. London: Jessica Kingsley Publishers.

Shonkoff, J. & Phillips, D. (2000). *From Neurons to Neighbourhoods: The Science of Early Childhood Development*. Washington, DC: National Academy Press.

Sibeon, R. (1990). 'Social work knowledge, social actors and deprofessionalisation.' In P. Abbott & C. Wallace (eds), *The Sociology of the Caring Professions*, Basingstoke: Falmer Press.

Skinner, B. F. (1971). *Beyond Freedom and Dignity*, New York: Knopf.

Smith, M. L., Glass, G. V. & Miller, T. I. (1980). *The Benefits of Psychotherapy*. Baltimore: Johns Hopkins Press.

Sparrow, J. (2009). 'Impact of emotions associated with reflecting upon the past.' *Reflective Practice*, vol. 10, no. 5, pp. 567–76.

Stuart, P. H. (2013). 'Social work profession: History.' In C. Franklin (ed.), *Encyclopedia of Social Work*, New York: National Association of Social Workers & Oxford University Press.

Sutherland, E. (1947). *Criminology*. Philadelphia: Lippincott.

Sutherland, E. & Cressey, D. (1978). *Criminology*. New York: Lippincott.

Sutherland, L. & Shepherd, P. (2002). 'A personality-based model of adolescent violence.' *British Journal of Criminology*, vol. 42, no. 2, pp. 433–41.

Taylor, B. J. (2006). *Reflective Practice: A Guide for Nurses and Midwives*, 2nd edn. Buckingham: Open University Press.

Taylor, F. W. (1911). *The Principles of Scientific Management*. New York: Harper Bros.

Taylor, R. & Harrell, A. (1996). *Physical Environment and Crime*. Washington, DC: US Department of Justice.

Thompson, N. & Pascal, J. (2012). 'Developing critically reflective practice.' *Reflective Practice: International and Multidisciplinary Perspectives*, vol. 13, no. 2, pp. 311–25.

Thompson, S., & Thompson, N. (2008). *The Critically Reflective Practitioner*. Basingstoke: Palgrave Macmillan.

Thornberry, T. (1987). 'Towards an interactional theory of delinquency.' *Criminology*, vol. 25, pp. 863–91.

Thornhill, R. & Palmer, C. (2000). *A Natural History of Rape: Biological Bases of Sexual Coercion*. Cambridge: MIT Press.

Thorpe, R. & Petruchenia, J. (1985). *Community Work or Social Change? An Australian Perspective*. Henley: Routledge & Kegan Paul.

Tomlinson, J. (1978). *Is Band-Aid Social Work Enough?* Darwin: Wobbly Press.

Toomelah Cooperative Ltd v Moree Plains Shire Council [1996] 1 AILR 407; (1996) 3(80) *Aboriginal Law Bulletin*, 27.

Trevithick, P. (2005). *Social Work Skills: A Practice Handbook*, Maidenhead: Open University Press.

—— (2008). 'Revisiting the knowledge base of social work: A framework for practice.' *British Journal of Social Work*, vol. 38, issue 6, pp. 1212–37.

—— (2012). *Social Work Skills and Knowledge: A Practice Handbook*. Maidenhead: Open University Press.

Trotter, C. (2006). *Working with Involuntary Clients: A Guide to Practice*. 2nd edn. London: Sage Publications.

Tuckman, B. (1965). 'Developmental sequence in small groups.' *Psychological Bulletin*, vol. 63, no. 6, pp. 384–99.

Vila, B. (1994). 'A general paradigm for understanding criminal behaviour: Extending evolutionary ecological theory.' *Criminology*, vol. 32, issue 3, pp. 311–59.

Vinson, T. (1999). *The Distribution of Social Advantage in Victoria and New South Wales*. Melbourne: Ignatius Centre.

—— (2004). *Community Adversity and Resilience: The Distribution of Social Disadvantage in Victoria and New South Wales and the Mediating Role of Social Cohesion*. Richmond, Vic: Jesuit Social Services.

Vygotsky, L. S. (1978). *Mind in Society*. Cambridge, MA: Harvard University Press.

Walter, M., Taylor, S. & Habibis, D. (2011). 'How white is social work in Australia?' *Australian Social Work*, vol. 64, no. 1, pp. 6–19.

Warren, R. L. (1963). *The Community in America*. Chicago: Rand McNally.

Watson, T. (1980). *Sociology, Work and Industry*. London: Routledge.

Webber, J. & Nathan, M. (2010). *Reflective Practice in Mental Health: Advancing Psychosocial Practice with Children, Adolescents and Adults*. London: Jessica Kingsley Publishers.

Weber, M. (1947). *The Theory of Social and Economic Organization*. New York: Free Press.

Weber-Pillwax, C. (2001). 'Indigenous research methodologies.' *Canadian Journal of Native Education*, vol. 25, no. 2, pp. 166–74.

Wheelan, S. (2005). *Group Processes: A Developmental Perspective*, 2nd edn. Boston: Allyn & Bacon.

White, V. (2006). *The State of Feminist Social Work*. New York: Routledge.

Wilson, E. O. (1975). *Sociobiology: The New Synthesis*. Cambridge, MA: Harvard University Press.

Wilson, G. (2013). 'Evidencing reflective practice in social work education: Theoretical uncertainties and practical challenges.' *British Journal of Social Work*, no. 43, no. 1, pp. 154–72.

Wonka, J. (2007). *Human Rights and Social Justice: Social Action and Service for the Helping and Health Professions*, Thousand Oaks, CA: Sage Publications.

Wood, J., Zeffane, R., Fromholtz, M. & Fitzgerald, J. (2006). *Organizational Behaviour: Core Concepts and Applications*, Melbourne: Wiley.

Yan, M. C. & Wong, Y. R. (2005). 'Rethinking self-awareness in cultural competence: Towards a dialogic self in cross-cultural social work.' *Families in Society: The Journal of Contemporary Human Services*, vol. 86, no. 2, pp. 181–8.

Young, J. (1971). 'The role of policies as amplifiers of deviance, negotiators of reality and translators of fantasy.' In S. Cohen (ed.), *Images of Deviance*. Harmondsworth: Penguin.

Zander, B. & Zander, R. (2000). *The Art of Possibility*. Boston: Harvard Business School Press.

Zastrow, C. (2003). *Introduction to Social Work and Social Welfare*. Belmont, CA: Thomson Learning.

—— (2006). *Social Work with Groups*. Pacific Grove, CA: Thomson.

—— (2010). *The Practice of Social Work: A Comprehensive Work Text*. Belmont, CA: Brooks/Cole.

Zubrzycki, J. (1999). 'The influence of the personal on the professional: A preliminary investigation of work and family issues for social workers'. *Australian Social Work*, vol. 52, no. 4, pp. 11–16.

Index

backward events 45
balance 132
behaviour
  antisocial behaviour and attitudes 96
  assault behaviour 79, 136
  behaviour patterns 70, 71
  behavioural approaches 99
  behavioural therapies 65, 107
  case study 66–8
  changes in 65
  codes of behaviour 191
  conflict—attitude and behaviour 111
  dysfunctional behaviour 65
  ethical professional behaviour 21
  'normal' social behaviour 108
  principled and accountable manner 23
  rationalisation of 86
  reckless/dangerous behaviour 133
  theories of 51, 52
  threatening/offending behaviour 66, 70, 86
being (concept) 5, 14, 21, 23, 38, 50, 52, 53, 54, 57–8,
    61, 80, 85, 87, 100, 189, 193, 194–5, 205, 207,
    210–13
  awareness raising 41, 126–7, 154
  to 'be' 83
  being-focused practice 212
  challenges to 88, 164
  child sexual abuse, importance in 81–2
  communities and 117–38
  dimensions of 48, 50–1
  disciplinary/interdisciplinary concept of 212
  dynamics 163–7
  evaluation and 132–3
  of groups 94, 107–8
  'home'; being a 'man' 83
  identification by skin names/clan
    association 137
  intergenerational disadvantage, creative
    responses to 134–6
  meaning of 29–31
  organisational being 191–2, 196
  PEOPLE model and 36–61, 146, 163,
    204, 210
  physical and organic perspectives 108, 122,
    124–5, 132, 133, 134
  of the practitioner—knower 47
  reflections on 81–4, 107–10, 131–8, 200–13
  in reflective practice context 64–88, 90, 117–38,
    142–67, 170–96
  as relates to purpose and objectives 131–2
  research undertaken as part of 209
  of researchers 161–3
  social work and 191–6, 201–4
  virtues and 31–4, 48, 204
  visualising and developing 110
Belbin Group/Team Questionnaire 98

Belbin's Team roles 95, 106
beliefs 30, 70
belonging 118
bias 31, 85, 195
Binaal Billa Regional Council 145–6, 158
  legal project 159–60
  Steering Committee 151
biographical management 40–1
bonding 53
Boud, David
  model's limitations 44
  reflective learning from experiences 44
boundaries 23
Bradshaw's taxonomy of need 127
brainstorming 108
Bringing Them Home [report] 182
brokering 72, 76, 130, 153, 156, 183
  brokers 124, 129
  intervention approaches 128–31
budgets 149–50, 160, 173, 185–6, 193
bureaucracy 64–88, 174, 189, 195, 210

capacity 128, 138, 173
capitalism 53
care (for others) 43, 173, 177–8, 190–1
case management theory 70
case managers/coordinators 72
case plans 73
casework 9, 10–11, 14, 70, 177–8, 183, 189
  casework models 13, 136, 138
  social casework 11
catastrophier approach 107
categorical imperative principle 203
central nervous system 51
centralisation 193
change 56, 72, 78, 82, 132, 142–67
  agents 166
  pro-social change 92–3
  social work research 142, 208
charity 82, 132, 133, 167, 192, 201
Charity Organisation Society (COS) model 9–10, 11
charity societies 9
Chicago School 53, 97
child protection 21, 70, 71, 173, 179, 187–9,
    194, 202
  Indigenous child protection worker 187–9
childhood sexual assault (CSA) 67, 80, 81–2
children
  child maltreatment and neglect 178
  child removal decisions 188
  child sex offenders 70
  childhood and risk 179–80
  in foster care, outcomes 71
  in urban centres 9
  well-being and protection of 21
  see also out-of-home-care

Christianity
  Christian Gospel 82
  evangelical Christianity 10
  missionaries 11
chromosomes 51
chronemics 51
cigarette smoking 127–8, 133
clients 23, 30, 69
cliques 94
codes of ethics 7–8, 20, 21, 23–4, 41, 149, 203,
    212–13
cognition 65
  cognitive behavioural approaches 65, 99
  cognitive behavioural therapy (CBT) 107
collaboration 54, 65, 72, 133, 192
  collaborative critical analyses 55
colleagues, responsibilities to 23
collective responsibility 8
colonisation 9, 195
Commission of Audit 149–50
commitment 24, 94, 161
common sense 27
communication 22, 23, 52, 94, 106–7, 155
community 53, 118, 119, 136
  Aboriginal/Indigenous communities 134, 137,
    143, 144, 151, 160, 208
  approaches 138
  being and 117–38
  capabilities 119–20
  case study 119–21
  characteristics 123–4, 132
  community counselling intervention
    approach 69
  community life 113
  community organisers 129, 130
  'community' term 118
  community theories 55
  definitions 118–19
  diversity of 126
  good of the larger community 204
  health of 123–4
  membership 125
  neglect of 192
  organic, dynamic and interrelated qualities 119
  reflective practice with 117–38
  rural and remote communities 121–31, 186–91
  of sentiment 136
  setting 51
  social systems, communal elements of 136
  well-being of 20
community development 20, 119–20, 125, 131,
    136, 145
community work 10, 11, 12–15, 19, 20, 118
  community identity 208
  declining communities 208
  frameworks and tools used 118–19

group work and 207–8
key concepts and models 118–19
project outcomes 120
specific and national objectives 120–1
thinking *versus* doing community work 207
top-down perspective 120, 193, 207, 209–10
community workers 131–8
competence 24, 33
competition, in groups 94
compliance 69
confidentiality 85–6, 93
conflict(s) 44, 56, 184
  attitude and behaviour 111
  conflicts of interest 23
  in groups 94–5, 107–8
  moral rules conflict 203
  tension and 176
confrontation 83
connectedness 53
conscientisation 127, 158, 195
consequences 10, 25, 203
consequentialism 31
consultation 153, 157
  continuum 154
  data analysis and findings 154
  data collection through 153–4
  with local government 153–4, 155–6
continuous learning 41
contracts 144
control 45, 53, 70, 92, 99, 107, 110, 118
conventions 70
convergent thinking 27
cooperation 69, 94
coordination/coordinators 124, 125, 129, 183
corrections 69
cost 159
counselling 69, 202
courage 162
covenants 144, 188
creative thinking *see* lateral thinking
creativity 27, 107, 128–31
criminological theories 96–7
criminologists 96, 97
criminology 70, 97
crises 65, 204
critical reflection 21, 23, 38, 42
  'critical science' link 39
  emancipatory domain of 45
critical reflective practice 38, 39–40, 202
  aspect—knower 47
  'critical' depth/breadth dimension 39
  'critical' term 38–9
critical thinking 21, 25–6, 41, 57, 70, 71,
    97–8, 204
Crown land 158–61
cues, artefactual and olfactory 51

emotions 44, 45, 52, 65
  dysfunctional emotions 65
  emotional support 69
  emotional/mental theories 52, 111, 122, 124–5, 132, 133, 134, 192, 193
  express and control, capacity for 51, 52
empathy 24, 27, 33, 83
employment/employees 156–8
  development and 156
  Equal Employment Opportunity Monitor 158
empowerment 11, 12–15, 130, 145, 149, 155–6, 161, 180, 183, 202, 208
enabling/enablers 124, 153, 183
endorphins 51
engagement 12, 54, 72, 126, 133, 143–4, 192, 208
Enlightenment/enlightenment 9, 43, 59
enuresis 69
environment 54–5, 59, 91, 96, 110, 149–50
  environmental scans 54–5, 57–8, 78, 125, 132, 177–8, 205
  social environment 52
epistemology 48, 164, 195
equality 43
equity 21, 150
ethics 21, 23, 31–4, 51–2, 149, 165, 202–3
  AASW codes of ethics 7–8, 20, 21, 23–4, 41, 149, 203, 212–13
  ethical issues 23
  ethical practice 23, 33
  indicators 23
ethnic values 53
ethnicity 150, 166–7
ethnobiographies 135, 145–6, 151
ethnographies 40, 130
eudaimonia 204
eugenics movement 97
European Reformation 43
evaluation 58–60, 71, 80, 132–3, 142, 190, 205
  conceptualisation of 58
  context, design limitations, foci 59
  cost-benefit evaluations 107
  doing and 79
  Harvard One-Minute Evaluation 95, 101–7
  methods 71, 73
  Post-it Note Evaluation/Minute Evaluation 95
  process and outcomes 59
  purpose 59
  questions for 58, 95
  reflective evaluation 60
  reporting and 125
  for results 60
  values and forces shaping 59
evidence 42
  evidence-based practice 180, 202
  standard against which evidence is assessed 180
evil 87

evolution 97, 167
excellence 204
existentialism 52, 53, 65
experience 51, 52, 87, 147, 156, 162, 189
  Boud's reflective learning from experiences 44
  experience–reflection–knowledge 43
  experiential exercises 93
  of participants 54
  social work leadership experiences 173–80
experimentation, exploratory nature 44
exploitation 40, 162

facilitation 76, 124
  of groups 125, 153, 183, 184
fairness see justice
faith 133, 167
families 64–88
  case study 66–8
  family dynamics, changing 78
  'family rules' 80
  family-based therapies 71
  'home'; being a 'man' 83
  nuclear families 72
  ways of being 'family' 72
  see also individual and family work
family workers 71–81
fatherhood 109
feelings 44, 45, 65, 94
femaleship 84
feminism 53, 202
flexibility 26
fluency 26
foreflecting 200–13
forgiveness 79
formal theories 85–6
forming 93, 96
fortitude 82, 133, 162, 167, 177, 192
foster care 71
Four Loves, The [book] 109
frameworks 25, 36–61, 70, 92–3, 120, 122, 200–13
freedom 43
friendly visitors 10
funding 119–20, 155, 173, 182

gang studies 137
  USA National Gang Centre 137
gemeinschaft 118
gender 17, 137
General Strain Theory 53
genuineness 27
geopolitical realities 155
globalisation 129, 211
goals 18, 56
'good works' 10
government 144, 153–4, 155–6, 157, 160
Grants Commission 152, 154, 157, 160

oppression 10, 17, 39, 41–2, 45, 85, 87, 107, 145, 162, 166–7, 188, 192, 193, 202
  of Aboriginal communities 138, 208
  agents of 209–10
  of Indigenous peoples 134
optimism 52, 53
organisations 53, 59, 174, 203
  Indigenous organisations 131
  interrelationships/intrarelationships 191
  mantra 191
  non-government organisations 119–20, 131
  as participants 53
  service organisations 133
  statutory responsibilities 173
  values and behaviour codes 191
  voluntary bodies 11, 201
orientation 124–5
originality 26
orphans 10
outcomes 79, 80, 138, 190
  case plans and 73
  for children in foster care 71
  developmental disability, influences of 71
  multiple 71
  outcomes 60, 142
  reflective practice—individuals and families 80–1
  variance 69
out-of-home-care (OOHC) 173, 177–8, 190–1, 193, 194, 196
  risk and short-term approach implications 180
outward reflective processes 45

pair-wise rankings 126–6
paradigms 97, 108, 109, 110, 146–7
paranoic approach 107
participants 49, 50–1, 54–5, 60, 121, 205
  acceptance of difference 53
  connectness to society assessment 53
  co-participants 145–6
  emotional/mental characteristics 51, 52, 122, 124–5, 132, 133, 134, 192, 193
  excluding from groupwork 92
  experience 54
  gaps/inconsistencies, noting 55
  physical/organic characteristics 51, 122, 124–5, 132, 133, 134
  priority on 49
  research participants, approach to 142
  situation of 54
  social workers as 52–3
  social/relational characteristics 51–2, 109, 122, 124–5, 132, 133, 134, 192
  spiritual/existential characteristics 52, 111, 122, 124–5, 132, 133, 134, 193
  thinking, doing and being, new ways 92–3, 122

  well-being of 50
  worldview and knowledge 50
participation 13, 118
  expectations 94–5
  in groups 94
  of women (value) 43
participatory diagramming 126–7, 145–6, 151
partnerships 18
past 51, 52, 87
  differentiating past from present 80
  past, present, future 66
pathologising (offenders) 70
peace-making 165
people 13, 18, 36–61, 122, 147
PEOPLE model 47–61, 146, 152, 163, 204, 205, 210
performing 93, 96
personality 30
petrol-sniffing 127
philosophy 25, 172
phronesis 204
physiognomists 96–7
planning 59, 65, 72, 73, 79, 80, 91
Platonic notions 204
policy 20, 59
policy practice 11
politics 50, 53
  political environment 149–50
  political voice 150
position 147
positivism 132, 146–7
  knowledge frameworks 202–3
post-fact analysis method 205
postmodernism 39–40, 97, 202
poverty 9, 17, 132, 134, 162, 178, 188, 192, 201, 202, 211
power 70, 99, 147, 164, 175
  bargaining power 155
  differentials 92–3, 195
  differentials/imbalances 78
  power relationships within environment 55
  power-sharing 49
  relations and structures 40
practical domain 45
practice 11, 17, 20, 21, 23, 33, 39, 41–2, 54, 180, 201, 202, 211–13
  with Aboriginal and Torres Strait Islander people 21
  action of 40–1
  basis 22
  being-focused practice 212
  binary focus 14, 29, 42, 182, 202–3, 211
  challenges 211
  clinically oriented practice 211
  contemporary social work practice 5–34
  context 21
  critical reflective practice 38, 45, 202

practice (cont.)
  cross-cultural practice 21
  depersonalising 211
  developmentally oriented practice 211
  emancipatory practice 41–2
  following the PEOPLE sequence 50
  forward practice 45
  frameworks 55
  future perspectives 200–13
  gender and 17
  habitual and heuristic practice 86–7
  improving/replicating 41
  informal/implicit theory and 85
  knowledge creation in 39–40, 202
  macro/micro practice 11, 12–15, 21
  one-to-one casework-based practice 11
  orientation 142
  past practice events 41
  policy practice 11, 12–15
  procedure-oriented and rule-bound
    practice 203
  pro-social change, to promote 82
  racism and 17
  reflection and 37, 38, 43–4, 60
  reflective practice see reflexive practice
  reflective social work practice model 36–61
  reflexive practice 21, 40–2
  remedial practice 211
  Schön's reflective practice 43–4
  strengths-based practice 11, 202
  theories for 44, 70, 84
  virtue ethics, relevance of 31
  virtue-led practice 204, 212
  see also individual (one-to-one) casework-based,
    medical/remedial/pathologically oriented
    practice
practice standards 22–3, 27, 33
practitioners
  being of the practitioner 47, 48
  client–social worker relationship 30
  content, thoughts of 25–6
  as environment shapers 110
  environmental scans 54–5
  gaps/inconsistencies, noting 55
  the knower 47
  outcome and impact focus 50
  as participants 52–3
  recognition of 16
  reflective practitioners 205
  responsibilities 23, 56
  roles and skills—doings 27–8, 72, 202
  sectors and settings 201, 202
  'social work self' 31
  spirituality factors 53
  virtue dimension of 48
prejudice 85

present 51, 52, 87
  differentiating past from present 80
privacy 85–6
private trusts 11
privatisation 108
privilege 147
problems/problem-solving 65, 125
  approach—systemic thinking 26
  in groups 94–5
  social work, significance to 57
processes 79, 172, 205
production 118
professional development 18–20, 22, 23, 71, 201
professional integrity see integrity
professionalisation 202–3, 211
professionalism 23
professions, competing 211
programs 59, 83, 99, 101, 128–9
  Getting Smashed program and video 129
  improvement, clarification and development 59
  Life Education vans 134
  symbolic reasons for 59
  urban programs 135–6
project development phase 125
pro-social change 82, 92–3
pro-social modelling 95, 96, 111, 145, 156, 163,
    176, 191
  research approaches 145–6
prosperity 201
proxemics 51
prudence 132, 133, 162, 165, 167, 192
psychoanalytical approaches 52
psychoanalytical therapies 65
psychodrama 65
psycho-social/psycho-sexual issues 83
psychotherapies 65
public speaking 76, 124, 125, 153, 183
punishment 98
purpose 52, 53, 131–2

qualitative data 151
questions/questioning
  Belbin Group/Team Questionnaire 98
  evaluation, questions for 58, 95
  reflection, questions for 43
  reflections through 43, 60

race 137, 150, 166–7
racism 17, 150, 162, 166–7
  non-racism 93
  racial divisions 132
  racial riots 123
Radical Social Work [book] 202
rankings 126–6
rapport 65
rates 158

rationalisation 86
rationality 9, 31
realities, current 54–5
reason/reasoning 9, 26–7, 31
recidivism rates 69, 98
reciprocity 82
reconciliation 97, 143, 149–50
reflection 57, 107, 167
  capacity for 51, 52
  critical reflection 21, 23, 38, 42
  experience–reflection–knowledge 43
  on individual and family worker 81–4
  levels 45
  questions/questioning and 43
  'reflect,' 'reflection' and 'reflective practice'
    terms 37–8
  reflective framework 48
  reflective processes 45
  reflective self-awareness 24, 33, 37
  reframing and 82
  Socrates' assertion 42
  on therapeutic group work 98–100
  on thinking, doing and being 191–6, 200–13
reflective learning 43
reflective practice 36–61, 202
  additions/refinements to theories 45
  being in 64–88, 90, 117–38, 142–67, 170–96
  continuous process 50
  doing—individuals and families 70
  evil, nature of 87
  external conditions and circumstances of 88
  formal and informal theory, changes in 85–6
  habitual and heuristic practice 86–7
  Hall of Experience 43
  meaning of 37–41
  outcomes—individuals and families 80–1
  personal and professional, influence of 87
  practice, on, in and for 38, 43–4, 45
  practice-based knowledge creation 41, 42, 43–4
  'reflect,' 'reflection' and 'reflective practice'
    terms 37–8
  reflective practice—individuals and families
    80–1, 205–6
  reflective practitioners 205
  significance and use of 41–2
  theoretical bases 42–3
  thinking and reflecting—individuals and
    families 68–71
reflective social work practice model 36–61
  application 48, 50, 204–11
  components 48–9
  critical progressive phases 48
  environmental scan 54–5
  evaluation and action 58–60, 142
  group work application 206–7
  limitations 48

objectives setting 56
participants, interaction 54
PEOPLE model and 205
physical considerations 51
principles 49–50
processes and labour/doing 57–8
reflective framework 48
thinking, doing and being 50, 122
reflective thinking 41, 70
reflexivity 21, 36–61
reframing 82, 83
reintegrative shaming 97
relapse prevention theory 70
relational capacity 80
relational dynamics 30
relationships
  ecomapping and 77
  environmental scans of 78
  interrelationships/intrarelationships 191
  non-land-based relationship aspects 144
  power relationships 55
  relationship-centred interaction 54
  therapeutic relationship 69
  trust/trusting relationships 80, 125
reliability 24, 33
religion 9, 52, 53
research 12, 20, 23, 51, 145, 155, 183, 184
  being of researchers 161–3
  for being-focused and virtue-led practice 212
  constructivist research 147
  conventional research 142
  critical reflective practice 39
  design 148–9, 151
  engagement in 208
  evaluation and action, research in terms of 142
  indigenous alternative approach 147–8
  Indigenous research principles 147–8
  influence on 40–1
  knowledge and skills 125, 208
  mixed methods approach 148–9, 151
  objective research 146
  outcomes 142
  participatory research methods 145, 149,
    151, 153
  partnerships 144
  pilot research 144–5
  process leading to change/action 154–63
  projects 143–4
  research ethics 149
  research literature 79
  research methodology 40, 145
  research participants 142
  researchers 16, 124, 145, 161–3, 166
  social work research 142, 208–9
  social work—research-oriented profession 142
  subject–object dualism 149

social work training *see* training
social workers *see* practitioners
socialisation 118
society 53, 108
sociocultural context (personal journey) 44
sociocultural diversity 164
Socio-Economic Index for Advantage
    (SEIFA) 178
sociology 97
solidarity 136
solution-focused approaches 65, 66
solvability 83
spirituality 50
    factors for social worker 53
sponteneity 30
staffing 177–8, 186–91, 190–1, 193
stakeholders 143–4, 176
standards
    accreditation standards 19, 21–2, 212–13
    minimum ethical standards 23
    practice standards 22–3
statistical mapping 120
stigmatisation 71
'Stolen Generations' inquiry 149–50
storming 93, 96
storytelling 130
strategies 57, 195
    for being-focused and virtue-led practice 212
strengths 12, 38
    strengths-based practice 11, 202
stress/stressors 79, 110
structural analysis 21
structural factors 9, 17
substance abuse 188
supervision 22, 23
support 57, 69, 125
    mutual support 118
sustainability 122, 130
systemic approaches 65
systemic thinking 26, 57, 69, 70, 71, 97–8
systems 72

task functions (groups) 95
teams/teamwork
    Belbin's Team roles 95, 106
    interdisciplinary professional teams 21
    research teams 145–9
technical domain 45
technological innovation 9
temperance 109, 132, 133, 162, 165, 192
territoriality 51
theories of state 55
theory 24, 25
    attachment theory 69
    of attitudes 51
    behavioural learning theories 51, 52

binary focus 14, 29, 42, 182, 202–3, 211
classical theories of management 174
community theories 55
control theory 53
criminological/criminology
    theories 70, 96–7
desistance theory 70
formal theories 52–3, 85–6
General Strain Theory 53
human relation theories 174
informal theories 85–6
interactional theories 70
knowledge and 43–4, 202
labelling theory 53, 97
practice, integrated with 44
practice-based theory 48, 53
relapse prevention theory 70
social learning theories 52, 55, 69
social process theories 52–3
symbolic interactionalist, postmodern
    theories 97
theories for practice 70
theories of state 55
theory–practice/practice–theory binary focus 14,
    29, 42, 182, 202–3, 211
therapy 69
    behavioural therapies 65
    brief therapies 65
    cognitive behavioural therapy (CBT) 65, 107
    existentialism 65
    family-based therapies 71
    humanistic therapies 65
    psychoanalytical therapies 65
    psychotherapies 65
    range of 202
    resource-intensive therapeutic work 180
    solution focused therapies 65
    systemic therapies 65
    therapeutic approaches 68
    therapeutic group work 98–100
thinking (concept) 14, 21, 23, 27, 33, 50, 54, 57–8, 61,
    100, 135, 167, 189, 193, 194, 211–13
    approaches 50
    assessment and 84
    capacity for 51, 52
    community development and 136
    components 24–5
    creative (lateral) thinking 26–7, 55, 57, 108,
        128–31, 133, 182, 205
    critical thinking 21, 25–6, 38, 41, 57, 70, 71, 97–8,
        133, 204
    deontology, domination by 31
    divergent and convergent thinking 27
    dynamics 163–7
    on individual and family work 44
    influences on 164